THERE'S A MAN
IN THE HOUSE

THERE'S A MAN IN THE HOUSE

* * *

Harlan Miller

"There is no solution—
seek it lovingly"

RANDOM HOUSE : New York

*To all the girls to whom I've promised
to dedicate my first book—but
most of all to Doris.*

Thanks and acknowledgment are extended to the LADIES' HOME JOURNAL and the DES MOINES REGISTER AND TRIBUNE for the use of their copyrighted material appearing in this book.

© Copyright, 1955, by Harlan Miller
All rights reserved under International
and Pan-American Copyright Conventions.
Published in New York by Random House, Inc.,
and simultaneously in Toronto, Canada, by
Random House of Canada, Limited.

Library of Congress Catalog Card Number: 55-10637
Manufactured in the United States of America
by H. Wolff, New York

PREFATORY NOTE

The best-known and most controversial man in Iowa is Harlan Miller

He is humorist, philosopher, storyteller, friend, gossip, critic and counselor to 1,000,000 Iowans who have been reading his daily column in *The Des Moines Register* for more than twenty years. He is loved, cussed and discussed, but always avidly read.

This book contains the best from his newspaper columns and from his regular feature in *Ladies' Home Journal*. I think all America will enjoy this varied collection of wise but amusing comments from one of the very ablest columnists writing today.

GARDNER COWLES
President, *Des Moines Register and Tribune*

CONTENTS

PREFATORY NOTE BY GARDNER COWLES: v

INTRODUCTION: xi

1. *There is no place like home*

    THEN & NOW: 2
      Our baby slips away—Whispers to bobby soxers—My mother never wasted an egg—Candor on our 20th—Father-in-law of the bridegroom

    DOG DAZE: 13
      I'd rather adopt a baby—I'd still rather adopt a baby—Inside a dog's mind

    COLLEGE DEPARTMENT: 19
      To capture a college child—College romance, the modern way

    FATHER & SON: 25
      Sonny Boy apologizes—Apology at bedtime—The father and son riddle

    FAMILY LEFTOVERS: 31
      To spank or not to spank—The theory of inconspicuous stowage—Don't move, say cheese

    FOR MEN ONLY 1

2. *The passing scene*

    PROLOGUE: 40
      Anybody miss their serenity?

    OUR TOWN: 42
      How to get a drink in Des Moines—A bad hat yells, me, me, me! —15 innovations for our town—In our town

    EAST COAST, WEST COAST: 51
      For New York armfuls of loose bloom—Carmel by the sea

    ST. PATRICK & THE CHATTERBOXES: 56
      Blarney on St. Patrick's Day—Bevy of chatterboxes

    MODERN DESIGN & MODERN WORKMEN: 61
      Furniture can ruin your morale—Brave new world—200 h.p. surrey —God bless my $20 carpenters

CANDY WAS DANDY: 68
I used to be a soda-squirt myself—Three for a penny

I ADVISE THE JUNE GRADUATE: 73
Free advice to the grads—50 hints to this year's class

RICH MAN, POOR MAN, BEGGAR MAN: 78
Man of the year—I spy on a rich man—$13 a week for 13 wintry weeks

FROM BOOM TO BOOM: 85
Ride on roller-coaster—The fall and rise of Mr. Jones

FOR MEN ONLY II

3. *Your children & mine*

PROLOGUE: 92
Portrait of a modern baby at 1 year

THE FIRST 5 YEARS: 94
At 3 he's still a plaything—At 5 she's still from Eden—VIP: Off to kindergarten

YOUR CHILD FROM 9 TO 12: 100
Biography of a 9-year-old—Girls are exquisite at 10—Foibles of a boy at 11—Portrait of a 12-year-old

THE LONG & SHORT OF IT: 109
Glimpse into a little boy's mind—Daydream: First day of school

FOR MEN ONLY III

4. *The presidents*

PROLOGUE: 116
Unknown bureaucrat

HARRY TRUMAN & 10 GREATEST PRESIDENTS: 119
Our 10 greatest presidents—Truman—one of our 10 greats?

FDR: 123
That man in the White House—FDR's museum: A shrine, too—Spotlight on FDR—At FDR's press conference

GEORGE WASHINGTON & THEODORE ROOSEVELT: 132
G. W.: My 1960 candidate—Teddy Roosevelt

FOR MEN ONLY IV

5. *Doctor, oh doctor*

PSYCHIATRIC DEPARTMENT: 138
    How you can psychoanalyze yourself—Puff-puff in a nervous era—If men die young, it's unfair to their widows

PHARMACEUTICAL SUPPLIES: 145
    Mystery in the medicine cabinet—Is penicillin your dish?

"DR. MILLER" PRESCRIBES: 150
    How to cure a cold—Sex in 10 easy lessons—Maybe you need trifocals

MEDICAL BRIC-A-BRAC: 156
    Mecca for the middle-aged—Planned parenthood preferred—Into the valley of the shadow—I take our young one to the dentist

FOR MEN ONLY V

6. *Sports illuminated*

FIELD & STREAM: 166
    Daddy goes a-hunting—Rendezvous with a duck—Miracle for duck hunters—Day of an Iowa nimrod—A fish called "Solitude"

ARE YOU A MAN OR A SPECTATOR SPORT?: 176
    Sport keeps me young—Shoot 20 baskets before dinner

TENNIS, ANYONE?: 181
    Don't throw your tennis racket away

DID I EVER TELL YOU WHEN I . . . ?: 184
    When a team catches fire—How did Connie Mack overlook me?

BULLFIGHT: 189
    Bezbul fan at a bullfight

FOR MEN ONLY VI

7. *Personal & otherwise*

PERSONAL: 194
    Big moments in your life

AND OTHERWISE!: 196
    Maybe I can be a better man next year—10 hour pilot—Try to mention your European trip!—My 25th reunion—I'll never escort 5 girls to El Morocco again—My Dad almost bought a ranch

FOR MEN ONLY VII

8. *Military life*

PROLOGUE: 212
Our unknown soldier

AFTER THE WAR IS OVER: 214
Right in the colonel's face—Heroes from Main Street—Old soldier looks back

UTAH & NORMANDY BEACHES: 220
First night ashore—Bedtime in Normandy

DRAFT AGE: 225
Army life won't ruin him—To a raw recruit: a little advice

FOR MEN ONLY VIII

9. *Husband & wife*

PROLOGUE: 232
Tips to a groom for his honeymoon

THE ALMOST PERFECT WIFE & OTHER LIKE TALES: 235
The almost perfect wife—Slightly imperfect husband—Man's doom in a brave new world—Your 2nd husband may be worse

WHO CAN WIN?: 243
How wives pamper husbands—Husband loose in a supermarket—Doctrine of alternative objectives

DO IT YOURSELF: 250
Husband: handyman in a crisis—How I do my chores

FOR MEN ONLY IX

10. *Men & women*

ST. VALENTINE'S DAY COMES & GOES: 256
To all secret loves—Valentines for old flames

CLOTHES MAKE THE MAN: 261
Revolt against the haberdasher—When a man dresses: 32 steps

CAESAR & NAPOLEON WERE SHORT: 266

FOR MEN ONLY X

11. *Literature is what you make it*

    MIDDLEBROW'S CHOICE: 272
        100 *poems to read aloud at picnics—My 50 favorite books from the Army's paperbacks*

    BOOKS & MORE BOOKS: 277
        10 *books for my desert isle—Bookless room: uncivilized?*

    MUSIC DEPARTMENT: 282
        Music soothes a savage

    FOR MEN ONLY XI

12. *Nature as I like it*

    THE FOUR SEASONS: 288
        Hurrah, another spring!—Midsummer rhapsody—Autumn comes to town—Late winter rhapsody

    WHY IMPROVE UPON?: 297
        What's wrong with crab grass?—What is so rare?

    EINSTEIN'S THEORY IN ONE EASY LESSON: 301

    EPILOGUE: 304

INTRODUCTION

Columnist's lament

If he writes in a light vein, he's just a trivial nitwit.
If he broaches something serious, he's getting "heavy" & wants to be a bigshot.
If he uses long words, he's trying to show off his vocabulary.
If he uses short words, he's just an uneducated ignoramus.
If he mentions people's names, he's trying to brag & curry favor.
If he doesn't mention their names, he's high-hat & secretive.
If he writes about night clubs & drinking, he's just a nighthawk & rounder.
If he doesn't discuss night life, he lives in an ivory tower.
If he uses the pronoun "I" frequently, he's an egotist & exaggerates his own importance.
If he uses the editorial "we," he's too pompous & formal.
If he never criticizes anybody, he's wishy-washy & a scaredy-cat.
If he does criticize somebody, he's "just taking a crack" & nurturing a private grudge.
If he plugs a worthy cause, he's a do-gooder & inclined to be tedious.
If he won't plug every worthy cause, he's a self-centered careerist.
If he shifts jobs, he's got a yen for the big towns & is restless & unstable.
If he stays on the same job, he hasn't got the stuff for advancement.
If he mentions his wife & kids, he's "exploiting his family" & imagines they're unusual.

If he never mentions his family, he's lukewarm about homelife.

If he uses a lot of contributions & quotations, he's lazy & easy to please.

If he uses few contributions, his mail must be light.

If he does some outside writing, he's money-mad & has illusions of grandeur.

If he doesn't do any outside writing, he's a wastrel & a flop.

If he reproaches a Democrat, he's a Republican reactionary.

If he rebukes a Republican, he's a New Dealer.

If he lives simply, he's a hermit & a failure.

If he lives comfortably, he's putting on the dog.

If he gets denounced, he's a public scold & a tactless pain-in-the-neck.

If he doesn't get denounced, it's because nobody pays any attention to him.

If he makes speeches, it's because he wants to be conspicuous.

If he declines to make speeches, he's a moron with nothing to say.

If he reminisces, he's getting to be an old fuddy-duddy.

If he pays any attention to the bobby-soxers, he's immature.

If he alludes to the war, he's capitalizing on his war record.

If he never mentions the war, he's still maladjusted.

If he uses slang & gags, he's going after the comic-strip trade.

If he uses plain English, he's passing himself off as a highbrow.

If he's in his office all the time, he doesn't get around enough.

If he's never in his office, he's hard to reach.

If he takes sides, he's biased.

If he doesn't take sides, he has no convictions.

If he advocates temperance, he's a sissy & a hypocrite.

If he prefers wine to whisky, he's in the pay of the breweries.

If he writes modestly, he's a phony & a Milquetoast.

If he writes confidently, he's swell-headed and feeling his oats.

* 1 *
There is no place like home

THEN & NOW

Our baby slips away

We, too, lost our first-born. I heard last night the anguish of a young couple who lost a son in childbirth; the tale brought back vividly our old anguish, that lump in my throat. And it reminded me of scores who wrote & phoned us then that they, too, had lost their first-born, were happy now with later children. Now this tragedy doesn't happen so often.

I'd chosen the doctor my friends swore was the best doctor in town. He turned out to be drawn & fatigued with overwork, as so many popular or fashionable doctors get. He smiled gently & wearily each time the b.w. saw him & told us there was nothing to worry about. "You're strong & healthy," he told her.

In the delivery room the atmosphere was almost gala. The obstetrics team was bright & cheerful, almost jocular, all except our elderly obstetrician. Three nurses & 2 doctors, & others dropping in. Was there a 3rd doctor? Part of the time, maybe. One was observing the baby's heartbeat.

Then the delivery began to drag. Sharp pains without much progress. Was this infant reluctant to plunge into life? A queer rhythm began, delay & tension. Suddenly the head doctor seemed wearier. "We may have to use the forceps," he muttered wearily.

I was in the delivery room because the b.w. had asked & urged me to be there. The doctors & nurses seemed to be tugging & swaying in a rhythm, like the rowers in an 8-oared race. The b.w.'s groans were inside me; I could feel her pain. I looked helplessly at the doctors. The younger one taking the infant's heartbeats seemed hypnotized for long minutes.

Suddenly he listened after a long lapse through his stethoscope & spoke: "The heartbeats have slowed down!" The head doctor called quickly for the forceps. It was a struggle, a race, an agony. With a powerful, long-drawn manipulation of the shiny instrument he extricated the baby. The delivery room quivered with tension & nerves.

He was late with the forceps. The baby lived only 20 minutes. Forceps a little sooner, a closer tab on its heartbeats with the stethoscope might have saved our first-born. I was numb & stunned. The b.w. was unconscious under the anesthetic. I staggered out into the early morning shadows of the corridor.

Later I stood with my father-in-law beside the b.w.'s bed. How would she take it? She was returning to consciousness. We looked at each other. How could we console her? Her eyes opened. She knew. She looked up at us & spoke softly: "We mustn't grieve," she said.

Years later, flying across the Atlantic, sitting beside the pilot up forward, an idea flashed into my brain which might have saved our first baby's life. The pilot had just showed me the checklist of 200 or more details he must check & confirm before each flight. . . . Why can't doctors have such a checklist? Like pilots, they aren't superhuman.

Phone calls & letters poured in for weeks. "Don't let it crush you," our friends said; acquaintances, strangers. "Don't be bitter." "Have another child immediately." "We thought we could never forget this first tragedy. But we did—almost."

A year later our daughter was born. Three years later, our older son. Nine years later, our youngest. They have fully replaced the boy we lost, & consoled us fully; but we have never forgotten. That lump in the throat sometimes returns.

I remember how my father-in-law & I stood in a dim room later, looking down at the dead baby. He was a handsome, well-formed boy, husky & strong. Would we ever have another? I bent down & kissed him. Oddly, I felt no bitterness about the little lapse, the little moment when the machinery quit in the hands of our physicians.

For I've never felt it fair to expect doctors or pilots to be superhuman, or infallible, or magical; who is? But as I thought about the story of the young couple who'd lost a son because of a mistake in the analysis of an X-ray photograph, I wondered how long the lump in their throats would keep coming back.

Whispers to bobby soxers

Your mother probably knows more about boy-friends & romance than you do. . . . After all, she's an alumna of the giddy 1920's & 1930's & helped invent the modern girl. Quiz her about her bobby-sox days, to get useful pointers. Read a book a week; beauty is perishable, but a lively mind lasts a lifetime.

Disguise your dismay & inhale your protests if confronted at the table by food you don't like. When the cooking is good, give with applause. Say something interesting & amusing at the table. . . . Some day you'll hold celebrities spellbound.

Practice charm on your kid brothers & sisters, without brass knuckles. They'll be uncles & aunts to *your* kids some day. Make pets of 'em, & they'll run your errands. Surprise 'em with a few minutes of your valuable time. Maybe they admire you secretly.

Treat your grandparents affectionately. Grandma was a bobby-soxer herself day-before-yesterday, & you'll be a grandmother, too, day-after-tomorrow. Acid test of a civilized bobby-soxer is her attitude toward her elders & her juniors.

Of Iowa's 117,000 genuine bobby-soxers, probably 117,000 are Dad's & Mommie's prize exhibits. Turn on that 100-watt smile at least 9 times a day at home! Treat 'em slightly as if they were Claudette Colbert & Spencer Tracy, & not as grandparents. They're not antiques; they feel *young* under their worries.

Five minutes is long enough for a phone conversation. Amazing thought: maybe someone wants to talk to your mother! Fold up the paper after you've read it, or maybe your future husband will have to teach you how.

Broaden your circle of acquaintances. Dazzle your shyer

classmates occasionally with a burst of personality; don't save it all for the Big Time Operators. Massage the old man's bald spot, & comment on Mom's clothes—not always adversely. Always give your teachers the big hello.

Confidentially, your parents *want* you to have fun. Your generation isn't as different from theirs as you imagine. Start fascinating 'em *more* than 5 minutes before you ask 'em for something.

Coax your mother to let you help with the mending. Catch your dad off guard occasionally by doing something for him. It'll help when you start *chiseling* a chance to use the car, or want something *big*. Chat casually with their friends, whose good opinion of you is priceless.

While you're still a *free* agent, it's a mistake to let 1 boy monopolize your time. Even if that means missing a date now & then. Affability & politeness begin at home—remember, it's your house, too, & there's no law forcing your mother to do *all* the work.

Cultivate a soft pleasant voice & keep your head up & shoulders back—these improve your beauty & charm as much as cosmetics. Shock your parents once in a while by preparing a meal. You might be stranded on a desert isle with Jeff Chandler or Rock Hudson some day, & maybe he can't cook.

It's silly to let yourself be baffled by cliques or secrets or affectations of others. Nobody is any more on the inside of things than you are, & very few of your high school bigshots are likely to be bigshots to you in 10 years. You probably seem as Big Time to others as they seem to you.

Everybody is full of doubts & uncertainties, & no one knows all the answers. For you, your father & mother come nearest. Try saying "Okay, Mom" without an argument occasionally.

A considerate, happy bobby-soxer can brighten a house more than $10,000 worth of interior decoration. Confide in your parents—they'll give you the low-down. Today's problems won't seem so weighty when you enter your next phase. You may be a bobby-soxer now, but you'll be wearing $2 nylons by & by.

My mother never wasted an egg

My mother was a good manager. I realize far more vividly today how skillfully she controlled our family finances. She kept us comfortable on my father's small earnings, & we were unaware of the struggle.

We always ate chicken at least once a week, though with 3 sisters I soon learned that as the only boy I always ate the wings & gizzard. I became so fond of chicken wings that to this day I esteem them a delicacy, though the b.w. argues they fatten.

From our hilltop overlooking the DM river we could see the fishermen on the muddy banks. Often my mother sent me when I was 8 with a dime or 15 cents to see what I could buy. I frequently came home with 2 or 3 sizable fish, fresh from the river.

I am not as fond of "big thick steaks" as most of our friends, & the reason is simple: We never had big thick steaks at our house; seldom any steak. And I get kidded because I like my meat well-done: My mother never served meat rare.

On the river banks I liked to loiter in the boats tied up at the thick, muddy, squashy shoreline. One day I tied a string of fish to an overhanging willow tree & they got loose & swam away while I played. Tragedy! I dreaded to go home. Luckily I found a fond uncle to lend me 15 cents.

My mother discovered that cracked eggs could be bought for much less, & since she was a great omelet beater, she went in for the freshly candled cracked eggs. As my dad kept a flock of hens, too, we often ate eggs 3 times a day. I still like eggs better'n steak.

Vegetable peddlers stopped at our front door every day, their wagons piled high. Many were farmers or farmwives from nearby farms. My mother was a shrewd judge of vegetables, & nobody could fool her about a muskmelon.

My father & mother were the first people in our neighborhood to go in for salads. We raised our own lettuce & tomatoes, & we usually ate salad once or twice every day. They were both strong for fruit, too; there was always a basket of cherries or apples in the kitchen, or dusty purple grapes. (They made good sweet wine, too.)

My mother was horrified at any waste of food. She gauged the quantities we needed accurately, & we all belonged to the "Clean Plate Club," & there were seldom any leftovers. But in summer we always ate ice cream at least once a week.

On certain edibles my mother refused to pinch pennies. She ranked a certain cocoa (& certain cereals & tinned salmon) as superior in quality, & gladly paid a few cents extra for those brands. Well, maybe not gladly; but she'd buy no other.

We had no luxury foods at our house, though. Mother was a great one for soups, & I've never tasted any better than her oatmeal & potato soup (a sort of Scotch broth) with shreds of meat & yolks of egg crumbled.

She made our clothes until my dad okayed my revolt, & how she could patch them! No matter how small her grocery & housekeeping allowance from my dad, she always managed to save a few dollars, & in a crisis he relied on these savings.

We never felt "poor," though; partly because my dad always saved a little money no matter how small his earnings. He bought the various houses we lived in & invested in a few others, & you never feel poor if you're saving a little money.

But somehow I absorbed a sort of "poor boy" complex through my pores in this atmosphere of frugality & thrift. I'm irked by lights left on, uneaten leftovers, clothes not hung up or discarded before worn out, refrigerators left open, houses too hot & other minor waste.

My mother always seemed to have money laid away for anything we really needed, but she never frittered any on nonsense. She wasn't responsible for my "poor boy" complex, either. That came later when I saw hard-earned money conspicuously wasted—usually by myself.

Maybe my dad's income wasn't so small; a dollar then bought $4 worth by today's prices. . . . But some incomes of today aren't as big as the people who spend 'em seem to think. . . . Anyhow, my "poor boy" complex helps me pick a chicken wing or chicken back reasonably clean, to this day.

Candor on our 20th

We celebrated our 20th wedding anniversary quietly. By agreement, I promised to give the b.w. a new stove, & she promised to give me a new refrigerator. (Same ones we'll give each other next year.) I also gave her yellow roses & a box of candy, of which I'll eat 3 pieces to her 1; the kids'll eat the rest.

If our 20-year marriage proves anything, it proves that 2 stubborn individuals can stay married 20 years even in these perilous times. Last night we confessed frankly to each other that we'd both had our doubts whether we'd ever reach the 10-year mark.

In our 6th year we counted up on our fingers one night over a cold supper in the kitchen & discovered 12 divorces among our DM friends. But those were the frenzied years. We aren't excessively fashionable, we aren't too social, & that makes it easier to enjoy evenings at home & family life.

I often get letters from skeptics demanding: "Don't you 2 ever quarrel? If so, why never mention it? Are you always so amiable & chummy with each other?" To which my unwritten response is: "Hell yes; we quarrel. Not very seriously. Just enough to serve notice on each other that we can't be stampeded."

I argue that 3 kisses a day (minimum) will almost guarantee a happy, amiable marriage. And I also recommend an occasional quarrel to cement a good marriage, if you follow a few simple rules:

1. Always begin a quarrel by looking at each other with amazement.
2. Quarrel in low voices.
3. Begin each rebuttal with "That's true, dearest, but—" switching to "Maybe that's true, darling—" if you're really angry.
4. If you throw anything, always aim to miss, & throw lamps or vases you don't like anyhow, preferably out the window or into the fireplace.
5. If you're sure you're right, stop arguing & lapse into a convincing silence.

6. If you say anything really rough, be sure to end the sentence with "precious."

7. Remember that the most dangerous quarrels are those about not living within your income.

8. Be ready with an exit line like "How about a walk around the block?" or "Let's go to the drugstore for a soda," or "Let's have a glass of milk & a hunk of cheese, you big cheese!"

Another way to end a quarrel is to remember something nasty about somebody your opposite quarreler doesn't like either. Either that, or (what I've found always works) recall the time the bellhop put all our luggage (9 pieces) on one of the trick beds at the hotel at Grinnell on the first night of our honeymoon, & the bed collapsed, to the mirth of all the hangers-on in the lobby, who got a play-by-play report from the bellboy.

On every wedding anniversary I feel that I owe a bonus to the Rev. Elmer Nelson Owen of St. Paul's Episcopal church here, the man who married us. I gave him what was almost my last cent—a $20 gold piece I'd been carrying as a good luck piece for several years. He went to a fashionable church in Boston & may well be a bishop by now.

Since our Great Date comes at this dawn-of-spring interlude, I'll persuade the b.w. to celebrate it each year with our first real outdoor picnic of the season. That is, I *think* I'll persuade her. But her reaction to weather is more genteel than mine, so we might have a knockdown & dragout quarrel about *that*.

Recently I read Ed Streeter's enchanting book called *Father of the Bride*, on the assumption that our 18-year-old b.g. might decide not to become a spinster after all. Besides some valuable hints on the silly role of fathers, it unveils a truth all husbands & wives ought to remember: The foibles & whims you think peculiar to your spouse & peculiarly baffling to you are commonplace whims & foibles; all other husbands & wives have 'em, too.

My real anniversary gift to the b.w. won't be the new stove, of course. It'll be another night at the hotel in Grinnell. The genial boniface has invited us to come down & be his guests overnight, but if they try any tricks with that trick bed, we'll have our safari cots along. We're better prepared for surprises than we were on our honeymoon.

Father-in-law of the bridegroom

When I first glanced at *Father of the Bride* again, soon after our daughter was married, it didn't seem so funny to me as it had been the first time I read it. My wounds were too raw. But now I can see once more the comedy in the father's role. I'm back to normal. So I can trust myself to give you 10 hints:

1. Try to bribe your daughter to reprieve you from a big expensive wedding. Offer her up to 90% of what it'll cost. Warn her that most of the presents ("loot") she'll get will be more fanciful than useful; that a "big" wedding will exhaust you & her & her mother & will undermine your faith in marriage. Jolly her young man about eloping, but don't let your voice break.

2. When she wins the argument & you succumb to her "big-wedding" plea, get her signature on the dotted line, & your son-in-law's, that she'll buy the wedding presents for all the relatives of all your guests who'll get married the next 20 years & will each require gifts, & send 'em as coming from him & her & her pa & ma.

3. It's far better to keep the expense of the reception down so you can afford to invite every friend you know. Around our town they figure $5 to $10 per guest for a "modern" wedding, and by the time your wife & daughter have listed hundreds of people you never heard of, you begin to feel terribly poor.

But if you skip any, you'll always be sorry.

4. You'll be agog & amused at all the complex records & bookkeeping of a stream-lined modern wedding: It requires at least 6 lists & 2 card indexes of guests; day-book & ledger records & card indexes of gifts as they arrive (plus memorizing 'em so you can allude to 'em lightly at the wedding); & of course thank-you notes forever.

5. I think a wedding reception in a hovel (if it's home) is better than one at Pierre's or the Plaza. . . . I got talked out of that, too: "It might rain!" I'd longed to hang lanterns around the tennis court. . . . The upshot was we had one downtown & then another on the tennis court, too, & didn't eat the last scrambled egg till 6 A.M. It didn't rain.

6. Don't argue with your wife if she wants to invite an

81-year-old boyhood chum of her great-grandfather while you want to add a 19-year-old red-haired coed. You just offer to mail the wedding invitations, pluck out the old sport's invitation from his envelope, & put it in an envelope you've addressed yourself.

7. Watch the womenfolk like a hawk when it comes to the wedding gown & the wedding photographs. There's gossip that for some recent weddings the females (left unguarded for a moment) have spent over $500 for the gown to be worn once & the photographs destined for the closet shelf year-after-next. In their own sweet way, women are suckers, too.

8. If you've had sense enough to go hunting with the bridegroom & get on the good side of him, maybe he'll support you in some of your unreasonable, tightwad demands. Otherwise you'll find that what he says to your daughter when you're not around will carry more weight in the wedding plans than your cries of agony, even if it is your dough.

9. The day'll come when you'll envy & admire the sensible pair who offered their intimate friends lemonade & macaroons in the church vestry room. Such strong-minded people don't give a hoot whether Maizie got 517 gifts to Penelope's mere 483, or whether it was the other way around.

10. To your intense astonishment, you'll wind up enjoying the whole silly spectacle even if you've had to pawn your shotgun or borrow the money. Especially if you've marched down the aisle with aplomb, & the wine cask hasn't run dry before 7 o'clock. You realize that what you spend on the wedding you simply deduct from what you'll leave 'em when you die.

About midnight it dawns on you that you-can't-take-it-with-you, & that this ceremony is more than the ostentatious show you've scorned so much. It's the going-away party for that little red-head you used to toss high in the air, & it's also a barbaric rite in honor of those little scamps who (you hope) will be arriving before too many years. Your wife's grandchildren.

As you can easily gather, I've just about got it paid for.

※ ※ ※

My wife has conceded a point. She says I'm entitled to complain about the grocery bill, or the accumulated leftovers in the icebox, or mention my fears that food is being wasted—but only on days when I take her downtown to dinner.

Junior can't make up his mind what he wants to study in college. But he *is* farsighted about one thing: he now reserves the family car for important dates as long as six weeks in advance. Gets a quicker "yes" that way.

"When I tell my husband it's time to mow the lawn," says Betty Comfort, exiling a too-purple petunia to the back fence, "he argues it ought to go to seed. But when I start to struggle dramatically with the lawn mower, thank goodness he's chivalrous enough to grab it from me!"

In our town the flight from the harem continues triumphant. Matrons who used to criticize a woman who invited a man in for a cup of tea now ask an old flame in for midmorning coffee with unfluttered aplomb. (No ruling yet from Emily Post.)

When I recognize some of my tools in a neighbor's garage, I usually seem more embarrassed than he does. Perhaps I'll have to be psychoanalyzed for a guilt complex.

Our daughter (somewhat to my consternation) has announced firmly that she intends to learn to cook this summer.
    "Have you run across a strong, handsome can opener?" I inquired frivolously.
    "You go on a diet, Daddy!" she retorted warmly.

I've been flabbergasted by our youngest's contention that it isn't fair to reprove him for doing something I haven't told him *not* to do. So we have a new pact: when he's about to do something he knows I wouldn't want him to do, he's to come to me and ask permission, and I'll tell him not to do it.

DOG DAZE

I'd rather adopt a baby

Frankly, our new dog Rex makes himself felt around the house about as much as any of our children in recent years. Maybe more, since our young began to play hard to catch. Unlike them, the Brittany spaniel watches our lips, our facial expressions & hangs on our every word. The children haven't done that since the age of 2.

If it came to a showdown, we'd rather send the dog away to college & have our children at home. Since this can't very well be arranged, Rex keeps us on edge almost as much as they did. He's a sensitive soul, modest & self-effacing, so we try harder than ever to interpret the exact nuance of every moan, whine & snuffle. Maybe I'd rather adopt a baby than a dog.

We call him Sexy Rexy in the privacy of our own back yard, after a certain Hollywood star whom he resembles remarkably. He is russet & white in color, 15 months old, a smallish dog, but lanky, & when he stretches out, he can stand on his hind legs with his forepaws on my necktie, clawing through my shirt at the hair on my chest.

Sexy Rexy arrived exactly 1 week ago today, early the morning after we'd stayed up till 3:30 A.M. listening to the politicians on TV. Sometimes it seems as if he'd been with us for years. Already, everyone in the household pays far more attention to him than they do to me.

He makes a small mouth & pathetic eyes at us, & we all love him. No matter how much we pet him & stroke him, how much we romp with him & walk him around the block, no matter how often we let him out & how often we let him in, no matter how carefully we feed him & improve the softness of his couch, we feel guiltily we aren't doing enough.

Actually, like a baby, he's an object lesson in the peculiar advantage of helplessness. He reminds me of Joseph Conrad's ailing colored sailor in *Children of the Sea*, who had the entire crew guiltily feeling sorry for him and trying to coddle him and make a pet of him.

And he reminds me also of the British officer I was teamed up with in the army, a stalwart, upstanding example of such triumphant helplessness that I found myself arranging for every jeep, every plane, every travel order & mess & billet, even at the British front. (I finally broke him down by asking genially if he were a spoiled only child.)

Rex is more obedient than our children. He's already learned not to come into the dining room; though I still can't persuade our youngest to use the side door. When I say "Down!" he takes his paws off my white shirt; but I can't make Q keep his paws out of my top drawer. When we blow a basketball whistle, he comes leaping across the pasture, faster than our children ever responded to the dinner gong.

After several experiments, Rex has chosen the couch in what we fondly call the "playroom" as his bed. It's the softest spot in the house, but he'd prefer to sleep 2 flights up in a bedroom. Our basement is acquiring a doggy smell and we keep the door closed. So he howls softly every evening & early morning for our sympathy.

This is especially embarrassing, because it may wake some of the neighbors. The spring Junior was born, one of the neighbors' dogs used to bark all night & wake up the b.w. She needed her sleep, & I phoned this neighbor once or twice at 5 A.M.

I've decided to phone all our neighbors that I've conveyed this delicate situation to Rex & warned him to be quiet between 8 P.M. & 8 A.M., the only hours he really likes to bark. I think he's beginning to understand that the honor & prestige of the family depend on his nocturnal silence.

Several times I've felt tempted to phone Vern Moore over at Dubuque & ask for some pointers on Rex's habits & foibles. He's a subdued, shy creature, on the nervous side, & sometimes I feel he underestimates his own charms.

He's a fool for the ladies, & in the presence of the opposite sex, self-consciousness seems to overwhelm him & he becomes covered with confusion. Well, he's still a newcomer in the neighborhood, & as soon as he finds out how friendly & easy-going we all are—including the 60 children & 30 dogs around our block—he'll be glad he came.

I'd still rather adopt a baby

Recently I've delved into several articles about dogs, & am shocked to report that at least two brilliant writers have tried to debunk the critters. One of these debunkers is Ring Lardner, a genial live-&-let-liver; he says he sees through the whole dog myth.

The other debunker is no less than Robert Louis Stevenson, a man who seldom owned fewer than 4 dogs. RLS after some elegant rambling concludes that the dog is a born liar, a snob, a sycophant & a fawner, but what of it? He still likes Fido.

I'm even more shocked because I find myself inclined to agree with both Ring Lardner and RLS. After meeting the mournful & reproachful eye of Sexy Rexy a thousand times at the back screen door, clawing at the screen 30 seconds after I'd let him out under orders to *stay* out for at least an hour, I began to suspect he wasn't sincere.

We used to have long debates in the 3rd and 4th grades about which was man's best friend, the dog or the horse. As I recall it, we were overly swayed by the fact that in Holland dogs pulled 2-wheeled milk carts.

What of horses that pulled ice & beer & coal wagons right in DM? Too commonplace. Usually the dog won the title, largely, I now suspect, because there were many more dogs than horses in our neighborhood.

Lardner thinks that many a man would never stop to pat a dog if he didn't hope somebody would see him & pass the word around that he's kind to animals & therefore a good egg in spite of all his faults: "He can't be all bad, he likes dogs."

Occasionally, when I've seen excessive affection lavished on a dog (especially by a lovely woman), I've thought secretly: "What a waste!" And does that warm emotion toward animals reduce, as some argue, the total amount of affection left for their fellow men? Maybe!

"The faults of the dog are many," says RLS, the great dog-lover. "He is vainer than man, singularly greedy of notice, singularly intolerant of ridicule, suspicious like the deaf, jealous to the degree of frenzy & radically devoid of truth."

RLS doesn't say a word about the noble watchdog or the noble shepherd dog, or about dogs which save little boys from drowning or give the alarm that the basement is on fire, or carry brandy to broken-down mountain climbers.

Frankly, as I've told the b.w. more than once, I think many people would find it more fun to adopt a baby than to own a dog, & no more trouble. Rex has always resented any attempts on my part to read a book in the evening, much as some wives disapprove of an innocent scanning of the morning paper at breakfast.

What's more, as a man who has at certain periods of my life seemed surrounded by flapping diapers, I'm convinced that babies smell better than dogs. There's a spirited argument between the b.w. & me whether the queer & persistent aroma in the basement is Rex or the oak firewood. For my money it's Rex.

It's out in the fields that Rex & most other dogs are at their noblest & best. With his head held high & alert, & 1 paw raised, Rex seems heroic. I used to think that the city was an unnatural habitat for dogs, until I heard that the Russians have banned dogs in Moscow. Now I'm convinced the city's okay for a dog.

"It is just this rage for consideration," argues the 4-dogged Stevenson, "that has betrayed the dog into his satellite position as the friend of man. The cat, an animal of franker appetites, preserves his independence. But the dog, 1 eye ever on the audience, in hot pursuit of admiration, has been wheedled into slavery."

Come, come, Stevenson, & you too, Lardner! What do you say about dogs which trot cross country several hundred miles to get back to their beloved masters? That stumps you, eh? Well, I'll tell you how *some* people explain it: that doggie's discovered the food's better at home. One DM dog lover loves 'em without illusion. He says that 1 good meal will lure his dog away to any new owner at least for a while.

Inside a dog's mind

Why do *they* eat 3 times a day & feed me only twice? I have to watch 'em yet! Do they think I'm made of iron? I just love to lick their hands, especially when they've been handling food. Never see 'em scratch the way I do. Maybe the sissies don't even have fleas!

Somebody oughta invent an indoor toilet for dogs. It's no bargain to go out in zero weather, at 11:30 at night. I don't see *them* doing it!

If I yip, or whine like a little baby, they really pay attention. Better'n barking, I'll say. They come tearing down the stairs to let me in. My chief objection to people is they don't have a nice odor like dogs. They eat between meals, too!

Shucks, the Big Boy gets vexed when I stick my head up under the book he's reading! What's wrong with that? It's more important to scratch my head than keep staring at that dumb book. He always growls a little, but he always comes across.

The young one's rougher with me than the others, but he's more fun, too. He's more like a puppy himself. I'm glad there are lots of dogs in the neighborhood. But they all want to play *their* way. Cute number, that blonde cocker next door. Standoffish, though.

I like most the ones that feed me. The women humor me more. The Big Boy certainly lays down the law. I suspect he's the one who thinks it's good for me to be outdoors a lot. Well, I like to snooze on the rug, but a good canter really puts me in the pink. It can be overdone though. Today he gave me a bone between meals, the old softie.

It wouldn't hurt *them* to eat only twice a day, either—or run around the block. When they step on my toes they weigh a ton. I must keep out of their way; sometimes they stumble around as if there weren't a dog within miles, the dopes. Dangerous to curl up between their feet, but I like it. Ho, hum, what's better than a dog's life?

Puzzles 'em when I whine to be let in & then to go out again in a few minutes when they open the door. They don't understand I need a vote of confidence every few minutes. Gotta be sure they still like me. If they didn't, where'd my next meal come from? But I had to cut out my cringing act; it didn't go over too well.

I know I'm not supposed to put my paws up on the furniture, but I can get away with a certain amount of it. They think I'm cute when I stand up with my fore-feet on the window-sill & look outdoors. Well, I've got to see what's going on. Blondie might be alone on the lawn.

Heard the Big Boy say a turtle would be a better watchdog! Zattso! If a stranger came in, would I raise hell! Do they expect me to bark on practice maneuvers? They sleep a little later Sunday, so I'll have to learn to drink less water Saturday night!

Yes, I know perfectly well I'm not supposed to enter the dining room when they're eating. But I can usually thrust my forepaws inside the room awhile before they give me a dirty look. Boy, it's great when they come home after a few hours away. I whoop & howl & jump all over 'em, & they're kinda flattered, too. He doesn't like his face licked, though; thinks it's unsanitary.

It's fun when they walk me around the block. They're kinda stuffy about it, but it makes me feel like a citizen in good standing. Always amuses 'em when I stop at so many different trees. Well, I've gotta check in at certain points, & once I have a routine I stick to it. I'm as sanitary as any dog I know.

Wish the Big Boy'd do his typewriting in the daytime. Who's he to thump that old machine right above my head after midnight? If he wakes me up he oughta at least let me come & see him. Wowie, did he get mad when I chewed up those letters he left on the floor. Sloppy, I call it! He covers everything with letters, papers, letters! He rubbed my nose in the scraps & thumped me with a newspaper, like clouting me with a feather. Didn't hurt, but I had to act depressed. I can read him like a book.

※ ※ ※

"To hear me tell it," confesses Peter Comfort, shooing a stray cherub off the top of his convertible, "I love all children. But I'm just a big liar. Some of 'em in our neighborhood couldn't terrify me more if they carried a tommy-gun."

It took twelve years to get a potato pancake in my own house, and now it looks like another twelve-year crusade before I get hash for breakfast. Calvin Coolidge could get hash for breakfast in the White House, but I've had to go as far as Florida! (Yet never a direct refusal!)

I don't know whether the young read Kinsey, but since I read his book I've had to smother an impulse to ask Junior to tell me all about sex.

You never know a man's true mettle until you see him play The Game. The acid test: make him act out a song title like "The Monkey's Serenade" and see if (1) he'll prance around your living room like a marmoset or (2) portray it with sheer intellect.

My wife divides into two groups our friends who're affluent enough to send their young off to summer camps: (1) those who say it's so good for the children and (2) those who admit they can't face the summer with their darlings at home.

I'm irresistibly tempted to imprint a surprise male touch on my wife's little formal garden. But I'm torn between shocking her with lowbrow hollyhocks or wowing her with a pair of elegant espaliered pear trees, flat against the garden wall.

COLLEGE DEPARTMENT

To capture a college child

I've tried a dozen tricks & stratagems to wangle a few extra glimpses of our young, home during the holidays, with only mixed success. We've even tried to get 'em up for breakfast. But I feel like Simon Legree; they need sleep.

Before they got home, I vowed to have a long walk in the woods with each of 'em separately; & one mass family hike. Maybe Patton could; I can't. They look at me in amazement at such a medieval & outlandish idea. Walk? On foot?! It went out with McKinley & Teddy Roosevelt.

If we lived on an isolated farm, it'd be easier. I'd merely disconnect a few wires in the car & muffle the phone. Far from the allure of Roosevelt shopping center. But even the offer of a musical comedy at KRNT theater barely copes with their chums.

Ah, a wily idea! Give 'em some chores to do, & work along with 'em. Then we can talk about things that matter. Too cold to wash the car. Lay a fire in the fireplace? The mention of chores gives 'em a weary look, like figures in a Salvador Dali picture.

Well, how about taking the cameras out in the yard to make some family snapshots? (In a year or 2 they'll be priceless.) They give me a wounded look, as if I'd suggested looking for 4-leaf clovers in a blizzard.

How about having lunch with me downtown? Great! Terrific! Dad, can you squeeze it in between 11:50 & 12:27? Gotta see 2 fellahs I haven't seen since last night.

We could shoot a few baskets in the backyard? Too cold? Oh, you'll warm up in a few minutes. By that time we're back in the house. Intimate conversation: "Was it more heroic for the state university to beat Notre Dame or for State College to beat Notre Dame's conquerors?"

Well, kids, save us an evening for a family dinner downtown. Sure! Great idea. What night? Shucks, I'm busy that night, but I can do it the next night. Oh, that's the night I'm busy, Dad. Could we eat by 5:30 & be through before 6? Or between 8:30 & 9 o'clock?

Maybe we can catch 'em for a cozy talk late at night, when they come in from a date? After midnight, in the kitchen, over milk & cookies or cornflakes? (We're sleepier than they are.) But maybe the yawns bring us closer.

They can't give us the slip at the big Yule dinner of all branches of the family. Committed to that. It turns out to be sacred to cousins, aunts & uncles. They're far down the table, discussing whether Sigma Nus are more intellectual than Betas, or vice versa.

A-ha, we have 5 reels of home movies (one a fascinating double exposure) they haven't seen. That'll captivate 'em, I'm sure? They're amazed at how young they were a year ago. And they're out of the house before I've taken down the screen.

We build a fire in the fireplace every night & our youngest turns out all the other lights. A hearth fire makes 'em thoughtful, but the phone keeps ringing. (The thoughts of youth are long long thoughts, but that's hearsay; I never hear 'em.)

Perhaps we can spend New Year's Eve together & let the rest of the world go by. We're willing to cancel our engagement for that night, & so is one of our juveniles. But the other seems heavily involved; maybe we can move the clock back at 2 A.M. & improvise a 2nd midnight.

We can toss a football in the yard, & that's good for 12 minutes, a sprained finger & no exchange of ideas. Ah, success! Junior's willing to go to a Prune Bowl basketball evening. But the Drake fieldhouse is hardly the place for a quiet chat.

If we're brazen enough we can barge in for a minute or two while our young & chums are conferring in the living room or playing the phonograph. Maybe TV'll keep 'em home.

It adds up slowly; a meal here, a tenacious few minutes pre-empted there. The fireside, the chores & the home movies bring 'em closest. When the 18 days slip by, we can still count the hours on our fingers, & our juveniles will still be a baffling mystery to us. Some day we'll take a long walk together.

College romance, the modern way

Recently I attended a genuine college wedding, the nuptials of a Tri Delt & a Sigma Nu. Both were still students, with fraternity brothers & sisters marching up the aisle, & a best man who flew out from Amherst College who'd been with the bridegroom in kindergarten.

Marriage & college overlap more & more in the mid-century; parents no longer even argue, much. This romance began on the campus. They met between classes, teamed up a year for campus parties & coke dates, even canoed & played tennis, began to kiss.

At the reception in the bride's house, the college pals & chums were ready with rice, old shoes, tin cans. But the resourceful best man outwitted 'em; a quick dash from the stairway landing to the kitchen, a car with motor running & brother-in-law at the wheel in the alley; they were off.

Somehow they wangled from studies a week's honeymoon toward the Ozarks. They visited the St. Louis Zoo, took each other's snapshots, spent a night on the shore of a lake, danced at a plush hotel, but made it back to classes without any cuts. Their "planning clipboard" for budgets & ideas was always with 'em.

Both of 'em graduate this year, both have jobs for the final semester. Back on the campus, they moved into one room of a medium-sized house with a 3-child family & the mellow grandpa who lives there, too. They have the run of the house, kitchen, icebox, TV, & feel entirely at home.

He works 24 hours a week at a hospital, but manages to get a few A's & B's in his studies. She is secretary to a psychologist on the faculty, & loves it. They're often bushed in the evening, but they're still 21 & full of zip & stamina.

This summer he goes into the Air Force for 2 or 3 years. They'll be in Texas first, then maybe Georgia or Arizona &, they hope, perhaps Germany or Japan. They'll travel light & store the "loot" of wedding gifts with both sets of parents.

He bought a used car with his savings, which began the year he was 6 years old, an economical 6-cylinder model. She gave up her mother's car she'd used around the campus. The bride still does his laundry (as she did before they were married) & he drives her to & from work.

This spring there was a flurry on the campus of "job interviews" with emissaries of big corporations. He got several offers to keep on ice till the Air Force is through with him, mostly some phase of "selling," & a free airplane trip east to see a company interested in him.

They toyed with the idea of buying a trailer, but reluctantly gave it up. Comfortable enough, but the places near airfields where they'd have to park it are often jammed & dreadful. So they'll live in base quarters or in the fringe of subsidized Air Force housing near the airfields.

A baby? Maybe. They didn't postpone marriage for old-fashioned "career" reasons, & they probably won't postpone that infant for long. If they'd met a year or 2 sooner they'd probably have had an infant watching 'em snatch their diplomas.

Their college is about halfway between her folks & his, & they spend a weekend a month with each; half collegiate, half newlywed. She has a married brother nearby, too, & he a married sister. They see them occasionally & get a glimpse of young life with a baby in the house.

Life is full up to the brim, & they're in it up to their chins. College, romance, army, career. Every problem shines with sharp facets & fascinations. They make a striking pair, she with her 1955 pony tail, he with his butch; with their books & music & dreams & theories, bless 'em.

Two or 3 years ago hot-war was often in his thoughts. Now it's cooled off to cold war, & he expects always to live with it. It might mean a 600 m.p.h. plunge for the jugular, the enemy's solar plexus; it might mean a bungalow & Blue Cross in the suburbs. They're ready. God bless 'em.

※ ※ ※

After I've paid $13.20 for a pair of New York theater tickets on our annual visit, and later find the stubs in my pants pocket, my opinion of the free fun at home soars. If those shows are worth $6.60, then my ten-year-old's performance is worth $5,000 a year.

"I'm not sure," says Peter Comfort, returning my rake and borrowing my snow shovel, "that the man whose wife spends her days playing bridge and canasta is any worse off than the wife whose husband serves on too many committees."

At last it has dawned on me how our teen-agers decide at which house they'll gather for the evening: they reconnoiter by phone till they've discovered where the grown-ups are least likely to be home.

I can't prove it, but I'll bet $1 my suspicions are sound. Wives in our circle have concluded that they get taken downtown for dinner oftener if they serve a dull meal or two every week.

Maybe Junior has sprouted an elfin sense of humor since he has been away at school. He devoted his last letter entirely to his desperate need for various sums of money, and signed off with: "I've tried to paint you a picture of life at school."

After a pilgrimage to the Hyde Park mansion my wife thinks that the Roosevelt-haters did a lot of needless worrying. "Any clever woman," she says, "could have told 'em that a house filled with those cherished heirlooms couldn't harbor a traitor-to-his-class."

Some of the wives in our town delight in overemphasis of their husbands' quaintness. If they were married to Einstein they'd treat him as an adorable old eccentric who hated to go to a barber and get his hair cut.

Our town's best-groomed man lives in a one-bathroom apartment, and now he's shopping for an old-fashioned washbowl and water pitcher. "No woman seems to understand," he complains, "that a man's bathroom routine may involve anywhere from thirteen to thirty-seven separate operations every morning."

I'm not quite positive whether I like meat loaf because it tastes good, or because it's easy to carve, or because it keeps the grocery bill down. (Also, it seems better cold at midnight than hot at dinner!)

My wife frowns on my colored shirts, but admires them on other men. Many times she's finessed me into a white shirt at the last minute. "You look so dressy in colored shirts," she says, "and other men look so dashing!"

Some of our town's wordliest people reveal their tenderness at Christmas. Like our neighbors who always invite a couple of childless newcomers to supper on Christmas Eve or Christmas Night.

FATHER & SON

Sonny Boy apologizes

Listen, Dad: I'm saying this to you as you lie asleep, sprawled out on your bed face down, your hair tousled, your shoes still on, snoring a little, not very cute, a nervous father.

I've just tip-toed into your room without knocking. Just a few minutes ago, as I was playing with my windup train on the grand piano, a painful wave of remorse swept over me. Had I been a good son? Had I made allowances for your limitations?

Guiltily I came to see if you were still awake. Here's what I'm thinking, Dad: I've been mean to you. When you told me to eat my egg while it was warm, I gave you a dirty look & said, "I'm sick of drooly old eggs, & maybe I like 'em cold."

Then you handed me the old line about how happy a little French child would be to get an egg every day & I said, "Tough bounce!" You looked at me oddly & started to say something. Then you changed your mind & turned away silently.

Later, near the front door, you said my T-shirt was too torn & dirty to wear to school & asked me to change it. I said, "I guess I know what I want to wear," & asked if you wanted to make me late to school. I changed it, but slammed the door.

Earlier, when I was looking at the funnies, you asked for part of the paper & I spoke sharply to you: "Gee, whiz, why can't we have 2 papers in this house?" You gave me a strange look & began to read that silly old Walter Lippmann instead of the funnies like a modern pa.

Then just before I put my dirty handprint on the newly painted front door, I kissed Mommie good-bye & you called "Good-bye, Son" & I growled, "Bye!" & ran across the iris & geraniums just to show you there are 2 sides to every question. I knew only too well how sensitive you are about those sickly iris.

When you came home from work & said, "Hello, Butch!" I didn't jump up into your arms, like the little boys in the picture books, but said, "Dad, you promised to take me out to see the planes," & you said you were too tired, & I said, "I'll bet you're not too tired to play tennis," & I saw that mute, hurt expression in your eyes.

At dinner I saw you trying to get in good with me by giving me the biggest piece of liver & I asked you why we couldn't have a new automobile with the gear lever on the steering wheel, like everybody else, & you doused your potatoes with too much pepper, which Mommie says is bad for you, & said you'd buy a new one in '59.

Then when some people dropped in I asked real loud why you don't hold your tummy in, & how could you afford to buy that new $12 golf club when Mommie can't have a new hat, & you turned pale & said, "Ha, Ha!" & it sounded hollow, & you didn't spank me; it was your day to be a modern father.

Before I went to bed I blew some soap bubbles with your briar pipe & left it in the driveway, & spilled some ink in your shirt drawer while looking for your gold cuff links to trade for Billy's frog, & you felt so badly you went into the pantry & drank some medicine.

Dad, there's a lump in my throat tonight, & I realize you're the best daddy you know how to be, even if you don't buy me 2 ice cream cones every day like Jimmy's dad does. You can't all be geniuses.

Tonight I realize that you've only been a daddy for a few years, & that you still have a lot to learn, & anyhow God doesn't guarantee that all daddys are bright. You didn't know I was still awake when you brushed your lips against my hair & stumbled out of the nursery blindly over my red metal truck.

It isn't that I don't love you, Dad. I guess I do when there isn't anything else going on. But I guess it's silly to expect you to be up on things like the younger generation. I'll try not to be impatient with you, or nervous, or bother you too much with my worries. I'll try to be a better son, Dad, though it would be a lot easier if you used a little horse sense.

Apology at bedtime

Listen, Son: I am saying this to you as you lie asleep, one little paw crumpled under your cheek, blond curls on your damp forehead.

I have just stolen into your room alone. Just a few minutes ago, as I sat reading my paper in the library, a hot, stifling wave of remorse swept over me. I could not resist it. Guiltily I came to your bedside.

These things I was thinking, Son; I had been cross. I scolded you as you were dressing for school because you gave your face just a dab with a towel.

I took you to task for not cleaning your shoes. I called out angrily when I found that you had thrown some of your things on the floor.

At breakfast, too, I found fault. You spilled things. You put your elbows on the table. You spread butter too thick on your bread.

As you started off to play & I made for my car, you turned & waved your little hand and called, "Good-bye, Daddy!" & I frowned and said in reply, "Straighten your shoulders!"

Then it began all over again the late afternoon. As I came up the hill I spied you down on your knees playing marbles. There were holes in your stockings. I humiliated you before your boy friends by making you march ahead of me back to the house.

"Stockings are expensive—and if you had to buy them you would be more careful." Imagine that, Son, from a father! Such stupid silly logic.

Do you remember, later, when I was reading in the library, how you came in, softly, timidly, with a sort of hurt look in your eyes? When I glanced up over my paper, impatient at the interruption, you hesitated at the door. "What is it you want?" I snapped.

You said nothing, but ran across, in one tempestuous plunge, & threw your arms around my neck & kissed me, again & again, & your small arms tightened with an affection that God had set blooming in your heart & which even neglect could not wither. And then you were gone, pattering up the stairs.

Well, son, it was shortly afterward that my paper slipped from my hands & a terrible sickening fear came over me. Suddenly I saw my horrible selfishness, & I felt sick at heart.

What has habit been doing to me? The habit of complaining, of finding fault, of reprimanding, all of these were my reward to you for being only a small boy.

It was not that I did not love you; it was that I expected too much of youth. I was measuring you by the yardstick of my own age. Son, I am sorry. . . . I'll try not to let my impatience, my nervousness, my worries, muddle or conceal my love for you.

The father and son riddle

In our family it was always the custom to conceal bad news as long as possible. When my favorite uncle died while I was overseas, it was kept from me till I got home a year later. Illnesses were disguised, financial reverses glossed over, & I even learned to hide football bruises from my dad.

Usually, if a member of the family or a dear relative were at death's door, news was kept from us children in hope of a miraculous recovery. If a relative died, we often learned of it a year or two later when somebody dropped a word inadvertently about flowers for the grave.

So far as I can remember, nobody in our clan ever went quite so far as the Russ Colombo or the Jolson families, who have concealed from a mother the death of a son for months and years. An Iowa friend of Colombo's tells me that, the last time he heard, Russ's mother thought he was touring England, though he'd been dead for years.

My wife & I were enjoying our first visit to lovely Hawaii, one place which surpasses all advance notices. We were smothered with leis, we rode over the Pali, we tried to surfboard in on the long Pacific swells, fresh pineapples were delivered automatically in our rooms several times a day, we flew over to see the great crater of Mona Loa. We also took hula lessons under pressure from Bruce & Beatrice, the dance-mad editors of the *Ladies' Home Journal*.

We came home in a private lanai suite on the Lurline, a small piece of deck all our own, with the best of traveling companions in the next suite. While in Hawaii we first discovered that Quentin would be born later that year. It was Dr. Pete Hulford, a Cherokee boy who made good in Hawaii & married into one of the Five Families, who broke the good news to us.

When we landed at San Francisco & went to our room at the hotel & were washing our faces before going up to the Top of the Mark for one of the world's 10 greatest views, a dignified managerial gentleman knocked at the door & gravely handed me a telegram with 3 stars. I looked at him questioningly, knew it was bad news, & opened it.

It contained bad news: my father had died 6 days before, & my mother & sisters had decided not to inform me until I returned to the mainland. For one thing, they didn't think I could return in time for the funeral. For another, they didn't want me to fly back the 2,000 miles over water. And there was the old family tradition.

They hadn't cabled me when he fell ill, & they hadn't cabled when he was taken to the hospital. In fact, with the ancient family optimism, they had counted on his recovery. I heard later that 30 minutes before he died he was spoofing my red-haired sister Ruth about her remarkable hair-do.

I took the telegram across the room & into a blind corner & stood there a moment, trying to realize that I'd never again see my father, never again talk with him. Then I walked over to the window & looked out toward the bay & the bridge & the bold slash of geography & history, calm & consoling. But it took a long time.

There I stood again last summer, with my 2 young sons, looking at the same imperial scene. I remembered the yellow telegram with the cryptic symbol of the 3 stars, & I wondered where they would be when the final day of farewell came to us.

And I remembered, too, how my wife softened the impact of the harsh & stunning news with exactly the right words & her soothing voice, & how our friends reminded me that another conversation with him could not have enhanced my priceless heritage of admiration & respect & love for him.

Mothers & daughters communicate with each other better than do fathers & sons. Over the household tasks & in the sweet intimacy of feminine moments, they pass along, sometimes almost wordlessly, their female secrets. And so they pass along a great deal of civilization's stability.

But sons & fathers do not talk so easily with each other. In all nature there is no stranger relationship than that of a father with his son. They should unfold their thoughts oftener to each other, sweep aside all the "thou shalt nots" & "Son, you'd better," & reveal more fully their mutual discoveries & uncertainties.

* * *

My revolt against big parties is apt to flare up on New Year's Eve. Too often at midnight I half reluctantly embrace a comparatively strange woman on the dance floor, unable to reach my own wife at the sentimental moment.

The breakage among my favorite phonograph records is incredible. I suspect Junior sails 'em across the room at the record player to prove he's an untrammeled soul. (Or maybe it's his criticism of my corny taste in music.)

An enlightened young mother we know has at last stumbled on a year-round use for their old swimming pool. She keeps it drained and uses it as a play pen for her tots.

Much as I rebel against the fashion of calling every girl who has two eyes and a nose "pretty," I confess I've never seen a homely girl on a skating pond.

FAMILY LEFTOVERS

To spank or not to spank

One of these days we're going to be forced to make up our minds (& so will you!) whether to be (1) modern, streamlined parents with a chromium-plated smile for everything our children do, or (2) on the stern, old-fashioned side, with modifications, like the ones who made us toe the mark, or (3) fuddy-duddy, resigned parents who've given up the struggle or (4) parents who valiantly play by ear.

By that time our children will probably be married, & it won't matter much. Maybe we can then kibitz a little, if we're silly, telling them how to raise their kids. At best it's only a mournful consolation to know that some day they'll be gnashing their teeth & talking brats & cherubs to themselves, when theirs go modern à la 1960.

I know some parents who've given up the good fight to save their young a lot of bruises by telling 'em, "Please do this" & "Don't do that." In today's world, despite oodles of labor-saving machinery & the 40-hour week, fathers & mothers seem more exhausted than ever before in all history. There's a great temptation to relax, to be either (1) modern or (3) fuddy-duddy. The difference is often invisible to the naked eye.

All these gloomy thoughts pop up naturally after one of the thrice-a-year jamborees when our high-spirited young, both high school and collegiate, relax from their studies. But uppermost in my mind is the strikingly classical case of the college boy out west whose father asked him not to fly in bad weather on a chartered plane.

So Pop, a worried darling, bought him a railroad ticket &

with Mom drove him to the station. The boy pretended to get on the train, no doubt chuckling, poor kid, at how old-fashioned fathers & mothers still are about flying. When they dragged his body out of the shattered plane, he still had the ticket in his pocket.

I could cite illustrations closer to Iowa. We parents know our youngsters slicker us in many ways. Fortunately, it's usually in smaller things that don't end so tragically. Sometimes the tragedy is merely deferred a long time. And in an amazingly large percentage of cases the boys & girls snap out of it by some miracle & emerge with common sense, despite us.

Alas, most of us have had no previous experience as parents. We're new at the job. We're inexperienced with 5-year-olds & with 10-year-olds & with 15-year-olds & with 20-year-olds. Maybe if we have 5 or 6 children we're a little wiser with the later models. But by that time we're as busy as a cat on a tin roof.

Anyhow, by the time we're entitled to the rank of Able Parent, 2nd class, the kids can protect themselves in the clinches. They can exert more pressure on us than we can on them, & we no longer enjoy a 15-round debate. (None of this, of course, applies to *my* children.)

Maybe we've overglamorized our children. All our homes are full of kids 14 to 19 who are miniature Alan Ladds or Jane Russells or Cary Grants or Martha Rayes, until they find out different. How're you going to handle a potential Alan Ladd?

There's something wryly comical about a parent trying to checkmate Darwin's law of survival of the fittest by giving his children little lectures & pep talks. When I'm a father, the clever boy thinks, no son of mine will get away with what I do!

But he will! Each of us in our own generation has our moment of glamor—young love, intimations of immortality, tunes that haunt you for a lifetime—before the realistic aftermath, & I suppose it will always be so. It may be irritating to our elders, but we have fun, as the young & dauntless.

Well, our parents didn't have to worry so much about the Russians & the atoms & the Chinese, & they were fresher & more vibrant in the clinches. They had more time & energy to be stern, & probably they were as hard as nails. But did they really think they could do it all with spankings?

The theory of inconspicuous stowage

Maybe this Yuletide is exactly the right season to toss my Theory of Inconspicuous Stowage fearlessly into the limelight. I'm giving it the green light, with top priority over the Sex Column, & even above my hints to Ike on how to handle Nixon, Taft & Mac. (Both Macs, I mean.)

Simultaneously, I'll fire a broadside into the rival Doctrine of Constant Clutter, which is the implacable enemy of my Theory of Inconspicuous Stowage. If you're a tidy husband or an untidy wife, this is timely; some love to clutter with impunity under the sanctity of Noel.

To condense it into words of one or more syllables: The Theory of Inconspicuous Stowage contends that obnoxious objects should be placed low in the room, or in out-of-the-way corners, or hidden underneath, & never placed above smaller objects, & edged out as soon as possible toward the basement or attic, & thence to defenseless relatives or a white elephant sale.

I can illustrate this best with an example. Somebody gave us (as a sort of practical joke, maybe) a piece of modernistic statuary. It resembled 3 donkey shins tied together, tripod shape, & topped with the breastbone of an ostrich or cassowary. The b.w., a gallant & kindly gal, placed it conspicuously atop a table in the living room.

Stranger, those sun-bleached donkey shinbones dominated the room. Every time I saw 'em I started to crawl on hands & knees across the great Australian desert. But the life-force is strong in me; I edged it down to a lower coffee table, then to the floor, then into a corner behind the waste-basket, then atop a cedar chest in Junior's room, then in a corner behind a bookcase, & when I give it to the DM art center, nobody'll miss it.

Maybe I could illustrate more simply with a big fat Sunday newspaper. When our boys read it, they always drape the sport section atop a vase of chrysanthemums, the comics above the telephone & the bowl of salted peanuts, the society section on a reading lamp, the Iowa news on the phonograph record rack on the TV set, & the farm section on the coffee pot.

So concealed, these things assume sinister & menacing

shapes, topheavy & about to tumble on your toe or on a fragile vase or ashtray & break it. What's more, your living room & the rest of the house then remind you of a hotel lobby or an auction sale. Or like a collaborator's sitting room in a captured village ransacked by the Liberators. Terrific mess.

If this Theory of Inconspicuous Stowage wins a Nobel Prize, that won't be more than it deserves. Old Man Nobel has been tossing his money at far less important discoveries. This'll dawn on you gradually between trivia about love & sex. I believe the great American malady is (1) buying the wrong thing & (2) putting it in the wrong place.

Also, I want to warn Ike that if he doesn't assert himself when he moves into the White House, there'll always be (1) a pile of clothes near the front door, for the cleaner to pick up, (2) a pile of laundry at the side door, waiting for the driver, (3) some ginger ale bottles on the back porch, (4) papers & magazines at the foot of the cellar steps, & (5) some mending & alterations in the kitchen hall, headed toward the seamstress.

Actually, there'll not be a day of the week, Ike, when there won't be a pile or a stack or a bundle of something waiting in some corner of each room in the White House: laundry to be sorted, gadgets to be repaired, upstairs waste-baskets to be emptied.

And if you try to hide 'em in closets, they'll end up on your desk in your den, Ike, maybe right on your desk, all of 'em, especially if somebody's dropping in for a rubber of bridge. You'll be spending half of your time wandering around the White House straightening up the magazines or taking the children's jackets off the chandelier & removing their shoes from the East Room.

Unless you want the White House tourists to see everything cluttered and cockeyed, better begin today to hide or give away or throw away the things singularly dedicated to clutter. Some modernists of the throw-it-on-the-floor school think if you're tidy you'd better see a psychiatrist. But if you don't keep your barracks tidy, General, the whole family needs a psychiatrist.

Don't move, say cheese

In about 1,000 snapshots, I suppose you're lucky if 3 or 4 come out looking half as good as the enlargements you see displayed in the windows. But you're fond of the others, too, as parents are of their homelier children.

One of my projects for these long winter evenings (never half long enough) is to cull out the snapshots of myself which I don't think fit to be passed on to posterity.

I don't want any grandchildren looking at any snapshot of me in the bye and bye & saying, "Gosh, but Grandpa was a funny-looking duck!" By careful censorship & culling I think I can enhance their opinion of me considerably.

Even the homeliest man occasionally faces a happy combination of light, shadow, angle & lens which results in a flattering likeness. I've even found one of myself in which I think I resemble Spencer Tracy.

Somewhat.

A little.

Not much.

So far the most satisfactory picture that I've run across taken by my own hand is one of the b.g. & Junior, standing on a pier at Martha's Vineyard, holding a string of small fish they've just caught. That was years ago, & I haven't seen 'em so elated about fish since.

The best snapshots of the b.w. (and probably of most girls) are the ones in bathing suits. There's one which hangs in both my bedroom & office, showing her sunbathing on a lonely beach in Florida, which is probably the prize. I hung it there to remind her that I *have* taken her on a good vacation occasionally. One picture is worth 1,000 words sometimes.

Even the snapshot on the beach at Rehobeth, Delaware, then only a few weeks before the birth of our youngest child, isn't libelous. By an accident of sunlight & angle, it makes her look slim and bridal, & it's one of my favorites. But as I study my wife's snapshots, it dawns on me again that she doesn't really enjoy having her picture taken.

Though by no means a repulsive creature, she often puts

on a strained look as if she were the unwilling captive of the camera fiend. One snapshot of her taken in the Ozarks is the most eloquent commentary imaginable on a childish husband who always wants to stop & take pictures!

We seem to have all the usual family snapshots. One of each infant standing naked in the backyard. One taking a plunge in a large tub alongside the tennis court. And here's one of our youngest, a flashlight shot, showing him seated on the you-know-what, looking startled & a trifle indignant, as he well might be. Nowadays he wouldn't permit it; he'd probably smash the camera.

After a reel of film has been exposed, I always realize, too late, that nothing is so wasteful as a series of unplanned snapshots taken at random in "cute" or banal poses. One simple, unposed, uncluttered shot is worth a dozen of the artful, stiff contrived pictures.

Ten or 20 years from now, when the children are grown & scattered, it'll be painful to look at some of these pictures: the b.g. in a white snowsuit at the age of 2, sitting on her grandfather's doorstep; Junior with a football at the age of 3; & our youngest with a snowshovel & a puppy at Arlington, Va., with a fine 3-year-old grin.

And those snapshots taken during our honeymoon, on the high rocks overlooking the ocean. Those aren't too easy to look at even now, as one realizes with futile resentment that the years have raced by too swiftly. How sophisticated we thought we were then, & how immature we appear now, reveling in those golden days!

I can understand why some people don't want to look at pictures of their dearly beloved ones, after too many years have passed, & the beloved ones perhaps have passed, too. I've heard widows & widowers talk of burning up stacks of fond memories, snapshots caught like the figures on the Grecian urn. But they seldom do.

* * *

Maybe the new trend toward music and art is an attempt to fill our lives with souvenirs that won't eventually clutter the big attics people no longer have.

"If I had a homely daughter," confides Betty Comfort, eying the neon tree lights of a newfangled neighbor, "I'd persuade her that an intelligent eye, a sweet mouth and a soft voice make a plain girl more charming than a pretty one."

We've been experimenting in our household with one of those new nylon shirts. It can be washed in two minutes, dries in an hour, and is too warm for a man to wear in an overheated room. But my lady's verdict is: "Hurrah! It needn't be ironed!"

Ever since our honeymoon my dauntless wife has needled me sweetly to drink milk before bedtime instead of ginger ale or bean soup or lobster bisque. She never gives up, and to my surprise I find myself unyieldingly drinking milk, oftener and oftener.

To my intense amazement, our youngest was recently voted the neatest boy at a session of his Cub Scout troop. They've either got him hypnotized or their definition of "neatness" is broader than mine.

One of our village belles met Monsieur Dior, of Paris, at a big-town party, and he complimented her gallantly on her gown. "How I wish," she says wistfully, "I could have replied that I'd just run it up on my sewing machine!"

Only after we bought our ten-year-old a set of tools did we remember that we bought an identical set for Junior six years ago, and that he had it impartially distributed around the neighborhood by New Year's Day.

A bright young psychiatrist from the state university who lectured in our town recently said casually that it's healthy for children to have other relatives around besides their parents. This may make aunts and grannies and uncles more fashionable than they've been since the nineties.

Older men at the club often deplore that their money sooner or later falls into the hands of their innocent and guileless widows.

I don't see how they can avoid it unless they marry women eight or ten years older.

What few men ever suspect or admit: that perhaps fortyish women get the same sort of lift from young men that fortyish men get from young women. (What, from those half-baked young scamps?)

* * *

FOR MEN ONLY [I]

When you encounter your wife accidentally downtown and are agog at how pretty she looks . . . when you find Junior at sixteen years reading late in bed a book you read all night when you were twenty-six . . . when your small one discerns that the stern tantrum you put on for his benefit is partly spurious, and jollies you out of it . . . when you discover accidentally that your daughter has pasted in her memory book a note you wrote her . . . when your wife confesses in a burst of candor that she values your judgment and relies on it even when she argues stubbornly against it . . . then you wonder why you've never put your marriage certificate in a silver frame, or maybe gold.

✶ 2 ✶
The passing scene

PROLOGUE

Anybody miss their serenity?

Who ate up all the serenity? Big chunks of it were lying around everywhere, not so long ago, coast to coast. If you worried only one-tenth as much as you do today, you could be serene. On Main Street, or in Newport. But who's serene today? Are you serene? The poor aren't serene because they want to be rich, & the rich feel so poor!

Once upon a time you knew the way to heaven. What filled the route with detours? Did Darwin do it, the rascal? No matter how much you worry, you can't get serene. Twenty or more men & women in our town with good jobs, enough money & people who love 'em have gotten so un-serene they've lately taken electric or insulin shock treatments.

Who hid the serenity, the serenity our fathers & grandfathers, the immigrants & pioneers, enjoyed so unconsciously? Did Freud? They'd have bet the odds were 100 to 1 they'd go to heaven & not to hell. But their sons enjoy quite a tour of hell before middle-age. The more security they have, the more insecure they feel.

Our forebears knew they'd save enough money to support 'em in their old age. Or their relatives would shelter 'em in the attic when they began to dodder. Or they'd find a comfy rocker in the poorhouse. (Real security there!) Retire at 60 on $150! Then why aren't people serene with $90,000 of almost ripe 20-pay life insurance? Shall you blame Jung or Adler, or those dratted psychiatrists?

Somebody mislaid the serenity. That's for sure. Maybe that hellion Karl Marx did it. Here we were, all swinging deliciously in a hammock, & crash! Somebody cut the ropes. The jazz band struck up & drowned out the hymns. (People began to wriggle nervously on their airfoam mattresses.)

I think maybe Robert Ingersoll, that wicked atheist, spilled some of the serenity. Maybe a few lawyers helped with their unwritten laws, & so did alienists who proved that murderers are really saintly characters carried away by a whim. (Or did Alex Bell kill serenity with his phone?)

Who embezzled the serenity? Did Jay Gould do it with watered stock, or eagle-eyed financiers with oversize mergers & inflation? Why won't your insurance policy dollar buy your widow as much as the dollar you paid in premiums?

The varmints who muddled & stole our serenity (if they're the ones) didn't get very far with it. What profiteth it a man if he makes a billion & his grandson pays 5½ millions in alimony to a blonde? Is Reno the fountain of youth? Does that win the blonde some serenity? If she doesn't read too many books on investment? Or consult too many psychoanalysts or fortune-tellers?

I'm positive that somebody stole our serenity! You positive, too? Did Debs do it? I laid it down right over there when I was 11 years old, & the next morning it was gone. Caught a glimpse of it 8 years later at Fontarabie, near Biarritz, & the year after that at Zoppot, a suburb of Danzig. Then kaput.

Are you quite sure the serenity is all gone? Some of my friends swear they still see chunks or slivers of it several times a year; some of 'em even have it around the house. They say the Kaiser never scared it away, nor even Hitler. Some of the youngsters claim they're salvaging theirs, after seeing their elders kick serenity around.

What happened to the serenity of the pioneer & the immigrant? Did Franklin Roosevelt snatch away their serenity? Or did the Joneses steal your serenity, always half a lap ahead of you? Can you keep up? Or are you just a big mixed-up kid? Confused by gadgets?

I daresay the serenity is still lying around somewhere. We'll stumble on it any day. On Times Square or Locust Street, or in your own backyard. From the right smile, the right tune, the inevitable poem. Nobody stole your serenity, chum, nobody stole mine. Did we kick it away? There's the serenity, right over there, next to the courage. O immigrants & pioneers!

✻ ✻ ✻

We've enjoyed our yearly scramble with the youngsters on sleds and toboggans on the golf links. This knits the family together and keeps us young so long as I can nurse my sprains and bruises in middle-aged secrecy.

Short of paying 'em time-and-a-half, the best of the fourteen ways I've tried to keep our young home an evening during vacations is (1) chores, (2) home movies, (3) a hearth fire or (4) as punishment for staying out too late the night before. (TV might do the trick—if ours were the only set in town!)

My wife has, though she hides it, a college master's degree. But she can't remember which of our trio do or don't like grilled cheese, creamed mushrooms, oysters, scrambled eggs, spinach or pea soup. (I may have a memorandum plaque engraved for the kitchen stove.)

OUR TOWN

How to get a drink in Des Moines

(Two men enter, wearing convention badges.)
    TOM: We must be getting close to town, Bill. Here's the cemetery.
    BILL: Yeah. Gee, this is my first visit to Iowa. I wonder if we can get a drink in DM. Is it legal?

TOM: Sure. It's just the same as Davenport, where I come from. You ain't got a liquor book, huh?

BILL: You mean cocktail recipes and stuff?

TOM: No. No! A *liquor* book. A *permit!* A permit to buy liquor.

BILL: No. What do I have to do to get one, prove I can drink?

TOM: No, it's just part of the law. I guess it proves you're 21 or something.

BILL: I don't look that old, huh? Maybe I *shave* too close.

TOM: Oh, hell. I don't know *why* you have to have a book. You just do.

BILL: And then I go into a bar & wave this book & order a hooker of bourbon, huh?

TOM: No, the bars can't sell liquor. It's illegal! They just sell beer.

BILL: Then what the hell am I doin' with a *liquor* book? I thought you said we could get a drink in this town.

TOM: Look: It's very simple. Let's start over.

BILL: Okay. I don't have a liquor book.

TOM: Yeah. You gotta have a liquor book. We don't start *that* far back.

BILL: I get a liquor book. Okay. Now what?

TOM: Okay. You go into the liquor store. The state owns it.

BILL: Here we are in the liquor store. I order a shot of bourbon.

TOM: No, you hafta get a *bottle* of bourbon.

BILL: A *bottle?* Look, I don't wanna get plastered. I just want a little shot of bourbon

TOM: They won't sell you less than a pint!

BILL: I ain't got that much money with me.

TOM: Oh, well, in that case we'll just stop at the Key Club near the hotel & have a quick snort. I've got a bottle at the club.

BILL: But you said the bars can't sell liquor.

TOM: They don't *sell* it to me. They just *serve* it to me. It's my booze, & I'm a member of the club. So that's legal.

BILL: How about me? I stand there & watch you nip at it?

TOM: No, you're my guest, so they can serve you one, too.

BILL: I show 'em my liquor book, huh?

TOM: No, you don't need the liquor book now.

BILL: Tear it up, huh? Hey, look. I changed my mind. I'll just have a bottle o' beer.

TOM: Huh, uh; not here, in the club. They can't sell beer. It ain't legal.

BILL: You told me that's *all* they *could* sell!

TOM: Yeah, they can sell beer, but they can't keep liquor where beer is sold, & they're keeping my liquor, so they can't sell beer!

(Bill, who has been doing a slow burn, rumpling his hat & tie, all during this dialogue, starts walking slowly away in the direction from which they entered.)

TOM: Hey, Bill! Where you goin'? Des Moines is *this* way!

BILL: You go ahead & go to the convention. I ain't smart enough. I'm goin' back to Omaha and get *plastered*!

(They exit on opposite sides.)

A bad hat yells, me, me, me!

At a recent gala party in DM I was frightened by 2 female hats. They happened to be worn by 2 ladies I fondly admire, so it hurt even worse to be embarrassed by their headgear. Especially since each had obviously gone all out to wow & intimidate.

I happen to know that some wives buy fantastic hats & then suffer a change of heart & hide 'em so their husbands won't see 'em. So I was deeply moved by a plea from a Cedar Rapids lady: "Please describe & analyze the kind of hats which embarrass the men? Or maybe the kind that don't?"

Well, I'll try. These 2 hats were incredible. One of 'em rose in tiers like a Chinese pagoda, overwhelming its owner's piquant face; I almost laughed out loud. The other one half-hid one of our towns' loveliest faces, as if the hat were more important.

This hat saddened me so I could hardly munch my 11th shrimp on a toothpick. (Even my wife doesn't suspect I'm so sensitive.) But I did munch on bravely, turning to look at hatless women or women with modest, unobtrusive hats.

Many women, I know, applaud zany hats. Especially when worn by girls they don't like, or by pretty women whose winsomeness is obscured by the hat. They'll praise an unbecoming hat with a fervor which all but convinces the wistful victim. A bad hat yells, "Me, Me, Me!"

I know a few women of melodramatic inclinations who deliberately buy hats which they hope will shock & stun their girl friends. What the hats will do to innocent men, they don't give a darn. I doubt that a fantastic, overweening hat ever won an admiring glance from a man. A good hat murmurs, "She, she, she!"

What, madam, is the function of a lady's hat? Is it not to frame her beauty, to focus the eye on her charms? Surely its purpose is not to conceal & distort her charm, to veil her beauty, to make her a clown & a laughing stock?

Hats can be becoming. One day at the Embassy Club I espied a young matron whom I'd always regarded as a comely wench, but who barely missed being really pretty. But on this day of days she wore a simple round cloth (or straw?) hat with downturned brim which framed her face so perfectly that it suddenly dawned on me: She's beautiful.

I happen to know that Des Moines' collection of local belles, the Junior League, will soon wear to a luncheon a barrage of bad hats they've never had the nerve to flaunt openly, which will be auctioned off for charity. Every woman of means has scores of such hats; so have some women whose husbands can't afford 'em.

Even my b.w., who has strongly curbed her melodramatic inclinations with hats, has accumulated some unworn hats over the years. Some saleswoman blarneyed her into buying 'em, but in the stark light of the morning-after at home, she realized she'd been tricked.

So I'll try to tell you, Lovella: Men are embarrassed by women's hats which are more disguise than attire. The gal's the thing; the heck with the hat. Would a man wear a cork-topper (pith helmet) to a cocktail party? Then why should a woman wear a Mata Hari hat to a cocktail party?

Marlene Dietrich has to wear those slinky hats, it's expected of her. Why should an innocent DM matron imitate her, especially if she's prettier than Marlene, as so many DM women are? Why should a sweet DM girl wear a hat that Ava Gardner might wear to dramatize a dive into a goldfish pond?

My analysis, Lovella, is this: The hat must not overshadow the woman. It must not be an architectural structure. It must not be an edifice. It must not have an air of desperation. It must be demure, it must be modest, it must yield to the lady herself.

An ugly, conspicuous, presumptuous hat detracts from a woman's good looks, it conceals her beauty. It yells, "Look at me!" A becoming hat says, "Look at her, isn't she cute?" I made a mental note to ask that girl at the Embassy Club where I could buy one for the b.w. But I lost my nerve. Next time, maybe.

15 *innovations for our town*

1. Some of DM's more fascinating houses & gardens might be opened to the public once a month for 25c. Money to go to the owners' favorite charity. I know 3 or 4 as interesting as Charleston's or Williamsburg's prides.

2. Open up a couple of really attractive rest rooms with rocking chairs where out-of-town shoppers could rest their feet. Or powder their noses. Or even DM shoppers. Several small towns have 'em.

3. Why not imitate Stockholm's idea of adorning downtown corners with enormous low concrete flower pots filled with flowers from the city greenhouses? Even in cold weather they add a touch that makes you like the Swedes more.

4. A few of the town's wealthier dowagers ought to establish salons (and I don't mean saloons) where young writers, painters & other intellectuals could drop in for coffee, inspiration, chatter, sandwiches & sympathy every 2nd Tuesday or 3rd Wednesday.

5. Why not an occasional band concert atop those pretty canopies that surround the R & T and Younkers fronts? Small, lightweight musicians, of course. No commercials, maybe.

6. Establish 1 or 2 bus tours of the city a day. Might

convince visitors we have prettier sections than our desolate river front or the regions around the depots & tracks.

7. I think the downtown executives are overlooking a bet in not sending their groggy staffs up to the roofs for a little exercise, fresh air & recreation once a day. (But then I once wanted Ike to put an obstacle course for staff officers outside *his* headquarters!)

8. DM ought to copy the "promenade" so popular in Europe & South America. Band plays in the center of a square; girls walk around it in one direction, boys in the other, while the music plays. Good exercise, & they get a peep at each other.

9. Why not give a prize to the motorist who gets the lucky number on his parking summons? Collect $2 instead of $1, but from *everybody*; put the extra buck in the kitty. Drawings once a week. Might pep up what's a dreary business at best.

10. Couldn't we do something to spruce up those sloppy police uniforms we impose on our gallant gendarmes? They don't have to be so somber; we could try out Northwest Mounted red, or maybe the French combination of scarlet & horizon blue.

11. Somebody ought to revive the city bridge tournament. Probably oughta be duplicate bridge, of course, to eliminate the lucky breaks. Big silver cup for the winner *plus* the right to park near fire plugs.

12. Why not build up DM as a glittering place to spend week ends? Lots of people have thought of that individually, but one fairish attraction on Saturday night & Sunday would bring in the cowboys from northern Missouri & southern Minnesota.

13. I'm unalterably opposed to conical paper cups for ice cream sundaes & sodas. They spoil the taste for me, & I serve notice that no matter what others do, I'm going to eat 'em only out of glasses.

14. Our green corner mailboxes are almost invisible. I'm in favor of painting 'em yellow, or maybe in stripes like a referee's shirt. And why doesn't the US put important notices & bulletins on 'em in a special frame?

15. I wish one of our downtown bazaars would establish a "gadget" dept. like a concentrated version of Lewis & Conger's in NY. Where does a man go when he wants a lucite what-is-it? My passion for gadgets is inexhaustible; I can clear out some old ones to make room for new ones.

In our town

In our town we boast 15 or 20 gilt-edged social circles, or maybe a hundred. Each is definitely the town's top-dog inner circle. Though they overlap, they're clearly distinguishable under a microscope. Here are a few, not necessarily in order of rank:

Old Family: Names appear in Tacitus Hussey's 19th century local history. Used to own first grist mill or early saloon; have managed to hang on to something. Quite a few are related; must be careful whom you mimic; might be 2nd cousin once removed.

Big Money: Need $50,000 income to be comfortable in this circle. But to enliven their lives they dip lower. Adhere sturdily to McKinley-Taft-Harding tenets. Not ritzy; act as common as an old shoe—a $52 shoe.

Literary: Read books other than best sellers. Tendency toward sweetish cocktails. Wear odd jackets & pants, collect antiques. Not afraid to discuss a book; but such talk freezes good gossip at mixed parties.

Sorority: Held together by wives branded with same Greek letters. Husbands resigned to meeting semi-annually men they rarely see otherwise, & secretly enjoy it; gets 'em away from normal circle composed of their business associates.

Drinking: They brag erroneously they can hold it better'n anybody; they compare hangovers. Regard others as fuddy-duddies. Tend to re-affiliate around 40, on doctor's orders.

Musical: Can recognize & hum Shostakovich's 7th Symphony. Own good phonographs, large collections of classical records; dabble in swing lore. Gather to listen to symphony & opera broadcasts; even go to flesh & blood concerts.

Drake: Studied under Profs. Morehouse, Herriott, Ross & Morrow; wear white hats at Relays & remember who was football captain in '16 & '31. Tend to form annual rings like trunk of a tree.

Whimsical: Apt to do handstands or flip-flops in living room, play practical jokes or The Game, or go to Omaha or Kansas City for parties. Wives very patient with husbands, don't try to dominate openly. Secretly envied by more staid circles.

Solid Citizen: Feel others (even Old Family) are a bit

flighty. Sedate gait, somber clothes, hats worn straight atop heads. Plenty of insurance; spiritual kinship with Elihu Root; occasionally discuss the waltz, tariff & Teddy Roosevelt.

Hunting Crowd: Fortissimo during shooting season & immediately after. Thrive on pheasant, duck & wild rice. Some own a duck press or know where to borrow one. Lusty, robust & good skin coloring. On hunting trips even do some hunting.

Fashionable: Some new money, but not indispensable. Re-do houses often & outstrip Park Avenue on new didoes. First with Audrey Hepburn hair-dos & nylon shirts & dacron suits.

Activity: Key men, sparkplugs & madame chairmen of noble crusades. They lead flying wedges in good causes; have hypnotic eye & can squeeze out frugal victim's hidden checkbooks. Costly but useful.

Intellectual: Can pursue an abstract idea through layers of "on the other hand." Predominantly masculine. Conversation gallops headlong till someone says, "We must define our terms." Then they relax, agree on gradualism & progress "at a biological pace."

Sociable: Feel lonely unless they see 19 different people every few evenings, or the same people several times a week. Make a pretty thing of gregariousness, prevent us from becoming solitary ruminants. Carry the banner for the classic view that social life is the ultimate goal of all human endeavor.

Recognize these few samples? With lodges & their auxiliaries, golf & other clubs, teamsters' & other unions, Junior League & PEO & the like, they keep the evenings tolerably lively, & prevent us from wasting too much time reading or sleeping. But they make us miss a lot of good movies & broadcasts.

✳ ✳ ✳

My neighbor who sells life insurance tells me (after a cautious look in all directions) that a man with a nagging wife ought to pay higher premiums; he's likely to die younger.

Once a month I remind my Glamour Girl that she owes her remarkable good looks, at her advanced years, to her lucky merger with such a solicitous husband. She hasn't thought it funny yet, and I'm beginning to wonder if it is.

The man next door confides that in his household the spenders of the family income seem to overshadow and outrank his humbler role as its earner. The only way he can attract attention is by buying, to everybody's surprise, a new suit.

I admire an arrangement the collegians have worked out at the state university. When a man graduates, he can, by hanging his pin on a sophomore or junior girl, virtually prevent her from having any dates on the campus till he's ready to marry her. (So far as I know, she can't do that to him.)

My ambition now is to watch Junior outgrow his garments so I can then snatch 'em away from him for myself, as he snatches mine. Score so far: two bow ties, one topcoat.

Either at church or at our road-show theater I can tell instantly whether a woman sitting in front of me is pretty or not. If her hair is frizzed, two to one she's hard on the eye.

Plain or fancy casual kissing on New Year's Eve and at Valentine parties has become so popular in our town that even the unpopular men have colds the better part of the winter.

Our ten-year-old often compares me, as a father, tactfully but unfavorably with a neighbor who makes alleged homemade spaghetti with meat sauce. (In self-defense I'll have to unearth a better brand of tinned spaghetti than he uses.)

My greatest victory with our sophomore daughter: she now admits that I had her boy friends of two or three years ago sized up correctly. (But she insists I'm all wet about some of her more recent admirers.)

My neighbor with the high-geared family confesses he dares no longer meet the proud, stern eye of his ancestor in the oil painting over his fireplace. "Downtown I'm something of a celebrity," he complains, "but at home I'm only the clown who signs the checks."

I'm ready to concede my Dream Girl's point that toasted English muffins at breakfast are elegant, but that only a churl would eat roast-beef hash at 8 A.M. (Still, I'm a churl only once or twice a year.)

EAST COAST, WEST COAST

For New York armfuls of loose bloom

I take back every mean thing I've ever said about New York. It is a kingly, imperial, majestic metropolis, far surpassing any other I've seen, & it belongs to every American. It's high time to re-examine our prejudices & to confess our pride.

We needle New York because it awes us. We needle New York to please our neighbors, to bolster our self-esteem, to avenge real or fancied slights, to atone for our follies & extravagances. But deep in our hearts we know New York is a miracle.

Every time I've visited New York, until recently, I've become again the overwhelmed teen-age boy of my first visit. Defiantly & stubbornly I've declined to be impressed, & while enjoying its pleasures I've hunted flaws in its magnificence.

Today I'm no longer afraid of New York's massiveness & my loneliness, & I see her at the height of her power—the last metropolis still unbeaten & unafraid, the freest city on earth, a fortress of courage, imagination & creativeness.

In the joy of my return to Iowa from the war, I wrote something faintly patronizing about New York. Someone sent the column to an Iowa boy on a warship in the Pacific, & he showed it to his shipmates from New York.

Soon I received a letter signed by a dozen gobs from New York. The gist of the letter was: "Izzatso?!! How come? Sez you!"

I wish those New York gobs could see this letter. At last I realize the error of my ways.

Paris has something that's still tentative & embryonic in New York, & there's a historic grandeur in Rome that New York can't attain for perhaps another thousand years. As for the others I've seen—London, Moscow, Vienna, Buenos Aires, Leningrad, Rio, Berlin, Stockholm, Copenhagen, Brussels, Amsterdam—each has its own magnificence, but not New York's.

New York is the most vigorous, most various, most untrammeled. It flings out its bridges, tunnels & highways with titanic abandon. It has more different kinds of people thinking more different kinds of thoughts & enmeshed in more different kinds of things. It's inner life has delicacy, subtlety & beauty, too.

New Yorkers are no longer provincial. On my first visit as a boy, a New York ticket agent asked me if Iowans weren't worried about Mexican border raids. Others seemed uncertain which side of the Rockies we lived on.

Since then New York has sent 1½ million men to 2 wars, & on this visit a New York taxi driver asked me if I were acquainted in Solon, Ia. "I visited one of my war buddies out there," he said. "Drove out in my cab. Great little place!"

New Yorkers, no longer quite so rushed as they used to be, are as friendly as people in an Iowa town of 2,000. They have a romantic interest in people from the great open spaces, people who have to do with cows & tractors.

We can learn a lot from them about tolerance. They are not suspicious of strangers, nor of strange foibles or rituals. A man in a turban or a silk hat scarcely gets a second glance unless he's advertising a new curry or seafood restaurant.

Her streets & buildings are incredibly clean. Every block for scores of miles of streets is a museum, an exposition, a world's fair. Too many of our best Iowa brains, alas, slip away & go off to help make New York greater.

Of course, I reserve the right to needle New York again in the future, just as I reserve the right to needle DM. For New York belongs to the republic, just as DM belongs to Iowa. But it'll be affectionate needling.

New York, I throw you armfuls of loose bloom. I kiss your brow, I hug you to my chest, I will defend you from captious critics. You are a wonderful town to visit. (But I still wouldn't want to live there!)

Carmel by the sea

Probably they eat more snails in Carmel, California, than anywhere else in the USA. It is a strange town, or village, as it likes to think of itself despite its 5,000 people. In some ways it is the strangest town I visited in the far west. In a way I wish every Iowa county seat could imitate Carmel a trifle.

Carmel is a little like Provincetown, on Cape Cod, but ritzier; more like Nantucket, without the sailing ship & harbor background. I couldn't find a mansion in the town. The houses are low & unostentatious unless their very simplicity is itself a sort of ostentation; low, dark, shrub-hidden.

They decline to put house numbers on their houses, in a brave stab at rural privacy. In turn, the government declines to deliver mail, until the houses are numbered. So there's a traffic jam near the PO every A.M. when the "Carmelites" go for their mail.

Both days we were there, it was foggy, & the inhabitants say it's foggy all summer & if they want to see the sun before 2 P.M. they have to drive 10 or 15 miles inland up the Carmel valley. But it seldom rains; they get a sort of spray or mist. They disdain to swim in the ocean (too much undertow), but use each other's swimming pools, some of 'em heated.

Probably the only ostentatious buildings in town are the public grade school, which resembles an expensive resort hotel & includes a delightful beamed auditorium, & the high school, which is somewhat like a high-priced dude ranch, with not one but two outdoor swimming pools.

In Carmel, they look down snobbishly on the snobs of Del Monte & the Monterey peninsula, where I'm told in spots it's virtually obligatory to build at least a $250,000 estate or stay away. Del Monte looks down on Carmel, too, but not very successfully; the Carmelites are people it isn't easy to snub.

I size up Carmel's residents—writers, artists, retired army &

navy officers, intellectuals, individualists, eccentrics, flower & garden & nature lovers, people of some means with fixed incomes— as people of great character who scorn to be swayed by such worldly considerations as sunshine, ocean swimming or mail deliveries; they want that Grade A village environment. And when they want to eat snails, nothing can stop 'em.

But you'll probably see no more $90 men's sport jackets anywhere else on earth except maybe at Newport & Southampton; in Carmel they buy good clothes. Carmel's shops are luxurious; they offer caviar, Sauce Robert, Hawaiian macadamia nuts, imported Graves & Rhine wines, tinned galantine of fowl (grouse & partridge); & such Frisco stores as Gump's & several New York stores keep rather drowsy branches open for prestige.

Across the bay you can see the famed Pebble Beach golf course, where a stranger with suitable credentials can play a round of golf for a total cost of around $12. But the Carmelites tend to look down on golf; anyhow, my host talked me out of 9 holes of golf (intended to impress the DM boys at the rathskeller) in favor of a dish of pizza on Monterey's sparkling wharf.

I'd rather walk along that wharf than play Pebble Beach anyhow, & save the $12. The fishermen bring in some fearful fish with eyes bulging out like scotch-taped marbles, but very tasty. Carmel has no saloons or bars, at least none I could find on a midnight stroll; the people strike me as proper, 2-cocktail people.

Carmel's flowers just about knock your eye out. The mist & fog, plus the afternoon sunshine, seem exactly right for the most lush & profuse growth of hedges & shrubs you ever saw, & begonias (in numberless varieties) & flowers of all sorts. Some inhabitants spend all their time (1) gardening & (2) shopping for souvenirs and antiques. They keep on gardening after dark under artificial lights.

Meanwhile, the writers & painters who gave the village its first shot in the arm seem to find its present atmosphere a shade too worldly, and are moving out a few miles to less stylish environs. They'd rather take their Bach at home on phonographs than dress up for Carmel's Bach concerts.

Carmel baffled me a little; maybe in a month I could fathom its secrets. But on the surface & off the cuff it's enchanting, & some day you might visit it yourself & shop at the Inn—run by a happy expatriate Iowan.

* * *

"I've almost convinced my wife it pays to be late to dinner parties," boasts Peter Comfort, hanging his dark overcoat out to air. "That way we miss one or two rounds of drinks before dinner and can still taste the food's flavor when we sit down to eat."

I gather that the public schools in our town don't have enough time to teach the kids to spell, because they've got to hurry and train 'em all how to be radio announcers and columnists.

The only woman in our block with two servants is regularly cut down to size by the young matron across the street, who entertains twice as well and twice as often without any servants.

Some of our town's sillier parents hope to elevate their brats to the aristocracy in one generation by never giving 'em any chores to do. (A child without chores is a part-time orphan and often a full-time pest.)

I guess I shouldn't have criticized Junior so flatly for spending eighteen minutes in my bathroom the other evening. I realized how wrong it was of me when he clocked me at thirty-five minutes immediately afterward.

The man next door tells me that in the hours he has to spend arguing with his teen-agers about their dates and homing hours, he could read fifty good books a year or see two good movies a week.

It's an uphill battle, but my Glamour Girl is trying to convince me that every time I eat eight ounces of something I like, it'll put an extra pound of weight on me.

It must be ten years since any boy in our block has earned a gold watch by not smoking till he was twenty-one. But you can occasionally get a juvenile genius to go a whole day without cigarettes by threatening to ground him from the family car.

ST. PATRICK &
THE CHATTERBOXES

Blarney on St. Patrick's Day

When I was a boy I always took it for granted that all the Irish were aristocrats. Next door to us lived a family of proud Irish, 9 of 'em in a 3-bedroom house, & they always acted as if the next mail would bring 'em a trunkful of gold.

I remember the one who was my age. He had invented a new way of running; you didn't have to move your legs, they moved themselves. He graciously taught me how. You kept erect from the waist up, & you merely let your legs swing independently with giant strides, especially downhill.

The Irish in our neighborhood were all good athletes. Whenever anybody on the vacant lot on University Avenue hit a home run with the bases full, it turned out he was Irish. At least if he was Irish, you soon heard about it. And they had me convinced that the 2 greatest ball players on earth were named O'Doul & O'Toole.

All the Irish girls were lovely. They had that faraway, soulful look in the eyes, as if elfin sprites whispered in their ears; or the merry look. Most of the pretty girls in our neighborhood were Irish—Myrtle Adair & Annabelle Douglas & Louise Ashley & Honore McCune & Louise Bullington. Something about 'em turned your head, & it was more fun to get your face slapped by them than to kiss ordinary girls.

The Irish were marvelous singers. The year Halley's comet swished through the skies, we gathered to watch it from the hillside overlooking the river. Till the moon set we sang "We Were

Sailing Along on Moonlight Bay" & songs like that. It was the Irish voices that echoed out boldest across the valley.

As fighters the Irish were terrific, too. Around our school yard it was widely assumed that an Irish boy could always lick a non-Irish boy approximately 15 pounds heavier. One minute he was gay & playful, the next minute he was trying with deadly intensity to give you a black eye. Whether he gave one or got one, he forgot the fight quickly & wanted to be friends again, until the question of pugilistic dominance arose once more. It usually did.

When the Jewish boys organized a baseball team, they called it the Irish Brigade, with the name in big letters on the chests of their cotton shirts. Once they even got Faber O'Hara to pitch for 'em. That was a day for the Irish minstrels. O'Hara had an out-curve clear over to the 3rd-base line & he hitched up his pants gallantly before & after every pitch, & he struck out 17 of Bert McGrane's Hillsiders. Or maybe that was another day & another team.

Around the Irish households there was often a magic touch of happiness. The kids were allowed to have more fun. We heard the family of 9 next door lived on $20 a week, but they didn't worry. Probably one of 'em is in the movies now & another has struck oil. In their houses there was more give & take. They were more relaxed. Naturally all the German, Jewish, Swedish, Italian & native (that is, 2nd generation) boys tried to date the Irish girls. And the Irish boys dated everybody.

The Irish were marvelous story-tellers, too. Years later, I was reminded of this on a short cruise on the liner America, her maiden voyage. On a hot night 3 Irish congressmen & 2 Irish judges kept us on deck all night reciting strange & comical tales more eloquently than any I've heard since. We were all in shorts & pajamas, & every story reminded 'em of a better one. Joe Casey the Great was moderator, & he dealt fairly with the Irish from Boston, Philly & New York. But he, himself, was from Boston, so he favored Boston a little.

Maybe all this sounds like a lot of blarney. No, it comes from the heart, a sober & envious tribute. The strain of Irish in our family is, alas, almost negligible. But not quite. Sometimes I remind our young that through their Great-Grandmother Owen they are descendants of Irish kings. If the Irish blarney us 364 days a year, why can't we blarney them on the natal day of Patrick the Saint? Long life & success to the Irish! Maybe I'll reprint this column every year by popular demand, especially from the Irish. The green necktie I'll wear tomorrow is no empty gesture.

Bevy of chatterboxes

Either people are getting long-winded or else our talent for conversation is dwindling. You hear more monologs & fewer conversations. Some people's idea of conversation is a 40-minute lecture without stereopticon slides.

I think civilized people should limit their flow of words. Conversation should be fired in short bursts; 50 or 100 words in a burst is enough. Anybody who talks steadily for more than a minute is in danger of boring somebody. He should let them spout too.

In a really fascinating conversation among 6 skilled talkers, I notice that in a 10-minute stretch the conversational ball changes hands 30 times. Nobody will carry it for more than 2 or 3 short sentences at a time, nor for more than 100 words, & each of the 6 will talk just about an equal fraction of the 10 minutes.

Even a man who's just back from an exciting trip to Africa, & who was chased by a lion into a ravishing blonde's boudoir in Cairo, shouldn't take an uninterrupted 15 or 30 minutes to tell about it. He should pause every 30 or 40 seconds & let somebody ask him a foolish question like "Were you frightened?" (Or even pause to let a nervous listener tell how a blonde chased *him* out of her boudoir in KC.)

People seem to get more garrulous around 40. Everybody wants to talk at once & nobody wants to listen. Almost nobody, I mean; usually the precious listeners are the most popular people in any circle.

I used to think that women were the worst; but I'll be hornswoggled if I don't encounter men occasionally who'd talk all evening if you didn't walk away from 'em & try to fence with the lonely redhead in the corner, or go out & whistle on the front steps.

But some women do make a bewilderingly fancy embroidery of the most ordinary conversation. You may love their voice & intonation, it may be sheer music, but you do wish it weren't non-stop. I know a woman who can recite the big adventure of her day —when she steps out her front door to pick up the morning paper— & make it seem like a Norse saga.

She'll give you the meteorological, botanical, psychological, fiscal, sociological, anthropological, misanthropic, introspective & poetic slant; what her mother-in-law might have said; which neighbor's house needs painting; & at the end of 40 minutes she'll be telling you what her kid brother said on D-day.

One trouble with these marathon mumblers is that something they say reminds you of a bright tidbit you're dying to get off, but by the time they're dried up, you've forgotten what it was you meant to say, & the upshot is that you feel mentally constipated & thwarted all evening.

I can say flatly that after somebody's held forth for an uninterrupted 60 seconds of discourse, it isn't rude to interrupt. You simply wedge in with "Sorry, but that reminds me of the time Calvin Coolidge said I was the prettiest girl at Smith college."

Some people are afflicted with "total recall." They can remember which girdle they were wearing when their hairdresser told 'em that Sophie Chumleigh's husband had been seen getting his fingers manicured by a Chicago blonde at the Drake hotel, & what the wind velocity was, & who was pitching.

I suggest you prune out some of the details. The point is, did the Cairo blonde shoot the lion, or did your uncle make the million $$$, or did you slap his face? If you sense any strong demand for details, you can elaborate later.

A good conversation should resemble a game of tennis doubles, with the ball skimming back & forth over the net, & occasionally being knocked out of the court or fluffed, & somebody slashing a brilliant stroke or falling flat on his face. Mixed doubles is even better; women add a lot—but better under 100 words in one rally.

But why am I telling you all this? Frankly, it isn't *your* long-windedness I'm worrying about. It's my own garrulousness. Me, who used to be the best listener in our Great State, now find myself on gala evenings afflicted with a baleful zeal to be heard. I'm going to have to put a stop to *that!*

※ ※ ※

Our neighborhood's crustiest father is secretly buying a house for his newlywed daughter and her husband. Unbeknownst to them, he owns the mortgage, while they strain to make the monthly payments. But at the end of eight years they get back both the canceled mortgage and their payments.

While they've argued for twelve years whether to give big parties or little ones, the most argumentative pair of socialites in our town have gradually become indebted to nearly 250 other couples. So the husband automatically loses; now it's going to take a big, $2,000 party.

The man next door confides that his coed daughter has passed a five-pound box of bonbons around her sorority house at the state university, and now all he has to do is borrow money for a wedding of the sort his friends expect.

When it got cold in my basement bathroom this winter, I shaved and showered occasionally in the bathroom on the second floor. But when I counted seventeen toothbrushes for the three people who use it, and they began to use my razor on their shins, I retreated quietly underground again.

I'm in Dutch with some of our eleven-year-old's chums because I confided to their dads that he gets no weekly allowance till all his chores are checked off. But I'm winning my way back into their favor by paying 'em to do part of his chores.

One woman in our crowd has discovered an important secret: that a wife can be domineering and disagreeable in a sweet, charming way and make her husband love it. (She'll become the most imitated woman in our town.)

After the gala season of turkey and baked meats, I've got my lady-love half convinced that meat loaf is better'n venison, and better cold than hot. (This oughta save us $7 a month on food!)

Over the bridge table the other day we talked our kids over and discovered a new note of cheer in our teen-agers' romances: that the average "exclusive dating" agreement between a bobby-soxer and her mate lasts only six months. (If they can stand it that long, we can.)

Junior had six youngsters in our living room the other night, high-schoolers and collegians, all half lost in the blind alley of the cold wars. My heart thumped and my throat got all clogged up for 'em. All I could mutter was that their fathers and grandfathers were in the same boat and most of 'em came through okay.

MODERN DESIGN & MODERN WORKMEN

Furniture can ruin your morale

Before I throw away the data I gleaned at a furniture show I saw recently in Chicago, maybe I'd better congratulate DM's furniture stores. They've come around gracefully at last to modern furniture. The other day I noticed half the furniture displayed on the first floor of a big DM store was light, modern, cheerful, gay & graceful.

When that attractive dark-haired girl married me, one of the many things we agreed on was modern furniture. Both of us detested the heavy, bulky, overstuffed, chunky, dark, overwhelming chairs & tables & sofas.

We bought what modern furniture we could find to start

housekeeping. Not much of it, because the b.w. spent most of our money on drapes. Some of those early pieces were "modernistic" rather than modern; we've got rid of many of 'em; & now some of the rest need replacing.

So we're looking around. Instead of dark, grim, heavy mahogany & walnut & deep-tinted oak, there's glass furniture, & blond coffee tables & wrought iron furniture as graceful as a dancer, & unpadded plywood chairs more comfortable than some of the old ones a foot thick.

Presumably it's safe to replace it now. The earlier years of our children & their chums were partly (but zealously!) dedicated to wrecking our furniture, just as some of 'em now attempt earnestly to leave their fingerprints all over our white walls. But they're older now & not so mad at the furniture.

When we used to ask the salesman for "modern" furniture, they'd look at us as if we were screwy newlyweds. "Here's a late design," they'd tell us, pointing to a Thing with carved wood, fringes, tassels, deep velour cloth & fat legs with conspicuous casters in 'em.

We tried to buy some modern lamps, & it was worse: I finally brought 3 of 'em back by airplane from Buenos Aires & Rio, where the modern era began 2 decades sooner. One of 'em still stands on my desk at home as I write. DM's stores have plenty of modern lamps now, when we're all lamped up.

We'd bought a circular, revolving, blond coffee table, & for 20 years the smallfry have tried to wreck it by revolving it with their feet, sitting on & resting their boots on it. It has survived, with only 3 trips to the repair shop. This modern furniture, though light & simple, is rugged.

I was in an unnatural, grumpy mood while ogling the furniture: Too much smoking & drinking in Chicago & over-emphasis on irregular meals, late hours, sales spiels; too much standing on one foot, trying to admire some of the phony & zany designs; heavy dinners at midnight, no breakfast till lunch.

Rebelliously, I kept an eye open for a light, airy rocking chair, preferably one with blond cane back & seat, but I never found one. I think Americans never needed the rocking chair more than they need it today, to relax & let off steam, swaying back & forth, a cure for the fidgets.

How can people be impervious to their surroundings? If their rooms are darkly colored & badly lit, if their furniture is ponderous, thick & clumsy, if their pictures and drapes are somber, banal, devoid of the light touch of joy, how can the owners be anything but tufted, fringed & tasseled?

I remember a chair I bought which seemed ideal for the b.w. to sit in & be beautiful: One of those high fanbacked chairs, but a modernistic version. I could never get her to sit in it. "Try it yourself," she'd say. I did; it was the most uncomfortable chair I've ever bought; its seat shifted when you tried to relax. (We've kept part of it as a TV foot-rest.)

What has become of the furniture salesman whose day was made if he sold you a 3-piece "overstuffed" living room "suite"? Or was it "set"? I think those 3-piece "suites" retarded American civilization by decades. It took 2 or 3 people to move 'em for the vacuum. . . . If you've still got those, turn 'em in on some cheerful, light, breezy furniture, & begin to live.

Brave new world—200 h.p. surrey

My new automobile is giving me more pleasure than I expected. It's clustered with new gadgets (or gadgets at least new to me), & from some of 'em I get more kick than a boy with a new air-rifle. (You've probably enjoyed these gadgets for years & became blasé.)

Maybe my favorite gadget (& the one I use least of all) is the knob mechanism which raises the radio antenna when you push the knob in, & lowers it when you pull the knob out. This gives me a sense of power, exactly why I don't know.

Next I like the divider arm-rest in the rear seat. Of course, I never sit in the middle of the rear seat, & when I do I forget about the arm rest (or don't want it between me & my companion). But I've never had one before, & I like the looks of it, & the idea.

I'm fond too of the big glove compartment, large enough to hold a thermos bottle & some sandwiches, or a baseball glove, or a medium-sized kitten. And the squirter that washes the windshield—though I've never used *that*, either.

You can't start this car unless your automatic gear shift lever is in neutral. And when you do start it (merely by pushing the ignition key down a little), 3 red lights flash on to warn you if anything is amiss: (1) if your hand-brake is on; (2) if your oil pressure is too low; (3) if your generator isn't charging.

This makes your instrument panel look like a small Xmas tree, so it's a gala occasion each time you start the car, besides making you wonder what's wrong. Also, I like it when the radio goes off as soon as you switch off your ignition. (But you can turn it over to battery.)

I mourn the fact that the car doesn't have automatic window openers & closers; next time, I hope. Nor is there an automatic cigarette lighter, but that doesn't bother me (on my 17th cigaretteless day).

But the map light is almost strong enough to read by, & once the b.w. turned it on when I was typing at dusk. (She was driving, not I, as one reader seemed to think, who denounced me as a highway menace, writing while driving!)

This is a 4-door car (I've never liked 2-door cars with a front seat to lean forward & squeeze past, except that it's good for kids) & it has a radio speaker behind the rear seat, on the rear ledge; & I enjoy the music better coming from behind. And the back seat warms up better, too, with its own heat outlet.

Originally I vowed I didn't like the automatic gear shift. I was happy to shift gears all my life. But since I've driven this car, I've changed my mind; this shiftless car (no clutch pedal) is pleasant. And I like the back-up lights which illuminate the driveway when I back out of the garage.

Probably the most complex gadget on this new car is the radio. I don't really understand it yet. When I'm trying to get KRNT (or some other Iowa station) I find myself listening suddenly to Natchez or Cheyenne or Dayton. It's a "signal seeker" radio, sensitive as a Spanish brunette.

With one eye on the page of directions, I'll try to explain: You push the selector bar the first time around & the nearest & most powerful stations come on, till you find one you like. Then you twist the knob to the 2nd position, & the stations slightly farther, slightly weaker, come on. You can set the knob 5 times until you've a choice of the weakest & farthest stations within reach. Complex enough for me!

After struggling for years with a hand-wound clock, I appreciate the first electric auto clock I've ever seen that really works. Of course, the buggy has its faults: The red dot which tells you your country lights are on is concealed by the steering wheel. But I'm not discussing the faults; & it does have trip-mileage reading on the speedometer, a pet of mine.

Maybe I've skipped a few things, but as soon as I've fixed the antenna raiser knob so it'll really work, everything'll be hunky-dory. What more do I want on my next car? Automatic brakes & steering? Power seats? The window raiser knobs? Maybe a pencil sharpener & a phone? I hope this car's comfort will make a more enthusiastic cross-country motorist of the b.w.!

God bless my $20 carpenters

Every few years I plunge into some remodeling project around the old homestead. Each time I do this I remind myself not to remodel any more for another few years. A man with a long memory, inclined to bear a grudge, wouldn't ever remodel again.

Legend has it that our house used to be the old Witmer farmhouse. In those days the farm stretched south down to the Rock Island tracks. Before that there must have been a buffalo wallow by the Raccoon. Nature was unspoiled, unremodeled.

I shudder to think what Farmer Witmer would think if he returned & saw what has happened to his farmhouse in the 17 or 18 remodelings during the 16 years we've lived there. Even Doc Stutsman's family (who lived here before we did) would be surprised, & Will Riddle would be goggle-eyed.

Each remodeling kills a summer. It may involve only a few days or a few weeks' work, but that work always spreads over several months. We've remodeled the garage, the driveway, the attic, the bathrooms, the fence, the tennis court, the living room & the basement. Each meant a summer of commotion & disquiet.

My only reward for all the disturbance is that each time I become acquainted with a delightful group of workmen. They are philosophers, humorists, raconteurs. Their attitude toward life is easy, unhurried & altogether enviable.

I remember one bricklayer, a silvery-haired gentleman with the bearing of a college professor or an elderly colonel. He treated his helper as a colonel might treat a promising second lieutenant. The helper, in turn, did all the small chores & handed him his plasma & surgical tools like a nurse at a delicate operation with a great surgeon.

Sometimes I go a little jittery when I see 5 or 6 workmen on the place & realize that their wages are totaling from $50 to $70 a day—with the work going forward as calmly as a slow-motion picture. But shucks, I always say to myself, who am I to challenge the leisurely processes of the American way of life?

I could be mildly caustic about some of my adventures in remodeling & some of the peculiar improvisations of workmen who play by ear. But on second thought maybe I'd better wait till after my last remodeling job is ended. No sense putting ideas into the heads of the next contingent.

One mystery about workmen troubles me. Why are they so hostile to such grass as tries to grow on our lawn? Where the grass grows lushest, that's where they like to pile their sand & earth, as widely scattered as possible, & their wheelbarrows, boards, tools, tarpaulins. Is there a Pulitzer prize for the man who kills the most grass?

From the statesmen & the streamlined executives, modern workmen have borrowed the conference method. It is not a rare sight to see one man, with a hammer or other tool poised, ready to drive a nail or something, but waiting while 3 other workmen discuss his next move from every angle & give him the benefit of their advice. Four heads, after all, are better than one.

Workmen are only human, & occasionally they make mistakes. Like other specialists, they get paid for their mistakes. But unlike a doctor whose patient dies, they also get a chance to do it over, & they get paid for that also, even if it's wrong, too. Yet always with consummate grace & charm—you can't help loving the way they do it. (Of course, you wear your teeth down a bit just gnashing 'em.)

They take a boyish pride in splashing concrete around where it'll sharpen your lawnmower. They start out to build a basketball goal & end up with a structure that resembles the Brooklyn bridge. You ask 'em to sink garbage cans inconspicuously in concrete, & they end up with what appears to be a monument to Epicurus.

But who can object to such mishaps when they reveal such rich personalities, such philosophical fortitude, such eagerness to comfort & console? Well, it's 4:20 & time to put our tools away & get ready to leave promptly at 4:30. Tomorrow is another 7-hour day with 8-hour pay.

✳ ✳ ✳

Under a hail of criticism, our neighborhood's most caustic bridge player refuses to use his new automatic card shuffler. "Shuffling cards is the only exercise I get in an evening of bridge," he explains bitterly. (He's the same one who's declined to learn canasta.)

"When we're not invited to a big party," muses Betty Comfort, sneaking some empty bottles into the garbage can, "we're half torn between the chagrin of being omitted and the luxury of staying home."

Our youngest has been needling me to move his electric train off the chilly sleeping porch to the third-floor (attic) bedroom. My dream-girl objects: she doesn't want him tramping above her bedroom at 7 A.M. It cost me $80 for a new radiator.

Our dominant fifth-grader has invented a new seating arrangement for dinner so we can watch television while eating. I've accepted it experimentally—one day a week—provided my back is always toward the screen, and only if he turns the sound off during certain repulsive programs.

CANDY WAS DANDY

I used to be a soda-squirt myself

A few ex-soda-squirts want that somewhat rude title abolished. At first it struck me as a silly crusade. What's wrong anyhow with the term "soda-squirt"? Suddenly I remembered I'd once been a soda-squirt myself, & then I winced a little at this all too realistic monicker.

Undeniably, a boy who squirts soda can justly be called a soda-squirt. When I think of my all too-few days behind the many-fauceted marble fountain, I see once again the indignant face of a boy called Joe Hoffman when he first tasted a malted milk I'd concocted for him—my first.

Joe was the pride & joy of a solvent family in our neighborhood which thought him anemic, so they financed him to a thick malted milk every day. On the afternoon when I first made Joe a malted milk, my first day on duty, I had reached the age of 14 and never tasted a malted milk.

On my princely allowance of 10 cents, I'd had other fish to fry. So I airily scooped some ice cream into the metal mixer, squirted in some bubble water, & set it on the buzzer. When Joe tasted it, his eyes grew wide with horror.

"Water!" he cried. "You've made my malted milk with water! Milk! I want milk!" Well, I'd absently confused his malted milk with a soda. So I made him an extra thick one with milk, & ate myself, with considerable relish, the one he'd rejected.

Druggists in those days regarded with anguish the quantities of ice cream their soda-squirts could consume. Eventually this led to the female soda-squirt, on the theory that a girl can't eat so much ice cream. And we always used the extra big scoop for our special friends.

Ours was a neighborhood drug store & we as soda-squirts thought it was honorable to eat a gallon or 2 of ice cream a day, but dishonorable to steal cash. Downtown, I learned from a colleague who squirted at 6th & Locust Street, such high ethics did not prevail.

The soda-squirts at Olson's thought of their boss as a soulless corporation, & bragged how they'd slide a half-dollar (or even a silver dollar!) off the marble counter & into the dish-water, where they'd retrieve it at leisure. Some of these fellahs are now high in American business.

To be strictly truthful, the attack on the term "soda-squirt" isn't really fomenting a spontaneous frenzy among former soda-squirts. It's a press agent's pipe-dream: He's organizing something called "The Ancient & Honorable Guild of Former Soda Dispensers," & he craftily hopes to use the members to restore the chocolate ice cream soda to its ancient popularity.

I suspect that if they weren't striving to be so desperately manly & grownup, most of Iowa's beer-drinkers in their later teens would prefer a chocolate soda to a beer. If you put behind the counter a few soda-squirts who looked more like Esther Williams or Tyrone Power, I can see the young customers wolfing down 8 or 10 sodas at a sitting, to impress the soda-squirts & each other.

Maybe the soda fountains ought to adopt the old saloon tradition of offering every 4th ice cream soda free "on the house." Some of the sundaes are getting so tiny that it's no feat at all to eat 3 or 4 at a sitting, even if you're an old man past 20.

Why is it that when you sit down at a soda fountain nowadays, the soda-squirt always seems to have something more important on his mind than the trivial chore of concocting you a marshmallow-butterscotch sundae or an Evashevski special?

Maybe that's why people call him a soda-squirt. Ah, it's marvelous training, being a soda-squirt, like being a newspaper front-door delivery magnate. In fact, I think the neighborhood druggists should rotate the job among a large squad of soda-squirts, each working 2 3-hour shifts a week.

I'd like to get behind the fountain just once more & fix up a thick malted milk for Joe Hoffman: a quart of ice cream, a quart of milk, 4 ounces of malted powder, a cup of chocolate flavor, and make him eat it with a knife. Let's stroll down to the drug store, shall we?

Three for a penny

I no longer eat as much candy as I'd like to. But I *can* hark back to the glorious days of my boyhood when the candy counter in the neighborhood grocery store was a shrine, & the sky was the limit —the sky, & the number of pennies I clutched in my moist warm hand.

What has become of the candies of yesteryear? Do obscure grocers still sell those tiny tin frying pans, containing a candied version of a fried egg, & a miniature tin spoon to scoop it out?

Can the youngest generation still buy those candy bananas with a stronger banana flavor than any real banana, lurid yellow in color & of a remarkable power to stretch a foot or more in length? What of the chocolate-covered dumbbells at the end of small bitter sticks.

These nostalgic memories cropped up last night when the b.w., in a reminiscent mood, told of the time she swallowed a tin whistle that came as a prize with a piece of candy. (Perhaps that long-vanished whistle accounts for some of the bird notes in her voice.)

I remember the licorice whistles of childhood; the long licorice tubes, 3 for a cent—although there was one store, blocks away, that sold 5 for a cent; the rock candy clustered around a string, that had to be chipped with a hammer; the jawbreakers black on the outside, magicked gradually to pink & yellow & white as the outer layers melted away.

I was more impatient in those days, & could never manipulate a jawbreaker or a dumbbell as slowly nor derive as extensive enjoyment from them as my chums. . . . There was a girl in the 4th grade who could nurse a jawbreaker along from recess time until school was out. But I was under a compulsion to crunch them swiftly & thus lost the joys of leisurely mastication.

Our younger set no long eat rock candy, even with their whisky, as it was taken by our forefathers; but they still puff with a worldly air at chocolate cigars and pipes & peppermint cigarettes. I doubt that they pass around those candy hearts which bore those tender legends "I love you" & "You're my tootsie-wootsie."

Youngsters of the Great State still munch patriotically at corn candy. But where are the fragrant red wine balls of yesteryear? And those little red cinnamon-flavored pills that stained our lips crimson are now used, so the b.w. tells me, to color cooked apples.

It's years since I've seen one of those pink or yellow marshmallow fish, or one of those soft, sticky ice cream cones made of marshmallow. And where are the lemon drops of long ago? How happy we were as we risked our teeth on those tenacious chocolate rolls for a cent that soon rose to a nickel confection & eventually became a dime bar!

Our gambling instinct was first aroused by squares of taffy & butterscotch. If the first one contained a pink slip instead of a white one, the next one was free, & so on. The day I won 5 of them for a penny still remains a red letter day. And the boy who won 11 for a cent was a 5th-grade hero for days, & was suspected of collusion with the grocer's son. Gone, so far as I know, are the old-fashioned jawbreakers, as tough & seductive a confection as ever chipped young teeth.

I can still remember the first nickel bar I ever bought, at the age of 10. It was a rich fudge with nutritious foreign substances imbedded, like tutti frutti. It haunted my dreams for a long time. That day I knew what it meant to be wealthy. And later, when lavish eras brought 10-cent candy bars, I knew poverty's pangs of envy.

My eyes I think were a trifle moist when I thought of those little tin frying pans with the artful candy egg. And I thought I noticed a catch in the b.w.'s voice as she recalled how those tiny spoons were apt to break before the egg was all scooped out.

How quickly fade from memory the gala moments of childhood, how soon erased are the easy joys of youth! Do you remember the pungent flavor of the crooked sticks of yellow wood tipped with lollypops—how you chewed it to shreds, bittersweet?

※ ※ ※

This winter I've beaten a strategic retreat from my old position that I'm the only one in the family who knows how to build a hearth fire. Junior and our youngest have had a chance to tote logs, and boast their skill, and we've had more fires in the fireplace than ever in our family history.

Our kitchen's remodeling has now been held up five years because my b.w. insists on cutting a new door into the dining room. I argue the two doors through the pantry are as good as they ever were, and if I'm stubborn enough I may yet save myself a couple of thousand.

All that giggling around our house turned out to be a scheme my wife and daughter were scheming: to present me with *four* separate and complete sets of house, car and office keys for my birthday. (And just because somebody has mislaid two sets of my keys this winter.)

I've tried hard to applaud our daughter's new short (*Short!*) hair bob, much as I've always admired her long red tresses. Secretly, though, I think it's first-degree mayhem when one of the talented girls around the sorority house goes on the loose with a pair of scissors.

"I've admired a row of seven fancy matching bottles on our bathroom shelf for twelve years," confides Peter Comfort, shoveling a path through a recalcitrant neighbor's snowdrifts, "till I discovered accidentally that there's never been anything in 'em. I've now retired 'em to the top shelf of the linen closet."

I ADVISE
THE JUNE GRADUATE

Free advice to the grads

My conscience hurts because this year I've declined to make graduation speeches at some 130 Iowa high schools. I simply don't like to make speeches. Maybe I can condense here today what I might have said, better than while squirming under the solemn eyes of a gym or auditorium full of pupils & parents.

Graduates: First, be sure to get snapshots of yourselves in cap & gown. Preferably standing in front of a lilac bush, or the high school door, or at your own front porch. Some day that snapshot will be worth $100 to you. (You might hold a pretty girl's hand if you can.)

Today you can begin to treat grownups as your equals, the way they treat each other. If you've felt superior to 'em, more knowing than they, banish that illusion. They also know a thing or two. And don't stay at the other extreme, where older people get you down & make you crawl into your shell. You're now a little older yourself.

Especially, begin to treat your father & mother like contemporaries. They'll enjoy it. Actually, they aren't much older than you. They've learned a lot by trial & error, & all they really want is to save you a few of the bruises where they still have scars.

I call especially on you sons to get closer to your fathers. The father-&-son relationship can be one of the most baffling in all nature. (Among highbrows & lowbrows, rich & poor alike.) Mothers & daughters work theirs out better. One of the beauties of farm life is that fathers & sons grow up closer together. You'll appreciate your dad more when you're 30, but why waste 12 years?

In graduation speeches I used to urge the shocked girls & boys to read a good book a week. Today I'll lower my sights & make it 10 pages of a good book every day. Reading isn't a chore; it's your rare privilege to match wits with the best minds, like chatting with a Big Brain you meet somewhere.

Keep a notebook in which you jot down the books & authors you read, with your own criticism & summary in 50 words. (Justice Oliver Wendell Holmes did that for 50 years.) Also read your newspaper & several magazines regularly. Patronize your nearest library. This is your world; don't let it mystify you; books help solve the puzzle, decipher the riddle.

Toss your major prejudices into the ashcan. (Cling to the little ones, if you must!) Most prejudices—against strangers, foreigners, religions, people hard to understand—are based on fear. But what have *you* got to be afraid of? You lucky stiff, you're an American! The higher the intelligence, the fewer the prejudices.

Go to college if you can. In most lives the college years are the greatest years, & the most fun. But if you can't, don't let it get you down; 100 good books can make you smarter than a college grad. Keep those high school ties; write letters if you're away; have a class reunion often.

I suggest that you adopt the view that life can be filled with ecstasy & rapture, even the simplest life. Any moron knows life plagues you with worries, distresses, ills & disappointments, & that at the end of it you die. Appetite is infinite, realization is limited. But joy & ecstasy are there for you; that's the only possible civilized view.

Be an individualist; cultivate your own sound viewpoints. Be a bit of a conformist, too—about 50-50. Don't let the views of the stuffy or pompous awe or stampede you. Differ, if you wish, but always politely. Politeness is diplomacy among individuals. Even at the wheel of a car, be polite.

Keep fit; don't abuse your body; there are no spare parts. Keep up your interest in sports & church. Nowadays we live more & more the life of the mind, but the mind doesn't do well in a sluggish body. Keep fit all 3 ways & you'll find plenty of that ecstasy & joy in your work & in your marriage. (No school board ever had an easier way to save the $50 fee for a speech than by reading this aloud in lieu of the commencement oration; & the ceremony ends 30 blissful minutes sooner!)

50 *hints to this year's class*

You'd think the ideal time to advise graduates is at graduation time. But teachers tell me it's better to give 'em The Word in the winter, when they're more apt to read it, talk it over, & perhaps even discuss it in class. So hold on to your freshman caps!

1. Keep a diary, so you can watch your own maturing. 2. Remember that good posture is more attractive & valuable than expensive clothes. 3. Treat your pa & ma as good friends who're a little older.

4. Save a little money; you'll feel freer with $100 laid away. 5. Read magazines & newspapers regularly, especially articles & editorials. 6. Pick up a variety of indoor & outdoor hobbies. 7. Even if it hurts, be polite to all, especially the rude.

8. Don't forget, under our system you're the equal of any man or woman alive. 9. Learn to play a musical instrument, if it's only a phonograph. 10. Speak in a soft voice with clear enunciation if you want to be listened to.

11. Others have no mystical secrets for success hidden from you. 12. Be particularly polite while driving a car, when the nervous beast in man raises its ugly head. 13. Why drink liquor, unless a doctor orders you to? 14. A good book every 2 weeks doubles your mental stature; you needn't read every page.

15. What you'd spend on cigarettes will pay the premiums on a $5,000 insurance policy. 16. Don't be afraid to be alone an hour or 2 frequently, a chance to think. 17. Write down your own rules of conduct & plans.

18. Begin to buy some land as young as possible, or a town lot for your house. 19. Study the dictionary & the encyclopedia; they're full of gems. 20. There's no organized opposition to your ambitions & dreams.

21. Accept your military service calmly—it's part of life, like marriage & measles. 22. In your favorite sex, loyalty, diligence,

good disposition & intelligence are as important as good looks or cleverness. 23. Keep a serene mask on your face & people will think you know the answers.

24. Bring your friends home, where you can be yourself & irk nobody outside the family. 25. Adopt outdoor sports you can pursue all your life. 26. Be poised & confident even if you're uncertain inside.

27. Don't be irked by your brothers & sisters; they can't help acting that way, & you may irk them, too. 28. Write letters to your friends; it stimulates your viewpoint & character; anyhow, it's civilized. 29. Read history & biography especially, to put your own life in perspective.

30. Cherish your chores & duties; work is a blissful refuge. 31. Become a real authority on one interesting topic, even if it's only left-handed Confederate generals. 32. Don't castigate yourself; God put you here as you are, a link in the chain of life.

33. Linger close to nature; plant something & watch it grow. 34. Remember who you are with pride, & don't humble yourself to second-raters. 35. Live within your means & don't envy the rich; a Cadillac doesn't guarantee happiness. 36. Cultivate humor & enough indifference.

37. You'll probably be happier where you grew up than in some distant city. 38. Discuss your problems with the wisest & most important people in town; they'll be flattered, & helpful. 39. Dodge the hysteria about the "crisis"; we'll always be under foreign strains, but let's not exaggerate.

40. Drop in & call on people; they enjoy it. 41. You needn't act tough & cocky; that's the attitude of boys & girls empty & afraid inside. 42. Don't be afraid to like people & show it. 43. No matter what your private views on religion, go to church; it's good for you.

44. If you're willing to work, the sky's the limit for your career. 45. Remember other people have problems & uncertainties, too. 46. If you're not sure what you want to do, try out a dozen different jobs. 47. Prowl often through the shelves of your nearest library.

48. Don't talk too much. 49. Confide your problems to a trusty confidante, as in confessional; it reduces the strain. 50. Re-

member: courage is the supreme virtue. And give me some advice some time!

* * *

Another moment when I doubt the male is the more sensible sex: at a party on a warm summer night, with the men's necks enwrapped in eight thicknesses of cloth and the gals in low-cut strapless dresses. (Of course, the men wanted to stay home half nude in the first place!)

Ah, as a father I can hear the bell toll: The deep thinkers assert the child has now replaced the father as the central figure in the American family. Soon I'll have to ask Junior for the use of the car.

I've never been prouder of our boys than during our vacation trip, when they made not one overture to paste tourist stickers on our car windows. When they made derisive comments on the obscured car windows of sticker enthusiasts, I glowed.

The man next door tells me the modern wedding is a sheer miracle of brave-new-world organization. "If the gals are handy with their lists and invitations," he says, "the newlyweds can begin marriage with such a clutter of gadgets and bric-a-brac as took their parents twenty years to pile up!"

Around the bridge table last night, I gathered there's now a grave doubt among the ladies whether a wife doesn't have to work harder spending her husband's income and writing the checks than he does earning it. (I can name a few instances where they're right!)

Let 'em pile high the laurels for John Dewey, but I can name four or five saintly old maid schoolma'ams in our town who contributed far more to my modern education (and to our children's!) than John's Freudian disciples.

"What baffles and scares us men," says our town's last surviving affluent bachelor, "is the modern female theory of conversation—if you can't think of five things to say, then just say the same thing five times!"

I'm still arguing gamely for a yellow oval rug to cover the middle of the twenty-year-old living-room carpet before it wears through. But the Lady of the House says it'd kill her drapes. (She can't hook me for new drapes, too!)

One of the college boys in our block pauses in his lawn mowing long enough to give me The Word: We're menaced by Russia because we ignored Schopenhauer's and Spengler's warnings and became a petticoat republic. I asked him if he'd seen any Russian girls lately; they look strong enough to take over in Moscow.

RICH MAN, POOR MAN, BEGGAR MAN

Man of the year

He didn't get his picture on the front cover of any magazine, but he's my 1955 Significant Man. You'd better watch him like a hawk. He's just had his shoes half-soled a third time, & since his wife told him what coffee costs, he's almost quit using it. But he always wears a clean white shirt, with a white collar.

He happens to be an Iowan, but he could be mistaken for an Oregonian or a man from Maine. His salary to the naked eye is just about what it was, but he's thrilled to hear that the republic is doing well. He now gets at least 5 shaves from every blade.

Often somebody tells him we're going through a sensational boom, but he hasn't bought a new hat since the war. He's a fuss-budget about paying all or part of his bills on the 9th of every month. But he's mystified to find that his grocery bill is twice what it was in 1940, because he's eating fewer & poorer victuals. Yet he takes a patriotic pride in the knowledge that the Great State raises one-tenth of the republic's food.

Still, he's a great kidder, & laughs a lot over his sandwich & coffee at lunch, so everyone'll think he's well off. But he hesitates to speed up the spiral of inflation by asking for a raise. In fact, his boss, before hopping the Rock Island for 2 months in Arizona, told him frankly the business outlook was mixed. White Collar Man!

He used to hope that he could retire at 65 & live with his wife on their insurance money ($150 a month for life!) but now he's resigned to keep working till he's 84. He always figured that if he died suddenly, his insurance would take care of his wife & kids, but he realizes that at present-day prices, they'd need twice as much insurance, & he can't afford it.

At his office he isn't the top man, but he does more plain hard work than any of the bosses or other executives. That's because they have to do a lot of promotional, exploratory, institutional, public relations, good will, civic, charitable, experimental & contact work, besides fronting for the firm on committees & going to conventions. Without him the company would flop, the payroll & employees would droop & the customers would lump it.

I know him well. He lives in a house toward the edge of town that isn't as big as it looks, & it doesn't look big. Once he was confident he could pay his children's way through Dartmouth & Vassar, but now he's urging 'em to try for scholarships at Drake & Grinnell. Once a week, as if he'd just thought of it, he asks his wife if there aren't plenty of vitamins in margarine.

Since he's discovered he can't buy a good lunch downtown for much less than $1, he often skips his lunch, or takes a walk, or sneaks a hot dog over on Mulberry St. He envies the nerve of the white collar workers who carry lunch pails. It takes several million like him to keep the republic running, & if they quit, it would snarl things up like a railroad strike. But his kind never strike, not the great middle class.

Once a week he examines the mounting grocery bill on its wallhook in the kitchen & then he lectures his wife about the leftovers. "We could eat crackers & milk once or twice a week," he argues. His house needs plenty of repairs & paint, inside & out, but all he can afford is one coat on the front wall, his own dauby handiwork if you look closely.

He worries about the foreign situation, too. "It's mighty white of us," he says, "to help Europe with wheat & meat," & he wishes the farmers could grow more & sell more & help feed our indigent hungry brethren among the infidels. He hears this'll cost every family of 4, $1,600 a year, but he can't quite see how they can squeeze that out of his hide. (But they do!)

His brave new world has been delayed a bit, & they've taken in a roomer at his house, just to help out on the housing shortage. His wife is a white collar man's wife & she's beginning to show signs of it prematurely. She used to phone for a plumber if the bathroom went haywire, but now she phones her husband first.

Actually, his take-home salary has been cut in half by inflation, & when he realizes it more clearly, he'll be unhappy & even angry. But so far he's behaved like the republic's backbone or bonehead or something, & that's why he's my Man of the Year. God bless him.

I spy on a rich man

He wakes 45 minutes later than he would at home & takes the first of his day's 5 baths. Then he swims 4 lengths of the pool & takes another shower to wash off the sticky salt. He edges into the dining room for breakfast 2 minutes before 10 A.M. closing. Not the $1 extra fee, nor the extra tip, stop him from breakfast in his $50-a-day room, only the same gnawing sense of sin that bothers hundreds of other millionaires along Florida's golden coast.

Of the 300 kinds of flowers & plants around the hotel, he recognizes only poinsettias & palms, & their luxuriance baffles him. As he passes the haberdasher's, he pauses to buy a $15 sport shirt he doesn't need, but fights off the seductions of the $22 blue suede shoes with yellow crepe soles. He dons his 3rd costume of the day for 9 holes of golf, then takes his 3rd bath.

He phones his office up north & learns the mail is slow.

After a 4th change of clothes he hustles his wife to the beach terrace barely in time for the buffet lunch, with dancing, pausing at the broker's an instant to see how his stocks are acting. So far he has driven his $100 a week hired car about 3 miles a day.

After lunch he dozes briefly in his $75 a week cabana, & makes a date with the man in the next cabana to go fishing in a $50 chartered craft tomorrow. Vaguely baffled, he changes clothes a 5th time for his ritualistic dip in the blue ocean. First he bets $50 on the nose (with the cabana bookie) on a horse named Athlete's Foot, a cinch in the 5th at Hialeah.

He's been on this Florida beach 21 days, & has spent exactly 23 minutes in the ocean. As he emerges with sand between his toes, his wife tells him pertly his rhumba is static & old-hat & he'd better brush it up with a few Arthur Murray lessons. He has a sinful pang that he's overtipping the cabana boy, or else undertipping him.

After his 4th shower bath he hurries to his room for a 6th change of clothes & a cocktail date. As he passes the tennis courts & sees men his age playing, he vows he'll take a tennis lesson. He can't get a table in the cocktail patio, so retires to the ignominy of the grill-bar, convinced his sins are catching up with him.

Someone tells him there ought to be a psychiatrist at every Florida resort. His wife has had the flowers changed in their room again. He learns that Athlete's Foot came in 5th, & swears to give up horses. Their dinner at their hotel is all paid for (American plan), but his wife has cut 'em in with a group going to dine at a nearby gambling club. "I'm paying for 4 dinners," he muses, "& no appetite for 1."

To his horror, his wife is the only girl in the crowd without a white ermine wrap. He makes a mental note to tell her to buy one. He has a spasm of sin-guilt & tells her to have her portrait done in crayons for $75 at the hotel.

The man in the lavender dinner jacket talks learnedly about the best taxidermist for stuffing sailfish, & our hero vows he'll get a stuffed sailfish if he has to buy an unclaimed one from the taxidermist. He tips the waiter $5 & feels better.

Somebody spots a celebrity, who resembles a stuffed dolphin. Can all these dubs be millionaires, too! He is dressed a little more formally than he'd like. After dinner the party scoots upstairs to play roulette, but he's back early to sit in the lobby & watch other guests walk past, with a fishy stare.

His oysters, lobster & filet mignon sit heavily on his midriff. He worries about his weight. Here's a telegram from his son asking for some money. But now it's time for the midnight snack, & he ambles in to munch cold duck, rock crab, cold turkey & a little pastry. He wonders where that man bought those yellow pants. Maybe some of 'em aren't really millionaires? Just well-to-do men paying for this holiday out of savings? He feels a vague sin-guilt at being so far from his desk.

$13 a week for 13 wintry weeks

Of all my newspaper assignments, perhaps the one I remember most happily & tenderly came at the end of my first year as a reporter. The great-hearted Rex Large told me to play Santa to the poorest families I could find in town.

I tackled it with enthusiasm, but with the stipulation that I needn't wear make-up. We explored the bottomlands with expert guides & finally chose the biggest, poorest families we could find— one had 11 children—about 102 souls in all. They all had souls, lurking in lean bodies; not much more.

We called 'em the Saddest 13—a trifle dramatic, but we had to be dramatic to lure the $$$$ in a lean year. And we adopted a slogan—$13 a Week for 13 Wintry Weeks—that gave our crusade a finite goal. (Then, $13 was equal to about $30 now.)

Shacks that seemed to be abandoned tool sheds at 50 yards turned out on closer inspection to be homes. Some big families lived in 1 or 2 rooms, like Dixie plantation workers. Most of 'em needed shoes.

When word got around, we were besieged. That $169 looked like a life annuity to some of the permanently destitute. The social service workers threw up a skirmish line, & saved us from pitfalls. (One importunate family turned out to have a bigger income than I.)

We gathered quickly that the charity workers thought we

weren't scientific. Bless 'em, we weren't. They wanted quite rightly to protect givers & receivers from each other. I emerged with a respect for the intricacies of charity. But if you want to unload a little largesse on some poor family, don't let me or science stop you.

I was amazed at the number of donations that flowed in from all over Iowa. About one-third of the money came in small sums from scores of little towns. They may say mean things about DM, but they have a soft spot in their hearts for the old capital city.

A valiant squad of cynical collegians from Drake & students home from the state university for the holidays helped out on Christmas Eve. We ranged far & wide (it was Drake's caustic, warm-hearted Keg Pendy who carried the heaviest baskets of food, toys & clothes through the mud & snow) until long after midnight, putting into eager hands the first of the thirteen $13 checks.

It was almost 2 A.M. when we got back to the Xmas eve party out in University place. The sardonic Harold Andrews stood on a stair landing overlooking the entrance hall, poured a clear, tangy liquid into a tumbler until it was half full, & drank in a gulp a toast to Santa Claus & to Tiny Tim.

I've often wished we could assemble the 12 most beautiful Iowa girls we chose that year (1 from each congressional district, 1 from DM) to see how life has done 'em. (We had 11 congressmen from Iowa in those days instead of only 8.) I'd also like to know what life did to—or for—the Saddest 13.

Where are they now? What ever happened to the baby with the hambone? I hope he hit the jackpot & became a vice-president of a bank, or an auto dealer, or a great surgeon, or at the very least obtained a lucrative beer agency.

Our follow-up system isn't all it should be. Whenever we choose a prize baby or a spelling champ or a beauty queen or a deserving family, we ought to hand 'em a self-addressed post card with a modest request: "In 20 years please mail this to us & tell us how you're getting along." What a series of fine follow-up stories we'd get!

Anyhow, good luck to all the campaigns, drives & crusades for the poor this Christmas. May your donations match your generous impulses! The experts in charity tell me that even if our national income reaches 300 billion inflated $$$$ a year, the poor will still be with us. At least one daughter from each poor family always works for the luckiest people in town when she grows up. In a town like DM they're less than a brassie shot away from your well-trodden path; we're neighbors, the saddest 13 & the gladdest.

※ ※ ※

The girl next door with the new baby confides that she never really understood male psychology until she noticed her infant's change of behavior before and after feeding. "After all," she says, "men are just babies!"

One of the new mothers in Enchanted Acres, where we visit occasionally, was bragging about her brilliant eight-week-old son. "When I put the nipple in his mouth," she reports proudly, "he throws his hands over his head as if to say 'Look, Ma, no hands!'"

Secretly I feel when I'm teaching our fifteen-year-old to drive that he'll be a better driver than I am. But that doesn't reduce my nervous tension nor muffle my wrath when he occasionally makes a blunder which I make frequently.

What shocked our little circle was not that Betty MacDonald said teen-age children don't hate their parents, "just feel absolute contempt for them"; it was that she still remembered it against them long after they were married.

Our club's deepest thinker at the luncheon round table is worried again about spinsters and bachelors. "If the government wants to run everything," he demands, "why doesn't it help the lonely 10 million men and women who'd like to get married, but don't know how to capture a victim?"

On the way to catch our bus, my mild neighbor with the three-car garage tells me he's puzzled about his weight. "Why do I usually gain weight when I go on a diet alone," he asks, "but invariably lose ten pounds when my wife diets?"

In the boom days of the 1920's some of our town's sportsmen built the hilliest eighteen-hole golf course in this region. Lately some of their sons prefer to play only nine holes on a more level course, with motorized scooters.

I was touched to find all my overseas Army letters to my daughter tucked away in a box of her mementos. I wrote to her as if I were wooing her, and those letters contain some of the most hair-raising tales of my adventures I've yet encountered. She was just a credulous tot.

FROM BOOM TO BOOM

Ride on a roller-coaster

1929. Last year for the Browns was the year of their lives. LeRoy, a conscientious & talented laborer, made $1,262 in 1928. Despite 4 tots, they could buy a radio, a $90 car (used) & furniture. This year he's working about 2½ days a week, & gets some help from the overseer of the poor.

    1930. LeRoy Brown knocks at the swells' doors for odd jobs. He can't quite average $10 weekly with his tools & paint brushes. Their Lester (2) is anemic. LeRoy used to dress up Saturday evenings & Sundays; now he wears overalls even to the movies.

    1931. He helps ailing Cora Brown with her housework, doesn't putter with his invention any more. After paying $312.50, they're evicted from their $2,200 cottage. The lady whose lawn he mows gave 'em some dresses & things for the kids, but nothing fits. He's only 26, but looks 40.

    1932. Brown's in dutch. He gashed his foot with a sickle & yelled at the social service girl who inspected their groceries: "Get out! You ain't doin' me no favors!" Then he smacked little Irene when she wanted an ice cream cone. He despises the "pinks" on the riverfront, but yelled at Hoover in the parade, "Where's the chicken in *my* pot?"

1933. In the Brown's shack between river & tracks now live his in-laws, & Uncle Jared, who pays $2.50 a week. Upstairs live Cora's sister & husband, with 6 kids. They quarrel about the use of the washtub under the colored picture of FDR in the kitchen. Cora's having another baby.

1934. Brown walks 58 blocks for his free groceries, spends half his time getting relief. Questionnaires interfere with his odd jobs. In zero weather he wheeled 100 pounds of coal home 3 miles in a borrowed wheelbarrow. The birth control people suggest contraceptives; he can't afford 'em, a week's supply cost as much as 6 porkchops or 2 movie tickets.

April, 1935. A quandary for Brown: If he takes the more frequent jobs, he's edged off relief. When a job peters out, he's got to yell & scuffle to get back on. But he likes to hold forth about government & economics with his buddies on a job: "Work or no work, a government can't let people starve!"

October, 1935. Relief workers tell Brown things are better. He works steadily on projects, often 3 days a week. "Roosevelt's trying to please the rich guys now," he says. But in arguments with his landlord he swears by FDR. Their new baby is the healthiest of all. He has only 1 friend not on relief.

February, 1936. This is Brown's smoothest winter on relief. No kinks in the machinery now; he can do a few odd jobs & still get free groceries. His kids think everybody's on relief except a few movie heroes & a few crooks. "We live better'n some, anyhow," he tells 'em. The Brown kids go after bread & corn syrup the way LeRoy ate cake as a boy.

April. Frequently the Browns yearn vaguely for maybe a fried chicken or a steak or a steady job. Brown gets mad when told his minor ailments are imaginary. He doubts he'll ever be strong enough for a full day's work. Cora's a wiry semi-invalid, weighs 87 pounds. A WPA maid helps her 2 days a week with the kids when he has a job.

July. Uncle Jared brought home a case of beer for their most glorious 4th. LeRoy putters in his garden: "You gotta have vegetables." Brown's 31, feels 50. He no longer expects to get rich, but he likes to tell his skeptical oldest boy about the glories of

Steady Work, as Gramp once talked about the good old days when Wild Game was abundant on the prairies.

October. "If the capitalists can't cut it," he says, "it's up to the government." One day he trudged around the municipal golf links with borrowed clubs. His dogged, melancholy devotion to FDR persists, & he suspects revolution is a get-rich-quick scheme of the Reds & crooks. "Look at the Russians!" he says eloquently. He carries a frazzled clipping to prove that if all the wealth were divvied up, each worker'd get only $17 a week. "Shucks!" he says. "We get almost that much on relief!"

LeRoy Brown earned $3,607.75 before taxes in 1949, & pinched himself; it had always been his dream to earn over $3,600 in one year. But he's puzzled why it didn't buy him more.

The fall and rise of Mr. Jones

1929. The Joneses have closed two-thirds of their triplex apartment on Park Avenue. They're letting 3 of their servants go. For Jane's coming-out party they're spending only $800 instead of the $12,000 they'd planned.

1930. Friends of the Joneses kid 'em about their decision to give up the apartment & live on their little yacht. Jane attends a fashionable secretarial school. What a lark for Bob to work in a filling station! Jones has turned his 16-cylinder car in for a Ford.

1931. No demand for stenogs, so Jane quit her business course & is modeling. The Joneses sold their yacht & have retreated to their farm in Connecticut. Mrs. Jones found an excellent seamstress & is making over her 1929 dresses.

1932. Mr. Jones has found a job as agent for air conditioners. They're taking a 2-room apartment in town; rented their farm to a farmer, on shares. They were excited to get a crate of eggs from a cousin in Iowa & tickled pink by a crate of oranges from Mrs. Jones' Florida brother. But Jones is still strong for Hoover.

1933. The Joneses are riding the subway. Haven't hailed a taxi for months. Bob's dropped out of Yale; his legacy from

Granny dried up. Jane's singing in a speakeasy. Mr. Jones is sardonic about rugged individualism. He sold his farm to a successful novelist for a song.

1934. Incredibly, the Joneses admit they actually *know* some people on relief! Mr. Jones, once a $40,000-a-year v. p., has grown slightly radical. Jane is engaged to a Fordham man, a fine chap in a liquor firm. The Joneses (the people you once kept up with) toss their bills into the waste-basket unopened. He's a fiend about turning off lights, smokes only 3 a day & argues for FDR & old age pensions.

January, 1935. Things are thawing. Mr. Jones pawned his $600 shotgun to buy a new $125 suit & get into the thick of things. He actually got a dividend check for $35 & blew it on a party at the Versailles.

March. When Jones made a little killing in the market, Mrs. Jones insisted on taking Jane away on a 45-day cruise. Cheaper than keeping house, she claims. Bob's in a broker's office. He says the depression really ended in 1932.

November. Jane's broken her engagement with the Fordham man & eloped with Bob's classmate who has a Washington job. Mr. Jones is pretty bitter about Roosevelt who, he says, is retarding recovery. He's back in harness at $15,000 a year & bonuses. Mrs. J. stopped in at Bergdorf-Goodman's, first time in 6 years.

February, 1936. The Joneses are going to be in Florida through Easter. Mr. Jones has gained 15 pounds & loses his temper when he thinks of what the farmers are getting away with. Mrs. Jones is having her face lifted to remove every trace of the depression.

April. Mr. Jones has bought his yacht back for only $5,000 more than he got for it in 1931! A slick deal. Mrs. J. is doing over their apartment in Beekman Place. They cleaned up $35,000 in Studebaker, & turned their 6-month-old Studebaker in on a 12-cylinder car.

May. Mrs. Jones has had a nervous breakdown & is off on a $4,000 round-the-world cruise. Jane is out in Reno; she has fallen for an orchestra leader. Mr. Jones made a speech at the League of Vice Presidents against old age pensions.

June. Cramped on his 46-foot cruiser, Mr. Jones has turned it in on a 58-foot boat. He asserts that all the Republicans need to do to win in November is to come out strong with a candidate who stands for rugged individualism. He sent a check for $500 to the Liberty League, with a note about "that man in the White House." His blood pressure is up again.

By request, I reprint this case history of a nice family in the 1930's. In 1949 Jones earned $53,606 after taxes. . . . They did much better than DM's Smiths, who got back up to $11,485 in 1949, or the LeRoy Browns, who reached $3,607.75 after spending the 1930's on relief.

※ ※ ※

At last our luncheon club's No. 1 cynic got a unanimous vote when he told the soup-and-sandwich philosophers at the big round table a man may forget a woman who says, "No," but never the enigmatic lady who says, "Maybe."

Maybe I'm mulish, but I argue the way my Dream Girl fixes her hair for a shower bath is more fetching than the way she does it after her shower. She just looks at me pityingly.

My neighbor around the corner is trying to talk his daughter out of a divorce. "It's the modern strain," he explains, bribing the neighborhood problem tots to get out of his flowers. "She talks psychoanalysis and even divorce now, when my wife would have been content to go home to mother for a week end."

My victory of the year: I talked the Boss Lady into creating our own fantastic sandwiches several meals a week all summer. "That's the nearest we come," says Junior, chomping a four-incher, "to the thrill of killing our own buffalo and eating the sweetbreads."

I caught my Dream Girl tossing together a delicious chicken-and-broccoli dish plucked from the *Ladies' Home Journal* and involving nine cans in all. When I opened the nine cans for her I felt like a frontiersman trapping a raccoon or shooting a deer or wild turkey.

My bridge partner in our monthly inter-family tussle claims she observes traces of snobbery in her husband. "For most parties he argues an electric shave is close enough," she reveals, "but for certain hosts he always shaves skintight with a new blade."

Since boyhood I've eaten the yolks of my fried eggs at home with a spoon. But I never quite dared it in public until I saw columnist Joe Alsop ("country club's voice of doom") do it boldly in Hotel Willard's main dining room.

I've tried (perhaps too successfully) to obey my grandmother's advice on table manners: to pretend a surface indifference to food but always to take two helpings.

* * *

FOR MEN ONLY [II]

When your son and daughter give you a sharp tussle at the bridge table the first time . . . and your wife says something scathing about somebody she didn't know you disliked . . . and you see your picture on Junior's dresser . . . and your youngest chokes up with compassion and pity for the helpless . . . then you know you've attained something you don't need to lock in a safe-deposit box, and you decide to invite your favorite bachelor to dinner.

✳ 3 ✳
Your children & mine

PROLOGUE

Portrait of a modern baby at 1 year

He will be only 46 years old in the year 2000, when you & I will be aged 10,000. When he yells he pauses briefly to watch the effect. He likes to pluck hair from my chest by handfuls. He now has 5 front teeth.

Like 60,000 other babies in the Great State just 1 year old, what an amazing change he's undergone. Now he even has a butch haircut. Like the governor, his quick grin flashes on like a silent light. At meals he grows more temperamental.

But sometimes he eats placidly as a clubman. As yet, no resentment against his fanciful costumes. Later, maybe— He crawls like a crab on a sandy beach, often sideways. Loves to play with books. Maybe a highbrow?

Soon, by family tradition, he must be photographed in his gramp's British leather kit-bag. His pa & ma reluctantly gave up their big awkward dog to shield him from pawing, tongue-licking, from a nibble—who knows? During his baptismal he chattered like a magpie.

Now he does 100 pull-ups a day via crib & furniture. He takes a tentative bite at a piece of bric-a-brac & looks at his ma to see if she'll scold. He's fond of his 15-year-old uncle, whom he recognizes as a half-kindred spirit.

Like a man of the world he now drinks his milk from a cup. A la teen-ager, he wears blue jeans & dislikes to wear shoes. When he stands up in his crib, he doesn't quite know how to sit down.

Favorite toy: a red rubber scalp massager. The more gooey the food, the better he likes it. He calls almost everybody "da-da," very broadminded. A soft practice golf-ball fished up from Lake Okoboji is his pet mobile.

So far he has no fear of people. His 3rd favorite toy is a plastic spiked soap holder. He's good-natured because he thinks everybody loves him. His "bye-bye" has several meanings, of which 2 or 3 are his own secrets.

He dislikes fuss & commotion around him. His thighs still have those infantile pneumatic folds. One chum a month older races him, a toddle vs. a crawl stroke, across carpet or lawn.

He enjoys being tossed in the air by his pa; no fear of falling. Pat lives on a suburban street of small picture-book houses inhabited by babies & their caretakers. He scuffles with a football, half puzzled by its illogical bounces.

To people who don't pounce on him suddenly, he reacts friendlier. On his face, complacence shines while he's diapered. He dotes on a tub bath & tries to drink from the faucet.

Nowadays he sleeps 12 hours a night, with 2 one-hour day naps. But he gets a lot done the other 10 hours. Since spring arrived, he's toyed with a softball, too. At the moment he's not so enthusiastic for milk as he was.

But later he'll want 3 quarts daily. His newest word is "Hi," which may or may not mean hello. After a week's absence he forgets his gramps, but in 1 minute he remembers 'em.

His mom boasts that he says a word that sounds like "duck." But no 5-syllable words yet, even to her alert ears. He's quadrupled his weight in 1 year, but then he didn't weigh much at birth.

He seems to like animals & children more'n adults, but recognizes neighbors flatteringly. Often he crawls swiftly in determined pursuit of a vertical walker. His smile is like a French general's kiss, complete with a medal.

He has a knack of watching your face, especially your eyes, & may become a good listener. Rare type among grownups nowadays. His mom could dive across a 30-foot room if he tried to bite a starfish. His favorite baby-foods repel an adult.

Every day he runs into people with babies which his mother freely acknowledges are probably smarter. But he has a cagey look on his face himself, too. I gather his pa & ma get more fun out of him than they would from a new car. He seems to like them, too.

THE FIRST 5 YEARS

At 3 he's still a plaything

He retaliates vigorously at any chastisement, & sometimes socks me promptly even when I merely threaten to disagree with him. Around the house he appears much more important than when seen downtown. He is capable of astonishing tenderness.

In an argument his jaw thrusts out pugnaciously, but his lips quiver as if he were fighting back tears. In another few months I'll stop inviting him to punch me in the nose; he hits too hard already.

He pretends to be bashful when little girls kiss him, but I notice he doesn't flinch. Thus far he has locked me into my study three times with the outside latch, while trying to get in when I had the key turned inside. He can dawdle with his food half an hour & then eat an amazingly big meal in 3 minutes.

On the seesaw in the backyard, it annoys him when the b.g. keeps him up in the air just high enough so his feet can't touch the ground. When he leaps out of bed it sounds like a guncrew hitting the deck. His favorite phrase: "Shoot all the people!"

Once he sneaked a sip of beer from a glass someone had set down & now it's the only thing he sees grownups eating or drinking that he won't demand. I hope his dislike of beer will endure until his twenties.

After declining to sleep any longer in a baby bed, he has **twice** fallen out of his big bed & was found asleep on the floor **clear** under the bed. Last year he opened the icebox & doused his hair with cod liver oil; this year he gets into the refrigerator after the honey jar & helps himself; so he seems smarter.

Once when I tapped his knuckles smartly, because he persisted in eating spaghetti with his fingers, he merely held out his hand to be kissed & kept on eating with the bare fingers of the other hand.

Sartorially he is in a tough spot, being forced to wear such of his sister's outgrown clothes as a man can wear without too much indignity; so he has once or twice been on the borderline of the ridiculous. Still he is infinitely handsomer than I thought he ever would be when I first saw him at the age of 5 minutes. His sister tends to be literary and imaginative; he is philosophically & mechanically inclined.

He is quite blond, & I wonder if girls still will be preferring dark men when he grows up. When he kisses anyone good night, he insists on kissing on both cheeks, like a Frenchman. He demands a bath every night, too, no matter how lazy the grownups are.

He is gullible enough to let the b.g. swap him out of almost anything he has that she wants—for little in return. To compel his parents to promote him from his high-chair to a regular chair he went on a hunger strike.

He still sleeps with his giant teddy bear. He searches in vain for 4-leaf clovers, while his sister finds 'em under his nose. For relaxation he spends an hour in the old roadster, pushing the pedals, shaking the levers, turning on the heater. If he only knew it, he'll probably have that same roadster to drive at college, or what's left of it.

At 5 she's still from Eden

Today is her fifth birthday. She is a more complex & mature personage than I was at 15. Almost 50,000 children celebrate their fifth birthday in the Great State this year. How the generations ripple & flow. Notably cautious, she fears nothing. She dislikes pink & blue, adores purple passionately.

Her most intimate chums are a white yarn puppy & a white fur kitty. She listens to long explanations more attentively than anyone else I know. Her suggestions on household arrangements or chores are amazingly practical: "If you build the shelf clear over to the wall, it'll hold more books."

When her mother & father go out in the evening she exacts a promise that they'll say good night when they return. She snatches things from her small brother as a matter of course, assuming that he's too young to appreciate them. At the drop of a hat she'll write you or recite the entire alphabet, or both. Grownups she treats as equals.

"When you spank me it doesn't make me sorry," she confides, "it just makes me angry." She comes into her dad's room every morning before 7:30, & asks if he wants anything besides tea & fruit for breakfast. "Won't you have an egg this morning?" she urges. She's clothes-conscious as a deb of 18, but no longer seems strange without her long red curls.

Occasionally she's a trifle prima-donnaish about visiting her grandparents, but most mornings of the week she assembles her luggage frantically & is off in an enthusiastic rush to lunch with them. Her stock joke: "They wouldn't give me anything to eat!" Zero weather is her dish. She's an unruffled left-hander.

Very romantic, she has considered almost every delivery boy & yard-worker as a potential husband. She will endure dizzy guff from any male other than from her brother or father. Once she let a 2-year-old boy knock her down several times in complete glee. Her fragility is gone; she's rounder & huskier. At sewing she is happy and adept.

Her delight at finding her mother's withered corsage beside her bed, mornings after a party, is boundless. She never harbors illwill for punishment, perhaps because her spankings are largely pantomime. Her most wounded rebuke: "You hurt my feelings!"

She pastes her favorite clippings on pieces of cardboard. Occasionally her hardboiled treatment of her brother relaxes in an amazing burst of tenderness. But it doesn't last long. Yet she finds him companionable when off guard. Her memory for details of 3 years ago excels her parents'.

She loves to watch her mother dressing up for a party. Occasionally she picks up a favorite object & asks, "Will you give me this when you die?" Reasoning with her is less strain than attempts at discipline. She always has that enviable Britannic fresh-bathed look.

Her mind is exploratory. "How do girls decide whether to go to college or to have babies?" She has the quickest ear for new words I've ever known; long ones like "magnificently" roll off her tongue. She still spurns dolls.

She's generous to a fault; loves to be read to; likes anything sweet, even lumps of sugar. Once she hears a word & asks how it's spelled, she never forgets it. Some mornings she crawls into bed with her father & prattles incessantly.

When hanging her favorite picture in her room, she lies down on her bed, to find where she can see it best on waking. Any altered detail in a room, any new garment or knick-knack, catches her eye instantly.

She swiftly masters the rudimentary operation of any new gadget around the house, & coaches her elders in its easy mastery. I have no misgivings about her ability to adapt herself to the brave-new-world she'll live in.

VIP: *Off to kindergarten*

He claims that with a good pair of pliers he could take the whole house apart. "And maybe the world!" We try to keep 'em hidden. Once a day he says, "Don't 'sturb me, I'm thinking about the poor children." His muraser is the thing that unrases.

He is talkative always, except at the table, where he's a good listener. When opposed in his pursuits, his strongest protest is "You make me *so* mad!" Like most 5-year-olds, his thinking is so straightforward as to abash many grownups. He invites his playmates in to raid pantry & icebox.

When caught in a misdemeanor, he is apt to blame the innocent boy next door. He asserts he likes the movies & dislikes the radio, but the first time he was taken to a movie he was bored & insisted on leaving in 20 minutes. But now he's a see-'em-twice movie addict.

In the midst of tightening the wires in an electric plug, he is apt to ask, "Do you really love me?" & then continue his soliloquies about his plans to be an electrical engineer. Occasionally he inquires whether Stalin is really dead. For a long time his favorite phonograph records were Johnny Mercer's "Glow Worm" & an ancient "Pistol Packing Mamma."

He is highly enthusiastic about his kindergarten teacher & says he "couldn't get along without her." Every day he raids the kindling pile under the back porch & nails pieces of wood together. When he struts, every part of his anatomy is in flux. His nose is so close to the TV screen that he can smell it!

While asleep, he often draws up one leg, knee-high, & crosses the other leg over it, a posture reminiscent of a hillbilly hayfield philosopher. He often cuts his flaming red hair himself between trips to the barber. With some vehemence, he denies that he's anybody's baby brother.

A great student of magazine pictures, he discovers details that escape his elders. He scorns a trike & wants no side-wheel on his bike.

When plumbing or electrical gadgets go bad, he offers to fix 'em for $2,000, but advocates phoning a plumber, because he likes to act as plumber's consultant. Once when a doctor, after tricking him into a face-down position, stuck a needle into his rear without warning, he turned his head & observed caustically, "Are you suposed to do that, Doctor?"

When he heard what venison costs, he began to set menacing traps of wire, nails & boards for rabbits & squirrels, & any day he's apt to catch a medium-sized garbage man. His questions are formidable: He points to the 7-inch thickness of the unabridged dictionary & asks, "How long would it take you, Dad, to read that clear through?"

At meals, he is the most leisurely eater in the family, but he gets a lot tucked away eventually. He is impatient to grow up, & weighs himself often on the bathroom scales, arguing that 42 pounds is quite a lot. When he watches his father shave, he demands one dab of lather on the tip of his nose as his inalienable right.

Occasionally he puts in a claim for this house for his very own when his mommie & daddy die. Then he adds, "But you're going to live 1,000 years, aren't you?" Sometimes he reminds his daddy, "You were afraid I'd be all grown up before you came back from overseas, weren't you?"

He likes to get letters, & demands pieces of paper with "something important wroten" on 'em. At bedtime he becomes irresistibly companionable, & likes to discuss things like tiling the basement bathroom, or farming, or remodeling the entire kitchen. He is delightfully chummy with his dad, but it's usually his mommie he leans on, in a pinch. He'd like to pipe chocolate milk all over the house & yard.

* * *

I assume the marriage counselors are coaching the brides on this moot question: If a girl won a boy while gowned in blue jeans, can she keep his love if she wears blue jeans at dinner?

'Tain't true that a man never learns anything after he's thirty years old. Just last week a friend told me that he shaves his chin first, while his blade is still sharp. I always shaved my right cheekbone first, but I tried his scheme and it works like magic.

I wish we could preserve and put up this sacred Christmas spirit in one-pound tin boxes, like holiday fruitcake, and open a box of it every profane month all year long. (And I wish we could give those Moscow go-getters a taste.)

The minute Junior got home from college for the holidays he asked me which girl in our neighborhood it was who's prettier in my opinion than Miss America. When I told him the names of three of 'em, he retorted scornfully, "Shucks, I knew *them* before they got their teeth straightened!"

Some of the men at the big round table at the club are old-fashioned: They think that if a girl accepts a mink coat from a man, she's slightly obligated. (Even if he's only her husband.) But does a girl who lets a man buy her a $5 steak expect to be kissed, or not?

Recently on a visit to New York I took my Dream Girl to see the

United Nations hideout. Now she wants to redo her bedroom more like those three big meeting rooms decorated by the three Scandinavian countries.

Every yellow school bus in the country should carry two or three loads of pupils, teachers and parents every summer vacation to see the UN! (With Coney Island for dessert.)

"A room without any books in it," asserts Peter Comfort dogmatically, tossing rock salt on his icy driveway, "is positively uncivilized!" (Under pressure from his wife, he muttered yes, he means a bathroom, too.)

Our neighborhood hardware man tells us that a wife should have her own pliers, hammer and screw driver, and leave her husband's alone. . . . Myself, I'm neutral, since I know now I can always find my tools either in our youngest's underwear drawer or in the compartment where my wife keeps the silver.

My ardent search for a modern rocking chair neared pay dirt when I spotted an aweome rocker in a 57th Street window. It rocks on solid wrought-iron curves, its blond body is stuffed with foam rubber. What a brave-new-world blend! Then I heard a rumor that it costs $135 or $235.

YOUR CHILD FROM 9 TO 12

Biography of a 9-year-old

He gets into more fights than you'd expect from the serenity of his face in repose. Usually he & his adversaries become warm pals. He is addicted to brief, curt telephone conversations in which he & his caller seem at cross-purposes.

He's still hovering on the edge of the sister-teasing phase. Approximately one-third of the foods paraded at our table are of dubious appeal to him. He is highly gregarious & likes to crowd into any closet where a family conference is going on.

Toward the game of tennis he's still lukewarm, though he swings a racket in the belief that distance is superior to accuracy. He can get more facts out of magazine & newspaper pictures than a college senior from a month of lectures.

He's apt to overestimate the importance of certain radio programs, & keeps his nose close to the sound box, as if trying to smell the hero's breath. Often he shows his indifference to money by declining to accept pay for doing his chores. But he's interested in the cost of everything except his monthly pair of shoes.

His tastes & opinions are amazingly sound & shrewd when he's willing to reveal 'em. So far as I know he has never slept past 7 A.M. He is getting over his passion for long pants & now seems willing to wear out his shorts.

On long walks he is excellent company, better than most grownups, & I enjoy him most in a twosome. When he philosophizes, he seems to view life from the standpoint of a slightly disillusioned man of the world. Some of his sayings belong in a book of quotations with gems from the best minds.

My favorite among his recent observations was the one on young love: "When you're young you fall in love with a lot of girls & want to marry 'em but when you grow older you forget about 'em and don't even see 'em any more."

He occasionally reminisces about things as if they had happened to him 90 years ago. Just about the time you decide to treat him more maturely, you discover that he's still a small boy. He adheres to the view of the human race he expressed when he was 3: "Gogar all the people," with a grimace.

He pores over a comic book as if it were a science text book, & his next favorite reading matter is the same "science" magazine that was my second choice when I was a boy. He seems to me to be smarter at 9 than I was at the age of 12, & more urbane than I was at 16.

He is quick to quarrel & quick to forgive, & 5 minutes after a stubborn argument in the attic or basement, we're arms around the neck again. Like most fathers, I often have the uncomfortable feeling that he's right & I'm wrong. He likes to douse his dark blond locks with the stuff I forget to use on my hair.

He seems to get along smoothly & easily with his pals except when they're fighting, & there's seldom a shortage of small boys around our place. But his views on girls are apt to be caustic, especially if he thinks he can get a rise out of his sister.

He concentrates heroically on occasion, & one of my favorite mental images of him is lying prone, aiming a .22 rifle at a target, with a fly crawling on the tip of his nose in the hot sun. He tackles his chores at top speed as if to hurry on to pleasanter activities.

Among sports he seems to prefer riding, shooting & swimming, far above football, baseball & tennis, which I think may be eminently sound. He keeps well up on the news & public affairs, & his views on affairs of the day seem sane & enlightened beyond that of many adults.

Often when you mention some novel or piquant tale to him, he'll reveal that he read it himself, & he certainly keeps abreast of the war news better as a 3rd-grader than I did in the first years of the first world war. All in all, as I think of him fondly, he seems a solid citizen of the world.

Girls are exquisite at 10

While the b.g. is still away at summer camp, so she can't tear my red hair out in retaliation, I want to jot down a few of her traits, so when I am old & gray I can remember, as all parents want to remember their daughter at the sacred & mystical age of 10; they're much alike.

At last she's slightly interested in dolls, because her playmates are. She loves to arrange flowers in bouquets, & gallops toward a violet as if it were a $1 bill. About a tubful of lukewarm water, she's not quite as enthusiastic as her 8-year-old brother & much less than the infant Quentin.

On the Bible, she's amazingly well-posted. Like the infant redhead, she's still cautious, apt to look before she sits. Sometimes the new words in her vocabulary, used glibly, are startling.

Her thoroughness in any project she undertakes shames her harum-scarum father.

Like her mother, she thinks the color purple is super. When I sneaked a peek at the encyclopedia to brush up on one of her questions, she told me gently she'd already looked there. She's very, very apologetic about cutting those bangs without permission.

Like her grandfather, she's the naturalist of the family, & was chagrined when she couldn't locate his famous wild bird egg collection at the state historical society. She uses the paper dolls her mother cut out in her girlhood eons ago.

From sweet reasonableness she can flare into a temper in 3 seconds, but rarely, she's quickly back to normal. When entrusted with an errand or chore, she can be efficient, if she thinks it's important. With a butterfly net, she's swift as Diana the huntress.

In spending her dimes, she's thrifty & sensible, buys what she needs. When wheedling for more, she's excruciatingly apologetic, usually prefacing it with: "I know your answer'll be no." Her most childish traits: irrepressible zeal for the funnies & the game of jacks.

She dotes on her baby brother, wishes he'd stay little. Unless her attitude changes remarkably, she's a cinch to win the traditional family watch & bonus for non-smoking & drinking till 21. Her school notebooks are pinafore neat, with crystalline round letters; but elsewhere her penmanship fluctuates almost daily.

We can't beguile her into taking music lessons, perhaps because we haven't found room for a piano. Beneath her jauntiness she's shy & modest & bursting with friendliness. When cajoled into doing her dance, she frowns clear through it.

She's fairly adept at disguising her interest in boys. Her shoes last twice as long as her brother's. She rejoices in her mother's perfumes & powders. When she overhears words about diet, she's stoic & heroic in renouncing her favorite fatteners. With her private museum, she's tidier than at anything else.

She can trade her brother out of anything, but in swaps with her friends she's an easy mark. She reads in bed every night, usually sneaking an extra 10 minutes. . . . When she wakes up after midnight, she herds me to bed if I've dozed off in my den, & turns out my light when I leave it on.

Despite a streak of impatience, she's a good organizer & planner, & likes to make lists of things to do. She'll be mighty happy to get back from camp in time for the state fair, where she'll view animals & babies with impartial interest. She wears her favorite dresses out while she outgrows the ones she won't wear.

She'll conceal her dismay at her brother's scorn for her bangs. She's becoming the fastest walker in the family, maybe because she's always eager to get to school. Exposed though she's been to modernity, progressive education & a chaotic world, she seems, praise be, much like the little girls of the last 40 years.

Foibles of a boy at 11

It still takes 45 minutes to make him go to bed in 10 minutes. He can stow away three 9-cent bananas in a flash. But his red hair & freckles are ingratiating & help him get away with more than he should. His vocabulary is somewhat fancy for an 11-year-old.

He gives our 30-some magazines a month a closer going-over than anybody else in the family. Recently he made a half-pint of lemon sherbet in the freezer, with ingredients worth about $1.10. His improvisations at spelling are wondrous.

Somehow he has developed a morbid interest in Cadillacs. Junior accuses him of overeating, & maybe Jr. has something there. He uses a dozen glass bricks in the decor of his bedroom. His 37th ambition: to be a movie director.

He loves to rearrange his room frequently. But it can go from incredible tidiness to complete squalor in 10 minutes. An excellent swimmer, he jumps into water holding his nose. At the drop of a hat, he'd remodel any house in town, & favors slum clearance.

Junior acknowledges him as his master at double-talk. He clings to an ostrich feather & a tiny dried, sun-bleached shrub he acquired out west, & they hang on his bedroom wall. When his bed is moved for dusting, a gold mine of lost knick-knacks & junk is revealed.

When he watches TV, he's apt to be leafing through Volume 17 of the encyclopedia, too. He likes to turn TV on & then go upstairs to run his electric train. This year his new hobby has been exploring our town via bus.

Apparently he enjoys a movie the 3rd time he sees it as much as the 1st time, even within a week or 2. He is allergic to chores & in fact to almost any exercise unless his father & brother join in. But he likes to swap punches with boxing gloves.

He loves to pound out neighborhood newspapers & columns on an old typewriter. Some of his favorite foods I'd never heard of at his age, like lobster tails & smoked oysters. Often I find him reading in bed at 7 A.M. with the *National Geographic*, the comics & *Popular Mechanics*.

I admire his taste in girls, & the prettiest blonde in his school has come to call. But he positively refused to take dancing lessons last year, half agreeing for this year, maybe. His ambition now is to be a patrol boy at his school & stand on the curb with crossed belts on his chest.

Occasionally he gets wrathful at the Russians' stupidity, & he often demands an ice cream cone just before dinner. He disapproves violently of smoking, & has been quite an influence in keeping me cigaretteless. His fondness for feeding the neighborhood kids inflates our grocery bill.

His ideas on clothes are stubborn & he sometimes puts on a tweed jacket for a hamburger at a drive-in. But usually he looks more like Huckleberry Finn. He loves to plunge into the deepest snowdrifts & often needs to be hung up to dry.

His reluctance to bathe vanishes when he steps into the tub, & it's hard to fish him out. Once, after a meal downtown, he watched the tipping closely, & later he bought a coke & tipped the waitress 10 cents. His athletic program this spring: to learn to be (1) a tennis player & (2) a homerun hitter.

He is polite to older people & inclines to treat 'em as equals. I estimate that he provides me in entertainment about 50 times what he costs me a year. Acts of injustice or unkindness move him to violent indignation.

In tune with his generation, he seems to think his every comment must be devastatingly funny or scathing. He loves to pound boards together with nails & strew nails in the driveway. He feels he should not be held accountable for what he did as a small boy last week.

He is an implacable foe of liquor, & ruthlessly mimics, with a curl of his lip, the "idiotic" grownups who drink what he calls "stupid highballs & cocktails." His feats with a snow-shovel this week were his best effort yet at chores. He shows promising signs of resembling his older brother. I hope he & I can keep each other young.

Portrait of a 12-year-old

His room is decorated with cuties from *Esquire,* with big cutout pipes stuck in the mouths of the pretty girls. He is a master of the terse phone conversation, & often settles more in 3 words than his sister in 30 minutes. Once or twice he has kissed his sister's girlfriends without warning.

He is fascinated by archery, & owns 3 long bows, though he can never find 'em all. He tells his mother what to wear when she's going to visit his school, & when she goes out of an evening he often tells her she looks nice. . . . He is opposed to divorce & what he calls "loose-legged families."

He has a resigned attitude toward his chores, which he performs swiftly & earnestly, & he doesn't seem sorry for himself. Among his favorite records are the Frankie Carle piano solos, & he is tolerant of both classic & swing music.

Before his 12th birthday he made an eloquent & masterly plea for a good dog. But when the doctor ruled that his younger brother was allergic to dogs, he agreed to deferment of the dog, without a murmur, until the allergy vanishes. He still adheres to his childhood motto: "If people bite me I bite people."

He bathes lengthily in hot water & I suspect reads in the tub. He has a moderate interest in baseball, a deeper feeling for football, thinks he'd like to become a golfer, but has a mild aversion to tennis, probably because there's a court in his backyard.

But he could swim a mile before he was 10, can sail a boat, has several shooting medals, & can ride a horse nonchalantly. He is good at arithmetic, but wrestles rather absent-mindedly with spelling, with a tendency to write "mush" for much.

His favorite costumes are somewhat impromptu, but he doesn't object to dressing up for dancing, when he even slicks his hair with water. There's never enough left of his clothes to save for his younger brother, & he can liquidate a new pair of shoes in a week.

He has a deep respect for money and money-makers, but can spend more money in an afternoon (in rather lordly fashion) than his father ever spent in 2 months at the same age. In conversation, he alternates corny grade school gags incongruously with fairly pertinent comments on the affairs of the day.

When reading fancy prose, like Booth Tarkington's, he plunges headlong through the long words, mauling the syllables, but the humor & sense don't escape him. At 12 he weighs almost as much as his mother does. . . . His personal library includes almost 200 books, & if he likes a book he withdraws it from the living room permanently.

Since the day it cost $5 to bind up his fractured thumb in a crowded doctor's office, he's dreamed of becoming a great surgeon. He is a tireless reader of books on house architecture & is strong for simple, gay & modern design.

His awkwardness is diminishing, but he still dives headlong up the stairs as if he were attacking a hill position. He turns cartwheels in the living room impressively, & rebels at the fact that some people live in gloomy, shabby houses.

He favors neat white bungalows. Recently he dabbled menacingly at chemistry, but his hobbies are often short-lived. He is an omnivorous reader of *Look* & *Life* & *Reader's Digest* & reads the newspapers from cover to cover. . . . His dislike for eggs irks his father more than almost any other trait.

A recent & credible report describes him as the best shot at camp from a sitting position. He dislikes peas, cooked onions & lima beans & is leery of homemade soups—they might have a touch of onion in 'em.

He thinks Roosevelt was as great a president as Lincoln & never remembers how he got the rips & tears in his clothes. In his more optimistic moments, his father hopes that with an excellent physique, a good mind & a gift for not saying too much, the lad is equipped for the brave new world ahead.

* * *

One thing the Girl of My Dreams and I don't argue about: four-lane toll roads. We both like 'em. . . . She thinks women ought to pester their state legislators to build more of 'em. (And we ought to sell some of our narrow old "concrete cowpaths" to the truck lines to use as one-way freight roads.)

"We have lots of fun when we visit the big town," says Betty Comfort, cunningly exposing 90-cent-a-pound steak fat for the winter birds. "I enjoy the window-shopping above all, while Peter peers shyly at the faces of the big-town babes."

I told my Dream Girl that "You Belong to Me" has the prettiest words of the year's popular songs, what with its silver plane over the ocean, and its jungle wet with rain. "And which girl does it remind you of?" she asked suspiciously. "You, my darling!" quoth I.

Our twelve-year-old has inherited my old-time bachelor fondness for eating in a cafeteria (buffet style); he likes to see it first. . . . But he and I now have a definite understanding. His dinner check mustn't be over 50 cents more'n mine or he goes without dessert.

When I heard that the new movie technique called Cinerama "plunges you into a startling new world," I told my wife that I hadn't realized how much it would mean to see Betty Grable's knees in three dimensions.

My plumpish friend next door confides that a modern wife qualifies as an expert diet and menu manipulator if she can bring in $30 worth of groceries without including a single item that makes her husband's eyes light up when he raids the icebox.

THE LONG & SHORT OF IT

Glimpse into a little boy's mind

All this furniture is too big for me. But no high-chair for me, please. It hurts my ears when Mommie bawls me out. Why do grownups think eggs are so good? If They think it's so good to go to bed early, then why don't *they*?

Daddy thinks he's so smart when he makes me pick up food I drop at the table. But he only remembers about once a week. I wish things didn't break so quick. Sometimes I want to be good but I just forget.

When grownups scold, They talk too long. They just say the same thing over & over different ways. Why does Daddy read at breakfast and won't let me? He acts like the king of the jungle. But he isn't bad to take a walk with in the dark.

Why do big boys always have dates just with girls? They act so silly. Some girls are just as much fun to play with as boys, though. They make such a fuss when I don't lace my shoes. They don't fall off, do they?

It isn't too easy to wash clean all over. Sometimes They find dirt when I thought I had it all off. The mirror's too high. When I ask 'em to do something with me, They think what they're doing is so important. It doesn't look so important to me.

But Mommie's the one to talk to when I really want something. Daddy tries to act so fierce when he thinks it's good for me. He claims he used to be a little boy himself, but it's hard to believe. If I'm good for a few minutes, maybe he'll take me to toyland.

It's just disgusting when They drink those awful cocktails. Smell worse'n medicine. But They even eat oysters, ugh! My new teachers turned out better than I expected. Why don't I hear all the noise They say I make early in the morning?

They go out to dinner too often. I don't notice it so much when They stay home, though. It feels so good when I ask Them to do something & They say yes without arguing or explaining why they can't. Once Dad said yes to me 3 times in a row!

Mommie's a lot sweeter after breakfast. I wish they'd invent a cocoa without a scum on it. My clothes get torn without any fault of mine, I'm just as vexed & puzzled as They are. When I've been sweeping the driveway all day, Mommie says it's been only 5 minutes.

When I look at the stars with Daddy, I certainly ask him some big questions! He doesn't know much more about the Moon than I do. But he surprises me sometimes. When I get sick, Mommie isn't as nervous as Daddy, but she puts me on a liquid diet right away.

After the teachers get through talking about life, I always want to do a lot of wonderful good when I grow up. If I had enough money I'd buy everybody a big farm & a modern house & an electric train. Daddy has promised me 5 times to take me out to the Drake Observatory & always forgets till the day after it's been open.

If I ever have a little boy (like Mommie's always saying), I'll know how to make him behave! By letting him do anything he wants to. But I'll never let my little boy get away with some of the things I get away with! Wonder what Daddy means when he says he's sorry for people whose kids are dumb *all* the time?

Daydream: First day of school

Take a good look at your new teacher, kids. When you're 50 years old & your own children ask you to name the most important 10 or 25 persons in your whole life, she may be one of 'em. Some day you may want to send her boxes of candy, or invite her to dinner.

Also take a good look at the other boys & girls in your class. Some of their faces will linger in your memory all your life. Long after they've vanished into faraway, gone off to Oregon or Texas, you'll wonder what became of 'em & what luck they squeezed out.

A few of 'em may live all their lives in your town. Every time you run into 'em, your subconscious mind will say: "There goes a chunk of my precious childhood."

You're all pretty grown-up anyhow, especially you in the 3rd & 4th grades, where you feel more grown-up than the bigshots in Callanan Junior or East High. How grown-up can you get? When you're 60 you won't feel as grown-up as a senior at Lincoln or Roosevelt or North does at 17.

Well, I hope you got the seat you wanted in your classroom or homeroom. Not too near the front, & not too far from the prettiest girl in class. Also, you want to sit next to your pal, or at least within a loud whisper or a soft shout. They used to make us stay after school for whispering!

Funny thing about your teacher. She seems awfully old to you. Well, she isn't quite that old. She may be only 4 or 5 years older than you if you're in high school & she's a young new teacher. Or even if you're in the 5th grade, she may be only 8 or 10 years older.

When I was in the 5th grade I had a beautiful teacher, big blue eyes & rosy cheeks & dimples, but I thought she was far too old for me. Maybe I was wrong. Ten years later I'd have been glad to take her out on a date, give or take a few years.

Actually, I had 2 or 3 teachers so attractive that I'd have been glad (only a few years later) to drive 'em out to a suburban café for a big thick steak or some lamb chops & a good intimate talk. And quite a few others who were past their first blooming but who must have been lovely indeed in their 20's & 30's.

Some day you'll be calling your teachers by their first names, & kidding 'em, & maybe telling 'em slightly off-color stories. Right now all they ask is that you concentrate on what they're trying to teach you. They don't want you to go out defenseless into a world dotted with gremlins & gogers.

Your reading & writing & arithmetic & spelling, your grammar, history & geography—they're all high-powered ammunition for your lifelong safari. Some word you learn, some fragment of history or geography may kill a big hippo for you some day, with a big valuable pearl in its belly.

I didn't think so when I was in school—our marvelous, free, equalitarian schools!—but each teacher is a genie with a magic lamp. It's a lamp you can rub many, many times & each time it'll grant you a wish. Aladdin never had it better on his best days.

Sure, sure—show off occasionally for the other brats in your class; show 'em what a hilarious cut-up you are. But don't leave school thinking that Havana is in the Hawaiian Islands, or Madagascar an island where they make 2-cylinder automobiles, up near Spitzbergen.

If you're one of the rare fish who don't need to learn anything in school, why, I apologize! This little outburst isn't meant for you. Maybe you're a born smart-aleck, destined to earn $10,000 a year by the time you're 21. Maybe you're heir to a gold mine or oil well or NY real estate or 1,000 acres of Iowa land.

But if you're just like the rest of us, you'll pay some attention to your teacher, study your lessons, complete your assignments on time & successfully. If you see a man earning $30,000 a year, then $25,000 of it he's earning with what he learned in the first 12 grades. And if he's earning $100,000 a year, chances are strong he learned to earn $90,000 of it before he got out of high school. College just put the $$$ sign in front of the figures.

* * *

Out of a clear sky my Dream Girl sprang the perfect Anglo-American dish on me for breakfast—pancakes with kippers. I congratulated her: "This brings the British closer than a thousand speeches."

One of our neighbors got a collect phone call from their boy in Korea; before they quit talking, the bill was $125. They didn't begrudge one dime; aim to subtract it from their clothes budget. "He's defending this neighborhood, too!" said the man next door.

"Those eastern girls' colleges turn out individualists!" muses Betty Comfort, waving to the mailman. "That young mother from Vassar thinks her baby'll be happier with circular diapers."

As our youngest soars into his seventh heaven with the last day of school in the offing, I remember how Last Day of School ranked above the 4th of July as a holy day, and just below Christmas.

Our town's No. 1 amateur theologian inquired over the bridge table how a man could believe in Darwin's theories and still use the affectionate phrase "God bless——" He beat a baffled retreat when the three other bridge players all professed beliefs in both the Almighty and Darwin.

I saw our town's most brilliant architect scowl and mutter to himself. "I've just talked with another client," he explained, "who wants me to design a hundred-foot ranch house for a fifty-foot lot."

"They used to send the maid away," says our town's most cynical matron, "if their son got fresh with her. Nowadays they might send the boy away and keep the maid."

FOR MEN ONLY [III]

When it's evident that your daughter will be as pretty as your wife . . . and Junior admits he's lost an argument, by introducing a new tangent with "Now, Dad, look at it this way" . . . and you discern that your ten-year-old has a soft spot in his heart for grannies and tiny children . . . and your wife catches you frowning into the mirror and assures you that you've still got more hair than most men . . . then you salute marriage as the Great Morale Builder, and wonder why you ever long to be the keeper of a remote and lonely lighthouse.

4

The presidents

PROLOGUE

Unknown bureaucrat

Alas, the average government clerk is far more intelligent than he need be to do his job, or any job he'll ever have. Before he has been in the capital a year, the romantic notions he once cherished, when he got his appointment, about becoming a big force in the government, have quite evaporated.

After a year he tells his Big Ideas to his wife, not the President.

Unless he is an especially alert chap, with a quick ear for office gossip & an inquisitive turn of mind, he has only the vaguest conception of what goes on in the big, top-level, corner offices in his own building. He knows only what he reads in the papers about policy & statecraft, though he may work two doors down the corridor from the chief.

To him his section boss is a Big Shot, whose little quirks & foibles assume an inordinate importance. Not only can he recommend promotion & pay, but his temperament colors the lives of his underlings. If he is a jovial fellow, his clerks may be 100 per cent happier on the same salary. Many anonymous bureau officials are heroes to their clerks, a tribute to their quality.

Long experience with the onslaughts of irate citizens on routine & the public treasury have taught the government clerk to cherish red tape with a passionate love. This is a reasonable passion. He realizes that barbed-wire entanglements of red tape, to be unwound only slowly & delicately, are the bastions of democracy, & all that protect the Republic from impatient special pleaders, pressure groups or greedy individuals with an axe to grind.

If his immediate boss ranks as a Big Shot, then his bureau chief is a demigod who dwells more than halfway up Olympus. The man at the head of the Cabinet department or agency in which he works is a fabulous Jovian creature whom the clerk has perhaps never seen at close range. Thus, to a man in Treasury or Agriculture, the remote Humphrey and Benson are apt to seem almost supernatural beings, divinities to be mentioned in hushed tones.

Despite his remoteness from the most awesome Swivel Chair in the building, the average government clerk does wield an almost impalpable influence on those above him. This is the influence of propinquity. Each clerk influences his superior a trifle, & this chain of influence throws sparks upward, by the substitution of a word in a form letter, the slight modulation of an attitude or an idea. He is, I should judge, ten times as influential as the average citizen.

So he is not quite a robot. He can tell you more comical & serio-comic stories about red tape & official delays in an hour than a lobbyist can in a day. He does not underestimate the importance of his own work, but he does it so well within his powers that he has enough left over to enjoy an aloof & critical attitude toward it. He realizes more clearly than most that the alternative to red tape is corruption, chaos & dictatorship; in a word, tyranny.

So he is an efficient buffer between the rights of the 165,-000,000 & the grievances and greed of the few. He knows that the rumbling laborious machinery of government often lays an egg long overdue, but it is not a half-raw 2-minute egg.

So far the American government worker hasn't (perhaps fortunately) realized his own strength. He has not formed a solid bloc of special privilege like the government functionaries of France. He resembles more the aloof minor faculty personage on a college campus, a little detached from the general commotion of the times. But his aloofness is a little deceptive. His influence is greater than it seems; it ripples out in overlapping circles to every family between the two oceans.

※ ※ ※

Behind any lilac bush in the neighborhood these days you can see 1953's high school and college grads being snapshot in their caps and gowns by their parents. A funny picture to laugh at now, which'll bring a lump to all their throats by-and-by.

I've ruled that if Junior uses the car occasionally, he should keep it washed and polished *all* the time. This makes me a sort of monster in the eyes of his chums whose dads are too tired to give 'em chores.

I still have daydreams, when I wonder what I'll be when I grow up. Most of the time (despite years of meditation) it's still left fielder on a big-league ball team.

Most of the men at the club agree that a husband deserves a night out every week or so. But the ones who're most enthusiastic are the same ones who're most jealous about letting their wives slip out an occasional evening.

Happiest of all grandparents in our town is the pair who recently drove three grandchildren to California and back. Maybe one solution for the Age 60-70 Blues would be to enroll grandmothers and even grandpapas in a college short course in baby-sitting.

Our town's most worldly parson put it up squarely to his parishioners in his last church bulletin. "Why don't you," he wrote, "spend one hour in church as a tithe for every ten you spend with radio and television?"

As a gracious (if slightly flamboyant) hostly gesture, I'm trying to learn how to serve Cherries Flambeau, blazing as they do at the Chambord or Ambassador East. But my vigilant Dream Girl spoils my act slightly; she's right on my heels with a fire extinguisher.

HARRY TRUMAN & 10 GREATEST PRESIDENTS

Our 10 greatest presidents

Who are America's 10 greatest presidents? I named my 10 choices recently. Since then I've performed research I should have tackled first. Now I am ready to amend my list of 10, & to salute the Great State's excellent judges of presidential greatness.

Probably the best list is the result of a study by Harvard's eminent Prof. Arthur Schlesinger. He quizzed 55 topnotch experts in history & government. They named 6 "greats" and 4 "near-greats," but omitted Truman from their calculations (*Life*, 1948) because he was still in office.

My own list brought both bombardment & praise. In historical sequence it includes Washington, Jefferson, Monroe, Madison, Jackson, Lincoln, Teddy Roosevelt, Wilson, Franklin Roosevelt & Truman. I included 2 I'd omit on 2nd thought, & omitted 2 I'd now include.

And now for the 55 experts' list, in their order of excellence. Great: Lincoln, Washington, Franklin Roosevelt, Wilson, Jefferson & Jackson. Near-great: Teddy Roosevelt, Cleveland, John Adams & Polk. My guess is that the events of Truman's last 4 years (1948-1952) might tempt these objective judges of history to include him now that he's an ex-president.

So I amend my own list to omit Monroe & Madison & to include Cleveland & Polk. It is my guess (& my devout hope) that at the end of Ike's regime, when he can be evaluated, I might conscientiously substitute his name for either Cleveland's or Polk's.

In my opinion, the blue-ribbon list submitted by a reader

is exactly like the 55 experts' list, except that he omits Adams & includes Truman: Washington, Jefferson, Jackson, Polk, Lincoln, Cleveland, T. Roosevelt, Wilson, F. D. Roosevelt & Truman.

My nominations for the 2 worst lists are: 1 from a small-town diehard, naming only Washington, Jefferson, Lincoln & T. Roosevelt from the experts' list, & including Taft, Harding, Coolidge & Hoover, all rated average or lower; & 1 from a village thunderbrow which names only 4 "great" presidents (Washington, Jefferson, Lincoln & Hoover) & argues that to name more would be "blasphemy."

Another excellent list (which I award 2nd place) comes from a scholarly recent grad of the state university of Iowa. His list is exactly like *Life's* except that instead of Cleveland he includes Monroe. Another high-ranking list is a professor's, which omits Truman & Polk but includes Monroe & Madison.

A magnanimous gesture from an erudite GOP judge substitutes Madison, McKinley & Ike for Adams, Polk & Cleveland, but ranks Truman in the upper half among our presidents. Another learned professor thinks we've only had 7 "greats": Washington, Lincoln, FDR, Jefferson, Jackson, TR & Woodrow Wilson.

A young soldier who twits me for including Truman among our mortal immortals includes Ike on his list but thinks baseball's Branch Rickey is the best man for the White House (for all I know he's right).

Despite state pride, Iowans seem to divide about 50-50 between our native son Hoover & neighbor Truman, the 2 living ex-presidents. (Maybe we'd better wait?)

I should add that *Life's* 55 experts divided the presidents into 5 groups: Great, Near-Great, Average, Below Average & Failures. The 2 failures: Grant & Harding. In our times we've been ruled (since World War I) by 1 failure (Harding); 1 below average (Coolidge) & 1 average president (Hoover). In the experts' opinion, that is.

One local servant thinks some great Americans who missed the presidency (like Hamilton, Clay, Gallatin, Webster, Lee & Bryan) were of loftier presidential caliber than quite a few who got elected. I'm not too sure about Bryan, Lee & Hamilton in this class, but I'd wager that hundreds of Americans of higher presidential caliber than 20 of our elected presidents couldn't possibly have been elected. And thousands of unknown Americans might (like Truman) have been surprisingly good presidents.

Truman—one of our 10 greats?

For a long time it was fashionable in some circles to sneer at Harry Truman, or to speak patronizingly of him. I hasten to disassociate myself from this juvenile, silly attitude, while he's still alive. I'd rank him among our 10 greatest American presidents, in his own cocky, homespun inimitable American way.

I'd planned to fly down to Kansas City for a chat; I never got acquainted with him. What makes this average American tick? It isn't easy for a president to be brilliant in the mid-20th century as things explode all around us. But I totaled his 12 triumphs with a pencil; they amaze me.

He once lost his temper with a music critic who made fun of his daughter's voice. My daughter has kept her musical aspirations, if any, a secret from me; but I'd resent it if anybody made fun of her voice. And he seems to be suffering from penicillin allergy, which once gave me a bad year; so my sympathy flows out to him.

What do the 3rd-highball Saturday night statesmen expect of a modest average American in a double-breasted suit? I don't think history will sneer at Truman. Out of his inner agony and his debonair courage, he made a dozen decisions which will still look formidable 50 years from now.

1. Truman pulled the trigger for the Hiroshima bomb, one of mankind's toughest decisions, to save 100,000 American lives.

2. He helped shore up our potential allies with billions in unpopular military aid.

3. He saved Greece from Communist onslaughts at its frontier & restored an ally.

4. He bolstered Turkey until her fierce warriors became our S. E. bastion.

5. Under him the Berlin Airlift set Russia back on her heels for the first time after the war, & stiffened western Germany.

6. With the help of bold liberals in France & the Catholic church in Italy, he helped save western Europe from the Reds.

7. Truman ordered manufacture of the H bomb over the sincere outcries of Scientist Oppenheimer.

8. During his regime we encircled Russia with a loop of bomber bases & aimed our Strategic Air Force at the Kremlin.

9. Despite opposition at home he negotiated successfully with Spain for bomber bases.

10. When the Reds chose Korea for their first "experimental" attack with arms, he promptly intervened.

11. When General MacArthur (a great hero) became a prima donna & defied his c.-in-c., hero-worshiper Truman gritted his teeth, fired him.

12. Somehow, for 7½ years he managed to avert the 3rd great war when Americans were betting on it.

He didn't act alone; but he was responsible.

I don't care whether a man wears a sport shirt or a double-breasted coat or plays the piano, that's an impressive list. Some of his decisions may turn out to have been mistaken. But each time a decision had to be made & he made one. The opposite decision might have been a mistake, too. These 12 stand up. A policy is better than no policy.

Maybe what impressed Americans more than anything else was his plucky, defiant campaign in 1948 against an able Republican who would probably have been a topnotch president.

I've long been an Ike man, but that doesn't blind me to Harry Truman's historic virtues. In American history he was a delightful surprise. An "average American," he was sometimes impulsive, hot-tempered, cocky; even dapper & off-the-cuff, his critics said. But he rose to heights.

If it's true that Harry Truman was just an "average American," then we're mighty lucky he turned out so well, & that average American character stands up so inspiringly in a crisis. If there are millions like Harry, we're even luckier.

✳ ✳ ✳

"I wish," complains Peter Comfort, lugging a sack of charcoal and his giant skillet across the yard, "I'd had sense enough to build my picnic fireplace so the smoke won't blow on Betty's clothesline. Or should I buy her a clothes dryer?"

How would you handle the ticklish problem that confronts our most affluent matron in the country-club section: should she get a new mink coat this year, or should she send her five children to summer camp this year and wait till next year for the fur? (Even the rich have their problems!)

One of our neighbors has a dog which stands up on its hind legs at the front door and bangs with the door knocker for admission. As nearly as I can discern, the neighborhood cherubs think it's a more intelligent animal than a Ph.D. or a Rhodes scholar.

F D R

That man in the White House

This is the day when, 10 years ago, people all over the world looked at each other with shocked surprise & said, "He's dead!" To some, the world seemed to stop for a moment. But not even a Franklin Roosevelt is indispensable, except perhaps for his own chaotic day.

I saw him & heard him speak perhaps 200 times, & I don't marvel that both J. P. Morgan & John L. Lewis detested him. He fought against tyranny from any direction. Ten years is hardly enough for the air to clear, & I suppose thousands of Americans will hate him until they die.

Some disliked him as a Groton aristocrat. One Iowan called him "little Lord Fauntleroy." Others, choleric & passionate with new wealth, called him a "traitor to his class."

I've tried to analyze why they hated him so. My best guess: A strong wind from the left was blowing across the world. As a good sailor, Roosevelt tried to reef the sails & batten down the hatches, to ride out the gale, a little closer to the wind. And it was easier to hate the skipper than to hate the wind. Especially when his seamanship hikes taxes & wins votes.

They attacked him for his little dog Fala. They attacked him because his son wanted to be a captain, too. They attacked him because his wife traveled a lot, & because one of his bright young men played the accordion. They attacked his cigarette holder & the Groton way he said "again." In retrospect these things seem so silly that I doubt any party will ever campaign on such an issue as "Steaks are too scarce!"

It was a petulant defense against a wind from the left that had long blown across the world. Like thumbing your nose at a hurricane. But the hurricane wasn't Roosevelt; it had begun to blow from the left before Roosevelt was born. Yet it was simpler to rail against "that man in the White House," as it had once been easier to call another man in the White House a "baboon."

Long ago a wise editor warned me that it's dangerous to practice irony or subtlety in a newspaper. Fortunately, such flights are rare for me, and I seldom use a 2-syllable word when I can think of a 1-syllable word. But recently I was reminded of this truth when I hinted that some of our fellow Iowans, if offered a chance to resurrect either Roosevelt or Hitler, might not choose Roosevelt.

You won't believe it, but I got reproachful letters: a fine way to speak of a great president, and they'd thought I admired Roosevelt! Not long ago I stubbed the same toe when I referred playfully to an army officer I once knew who always tried to behave like Black Jack Pershing at Shiloh. Several keen students of history reminded me promptly, with learned hauteur, that Pershing never fought at Shiloh. Well, I probably meant Ticonderoga.

To avoid misunderstanding, I might as well say it in plain words: After 10 years, with all the human frailties I saw in FDR in 200 glimpses, I more than ever deem him one of our 3 greatest presidents. Perhaps greater than Washington. Perhaps the peer of Lincoln. But certainly in their great company.

Some of the best of the Roosevelt-haters are beginning to

forgive him. Gradually the brighter ones among them see that but for him capitalism, private initiative, rugged individualism, freedom itself might have perished in our time. His good seamanship gave us all a fighting chance.

So once a year I say a few words about Roosevelt, to remind our fellow bellyachers that it wasn't easy to chart such a skillful course between Pierpont Morgan & John L. Lewis as to win the hatred of both. FDR is a symbol to rally around; he's a test & a shibboleth. Men who still hate him are questionable pilots. After all, he caught more hell for giving England 50 old destroyers than Truman & Paul Hoffman & Averell Harriman & Ike catch today for giving our allies billions. We're catching up with FDR.

FDR's museum: A shrine, too

Across the road from the Roosevelt home at Hyde Park stands a new Howard Johnson café (white & red-roofed) which offers 28 different kinds of ice cream to the pilgrims. It also offers hamburgers & other dainties. Business is excellent because so far more than 1,500,000 people have stopped to see FDR's grave.

The Roosevelt mansion is really out in the country, a good half mile from the first cluster of houses in Hyde Park village, out in the rural fringe of its corporate limits, 8 miles from Poughkeepsie's big bridge.

You can't see the hamburger stand from the house, nor the house from the hamburger stand, because the house is 200 yards in, between the north-south Highway 9 & the Hudson River in the middle distance & concealed by trees, like the river. A few steps from the proud emporium of the 28 ice creams now stands a movie theater in the open fields, not a drive-in, & it's called The Roosevelt.

Recently we visited the Roosevelt house, which the family gave to the government, lock, stock & barrel. We also visited the new stone library or archives building, filled with FDR's souvenirs, curios & his great collection of papers. These are really 2 museums in 1, & we lingered till almost dusk.

There are so many FDR curios in the library that they

can't all be shown at once. They're simply rotated from time to time. The museum could easily spare a good exhibition to send out to DM for the Iowa state fair next year, & never miss 'em for a month.

It must have annoyed the Roosevelt kids, or certainly the grandchildren, to see FDR & Eleanor give all that stuff to the USA. I can picture the tots brandishing the gorgeous bejeweled gold swords from Arabia & teasing to keep 'em in the family. But the Roosevelts have given the library even the postage stamps they accepted as official gifts.

A few steps from the gold swords is a slim orchestral baton from orchestra leader Cab Calloway, & the solid gold inkwell from King George VI. It's probably one of the world's sillier inkwells, a large square gold box with a tiny glass inkwell inside it. Nearby is the most modern sort of gold pen & pencil set, & I marvel one of the boys didn't glom onto that; it was on his desk when he died.

I imagine the Queen must have said to the King, "George, we've got to take the Roosevelts something, & in the present-&-white-elephant-drawer we've got that old inkwell somebody gave us years ago. . . ." Not far away is the flattened bullet Zangara shot at FDR in Florida, presented by Detective Bill Sinnott, from whose head it was removed.

For my two-bits (the price of admission) the most interesting exhibit is a sample of the documents filed in the library rooms where only researchers with an admission card can penetrate. It's a note from Ray Moley writen in 1933 to Marvin McIntyre, suggesting that maybe Marvin better tell the president that some Big Brain thinks we'd better be careful how fast we open state banks as well as national banks.

Yes, there's a sprig of orange blossom from Eleanor's wedding bouquet, & FDR's cradle & rocking horse, & one of the light, Spartan, none-too-comfortable wheel chairs he used (not so luxurious as those at Smouse school for children in DM); & the 8-inch cigarette holder; & in a box on his desk (as well as in an automatic lighter of his Ford touring car) some old withered cigarettes he never got smoked.

In the basement is the huge ice boat on which he raced 100 mph on the frozen Hudson as a boy, & the Russian sleigh his father bought for $15 in Paris, & the ugly sphinxlike caricature Jim

Preston made for the 1938 Gridiron, when FDR wasn't saying whether he'd run in 1940, & the flood of grotesque knickknacks with which the world showered him so affectionately.

It's a curious thing that while 1,500,000 have visited his grave free, only 1,100,000 have sauntered through his house. . . . I'll write about the house another time. One must be careful, or Roosevelt-haters say you're an FDR-worshiper while Roosevelt-lovers call you irreverent. . . . Didn't the other 400,000 have the two-bits?

Spotlight on FDR

At close range President Roosevelt seems almost as robustly human as Wallace Beery, in a well-bred way. His broad sentimental streak is revealed in a desk cluttered with knickknacks & mementos which would give Herbert Hoover the jitters.

He has a strong sartorial flair—likes to wear odd jackets, tweeds of unconventional hue. One of his Norfolk coats is of a greenish tinted tweed. Yet he is no precisionist in the knotting of his neckties.

Occasionally he still reverts to the high starched collars, meeting closely in front, familiar in his earliest pictures as Assistant Secretary of the Navy & as candidate for vice-president.

In his strong-jawed face remain vestiges of perhaps the handsomest chiseled features ever seen on the national stage in modern American politics. But this souvenir of the days when he was the Adonis of the Capital is now muscularly overlain with a bronzed patina & seamy ruggedness. His good looks were a handicap he had to overcome.

His face might be a sea captain's, a rancher's, a country squire's—almost anything but a lawyer's face. But it has a mobility & sensitiveness rare in the bronzed outdoor type, given to flexible mannerisms which make him a setup for mimics.

In his voice there is a noticeable note of the didactic. There is undeniably a touch of the schoolmaster about Mr. Roosevelt, which reminds you of Woodrow Wilson. Perhaps this is partially because the journalists whom he lectures twice a week (and his advisers, no doubt) give off such a youthful, flattering aura of eagerness to know, of trying to cope with the unfathomable.

He loves to deliver little homilies with a strong historic flavor—& a pointed moral. There's a bit of a bite in some of his repartee, reminiscent of a crusty professor with a vein of humor keyed to smacking down a frolicsome sophomore. . . . Like some professors, he often underestimates the worldly wisdom of his classes.

He breaks into a smile with incandescent suddenness & an expectant upward lilt, as if confident his audience will chuckle with him. It usually does, with hair-trigger reaction. In his press conferences & speeches his humorous sallies, usually aimed at his adversaries' tender spots, bubble out as if calculated to displace 10 times their weight in heavy persuasion. If the answering laugh is muffled or slow in coming, he's apt to remind the journalists: "This is funny!"—or repeat his jest.

He is a big man among big men. His great physique is conspicuous among such giants as Jesse Jones & Jim Farley—& the robust Farley, incidentally, looks a trifle sartorial and roly-poly beside him. To the elder pundits like Mark Sullivan, his tone must occasionally seem a shade patronizing.

It is difficult to imagine anyone else dominating the conversation in Mr. Roosevelt's presence, even if FDR were not President. He has an amazing mélange of knowledge on tap, sufficient in depth to embellish his utterances with a kaleidoscopic variety of analogies & similes, all sorts of figures of speech. And in his persuasive & expository passages he relies valiantly on the total validity of his analogies, though they are not inevitably on all fours. But they sparkle, & few people have the courage to prick his conversational bubbles.

He is the most inveterate optimist of this era, subtle & Machiavellian. You wonder if he ever succumbs to private misgivings; you guess he never does. He seems so confident that Tommy Corcoran's statutes can outlive Tommy Jefferson's Constitution. He has been through the worst of troubles, & he fears neither death nor taxes.

At FDR's press conference

The Oval Room, in which President Roosevelt receives his callers & does most of his work, with its greenish hues & its indirect lighting around the tops of the walls, gives a little the impression of a goldfish bowl or an aquarium.

Its profusion of marine engravings, prints, ship models & curios, its tall windows, opening graciously toward the porches, terraces & gardens, leave it little of an office or workroom atmosphere. It is very relaxing.

The Cabinet Room is a more somber setting for solemn thinking, though probably more talking than thinking occurs there. The President's office doesn't exactly mirror his personality; I think it is more an accidental flowering of hobbies, tastes & the exigencies of architecture & decoration.

Most of Mr. Roosevelt's top aides have bigger desks than his; it is neither large nor ponderous. Were it five times as large, it probably would be equally crowded with the unique curios & objets d'art which he collects and which are showered upon him, for which he seems to feel a genuine attachment.

Mrs. Roosevelt's serialized memoirs reveal a number of important things about him & shatter quite a few legends. On their honeymoon he was an inveterate prowler in book & print shops. Personally he is quite frugal, habitually counting the dimes if not the pennies.

They reveal also that she holds him in the moderate awe which is only proper in a wife toward her husband. He is definitely the master of his household, & very positive in his personal predilections, but completely tolerant & reasonable toward the individual quirks of his wife & children.

Actually, Mrs. Roosevelt knocks the props from under Alice Longworth's famous witticism that "Franklin is one-third mush & two-thirds Eleanor." For once Princess Alice let her flair for the bon mot run away with her keen realism.

There is no mush in the President's personality. He has, on the contrary, an indomitable streak of patient stubbornness in his make-up, fortified by a streak of stubborn patience. (In him a half-forgotten grain of sand like NRA or packing the Supreme Court becomes, by accretion, a cherished pearl.) He can ride an uppercut & come back swinging.

Even with his prodigious memory, Mr. Roosevelt makes no pretense of remembering the mountains of detail which encumber his job. He leaves these to aides, who vie in prompting him during press conferences. Actually, he enjoys flabbergasting a reporter with a positive, emphatic assertion that he knows nothing about something that seems pregnant with importance to the questioner: "I haven't even heard of it!"

He also gets a chuckle out of the "no one tells me anything" pose. He is quite obviously fond of people, enjoys the interplay & flavor of personalities, & is a connoisseur of the whimsies & foibles of those around him. These he searches out with a rather robust ju-jitsu wit. His quips might draw blood oftener if they weren't usually so palpably amiable.

At his own dinner table the President is apt to ask his guests embarrassing questions. He takes occasional potshots across the table at what he thinks are their economic prejudices. But Mrs. R. is on the job every minute, softening the punches.

In many people who come near him, Mr. Roosevelt inspires a smiling, delighted affection. Against this magnetism (to which I have seen hostile millionaires succumb) his callers must fight consciously. Some of his bitterest critics might succumb to his personality—& to the loftiness of his purpose—& work shoulder to shoulder with him, if he'd let them.

✳ ✳ ✳

Shall I tell our town's nervous retail tycoons how to solve the downtown traffic jam? Simple: let husbands ride the bus downtown, let the eager little woman use the car—if she'll promise not to drive it downtown herself! (But the tycoons *want* her downtown!)

With her room-cooler, my Lady Love is the most popular member of the family on a 100° summer day. She welcomes us to her room graciously with our books, letters and arguments, and even digs up an ancient box of bonbons.

"A smart insurance fellah downtown," confides Peter Comfort, tossing a garter snake over the fence, "warns me to increase the insurance on my house. I paid $7,000 for it eighteen years ago, I've remodeled it nineteen times, and there's $14,000 insurance on it already, but I've been offered $21,000 and he says it'd cost me $35,000 to replace it!"

Since the little brown dachshund in the next block got knocked over by a car he was chasing, our youngest has held a solemn funeral for it, written a three-act tragedy on the theme, and now wants our neighbor the governor to declare an annual day of mourning.

Among our town's rich originals we boast one individualist who hates disorderly medicine cabinets. When he finds one in a friend's house, he takes out its contents, wraps 'em in a bath towel, and hides it under his hostess' pillow as a hint.

An out-of-towner trapped himself into telling an indelicate (!) story in front of mixed company; nobody laughed except one or two nervous women. What could the disgusted husbands do? They merely glowered, stony. It fell flat. Later the raconteur sent flowers to each woman who'd heard him.

Letters to mothers from June brides on their July honeymoons have started gossip in our town. Apparently some bridegrooms who were as meek as lambs before the wedding are prone to argue on anything after the third day of the wedding trip.

GEORGE WASHINGTON & THEODORE ROOSEVELT

G. W.: *My 1960 candidate*

Washington never wore long pants; Madison was the first president to abandon knee breeches. He never said "entangling alliances with none"—'twas Jefferson. GW owned 60,000 acres of land.

His Martha bore 4 children to her first husband; 2 died. Robert E. Lee married GW's stepson's granddaughter. GW never used tobacco, except maybe snuff; but he drank moderately & danced gayly. He swore at one Lee.

GW weighed 210 pounds in middle age, never wore a wig. He attended 40 different churches of various denominations, vowed to go to church at least once a month. But in 6 months of 1773 he made it only twice. His family motto wasn't wishy-washy: "The end justifies the means."

As army c.-in-c. GW refused salary, filed expense accounts. He vetoed only 2 bills in 8 years. Didn't sign the Declaration; he was fighting in the field. Martha was only 8 months older'n he.

Probably Washington would have lost the war without French aid. He quit raising tobacco, it ruined his soil. He sat for portraits by 19 painters & 2 sculptors. GW insisted that his personal guards be between 5 feet 8 & 5 feet 10.

Washington declined to let the House see important diplomatic papers. His favorite general, Nathanael Greene, was a fighting Quaker (& an ancestor of my indomitable wife). At either river in the dollar legend, it's physically impossible to throw one across.

GW covered more territory on horseback than Buffalo Bill.

He missed 8 straight Christmases at Mt. Vernon. The British offered a $16-to-$24 bribe to GW's soldiers who deserted with muskets. He sold his stock in the Bank of England.

Washington's 2nd inaugural address is the shortest in our history—135 words: he read it in less than 2 minutes. A soldierly mark for Ike to shoot at in '56. George wrote between 18,000 & 20,000 letters—half of 'em dictated. In 1793 he saw a balloon fly.

His spelling improved as he grew older, till it was as good as Jefferson's, who called GW's mind "great & powerful without being of the first order." He never studied Latin. Once he spoke sharply to Hamilton, his aide, & Alex resigned. Even during the war he read a solid book a fortnight.

Two sets of GW's primitive false teeth survive. . . . His face was slightly pockmarked. He read Pope & Fielding. He issued 4 orders against profanity. It took reports by 14 generals to convince GW that Major André was a spy, and should be hanged.

In his first campaign for the legislature, he was defeated. Next time he passed out more whisky. Of his 6 pallbearers, 5 were Masons. Martha spent February to June at Valley Forge (Mamie never got overseas). His first military rank was Major, at age 20 & $700 a year.

GW saw his first play at Barbadoes, West Indies, on his only trip abroad. He preferred rum to whisky, & if it was good enough for our country's father, it's good enough for unhypocritical little me. It isn't known whether his mother ever called his father Gus (for Augustine). He once hunted buffalo, helped kill 5.

He wore specs for reading. Freed his slaves by his will effective at his wife's death. Never lived in the White House. Loved to go to the theater. Gambled for small stakes. Hunted 2 or 3 times a week. Refused his nephew a US job.

GW's writings compared with Caesar's & Napoleon's in quality & historic value. He was worth about $780,000 at death. At Yorktown we lost 23 men, the French, 50. His pew cost him $146 for life. Some books he borrowed in 1783 were still among the 884 on his shelves 16 years later.

His biggest army was 23,000. Mt. Vernon is 96 feet by 30, shorter than several local ranch houses, but 2 stories high. His letters are masterpieces. *What a man he was!* Five times in US history we've been lucky enough to have the right president in a critical era.

Teddy Roosevelt

If you gentlemen suffer from a famine of good movie stories, why not make a film about Teddy Roosevelt, my boyhood idol? Here's a thumbnail scenario of filmworthy episodes in his lusty career. As you'd say at the Brown Derby, while paying $10,000 for a stinkeroo scenario over a dish of chopped liver, it's got everything.

(1) He was 7 when the Civil War ended, peeved because he couldn't get into it. (2) When he got out of Harvard he was frail, & spent 2 years on a western ranch. (3) Cowboys, Indians, big game hunting, horse opera. (4) In his early 30's as New York's police commissioner he sleuthed in a black cloak, hat pulled over his eyes.

(5) He bullied his 6 kids into point-to-point follow-your-leader treks around Oyster Bay, through ponds & over walls & haystacks. A bit of slapstick. (6) One favorite relaxation: diving off a 90-foot cliff into the ocean. Terrific shot; imagine Spencer Tracy, with double & stand-in.

(7) At 40 he organized the Rough Riders, sewed 11 pairs of specs into his uniform so he could see his way in the cavalry charge up San Juan Hill. (8) There is controversy whether the Spaniards ran before or after Teddy's headlong attack.

(9) Teddy became President before he was 43, when McKinley was shot. His youth didn't bother him. (10) He browbeat the Japs & Russians into making peace, & (11) the White House "kitchen cabinet," forcing reluctant middle-aged men to kick a football & play tennis with him. (Comic stuff!)

(12) Soon he took after the "interests," bludgeoned 'em with his big stick, & (though a Republican) was denounced as a traitor to his class. (13) He organized the Ananias Club as a convenient shooting gallery with his foes as targets, & (14) popularized "Bully!" "Delighted!" & the Big Grin.

(15) He sloganed "Tread softly, but carry a big stick,"

didn't tread very softly himself. (16) He finagled a strip of jungle from Panama for the Canal, & (17) sent the American fleet around the world, a fine piece of Yankee publicity, to show the world our voice had changed from soprano to deep bass.

(18) Teddy imagined our colonels & generals soft & chair-galled, so he ordered 'em to ride a horse 90 miles in 3 days, to prove themselves physically fit for promotion. (19) To show 'em he didn't mean to be petty he rode 100 miles himself (in 1 day, I think) through nasty weather. (Close-up shot of fiftyish president bouncing on horseback.)

(20) After he'd squeezed Taft into the presidency as his successor, off he went to Africa to shoot the wild whiffenpoop. (21) When he emerged from the jungle he took time out to give the Kaiser a piece of his mind, & (22) had some left over for the King of England.

Refreshed by all this he (23) got peeved at Bill Taft, (24) became a Bull Moose to run against him in 1912, & (25) after someone put a bullet in him, succeeded in getting Woodrow Wilson elected. To relax from his campaign he (26) went to the Amazon jungles to hunt & explore, & got his feet wet in the River of Doubt.

I forgot to mention that he (27) won the Nobel Peace Prize, incidentally. (28) In 1917 he wanted to organize a Rough Rider division of unmechanized cavalry & lead it to France, but Woodrow Wilson said no; thought it might make him a presidential possibility again in 1920. So (29) he sulked at editing a magazine.

All 4 of his sons (30) were in World War I; Quentin Roosevelt (for whom we named our son) was killed in aerial combat; & (31) Teddy Jr. died as a brigadier general in World War II. Teddy himself died in his sleep in 1919, embittered because he hadn't got to France. What a family, what a career! My favorite American president, & one of the 10 greatest.

Maybe all this is too long for one movie; maybe it'd make a $5,000,000 3-hour Technicolor epic. Certainly it might make a florid American opera. . . . Teddy had 2 fine romances, & Daughter Alice Longworth (the White House "princess") might pep the film up. On second thought, gentlemen, I think this rough script is worth $150,000, but you can have it for less, if you promise a really deft picture, & let me help pick director, hero & heroine.

※ ※ ※

I've agreed to a new compromise on vacation luggage with the girl on the upper half of the teeter-totter in our house: one big bag for each; one small bag in common; and she picks her favorite three costumes for me and I choose three for her to wear.

We've figured out a vacation trip that'll keep our womenfolk happy and yet satisfy my two boys' yearning to rough it: we'll leave the ladies at a 400-room resort hotel with a two-acre lobby on the edge of the mountains, and camp ourselves up near the timber line, emerging every few days to take a bath in their palatial quarters.

"Some women," drawls Betty Comfort, drying her hair in the back-yard sun, "aren't happy unless they've got several of their dearest women friends glaring jealously at them and watching their husbands like hawks."

※ ※ ※

FOR MEN ONLY [IV]

When the day comes that you can borrow Junior's dinner jacket, instead of vice versa . . . and you and your daughter exchange a few sparks and make up quickly as redheads must . . . or your youngest protests when you razz and belittle your own mental powers . . . and your beloved wife passes you into the doghouse a dish of your pet lentil soup . . . when the tasty mulligan stew of family life runneth over . . . you take your politics more calmly, confident that, whoever's elected, a happy home is the best blessed sanctuary.

✻ 5 ✻
Doctor, oh doctor

PSYCHIATRIC DEPARTMENT

How you can psychoanalyze yourself

Like this: Why do I lock so many drawers & doors, & leave keys helpfully nearby? Prop up a written warning against midnight snacks on the kitchen table while I raid the icebox? Think of my wife's intimate girl friends as sisters?

Just write your foibles down & study 'em. I never really feel comfortable in anything but a white shirt. Why? . . . Invariably I'm infinitely more relaxed in tan shoes than in black. Quite inexplicably, I now dislike beans, once my favorite dish. (Do this at least twice a year—good for you!)

All these quirks may be important: I fight sleep often for 90 minutes, rereading a page after I'm too sleepy to comprehend it. Enjoy the same people more at my own house than at theirs. Feel like an intruder when I'm late at a party. There's a secret meaning there.

I use 9 different kinds of tooth pastes & tooth powders, to get all their secret virtues. Detest both shaving soap, which my father used, as old-fashioned, & brushless shaving cream, as newfangled & unsatisfactory. Some deep significance, maybe?

For $5,000 a psychoanalyst probably could find out why I leave a dry washcloth near the phone to keep from being electrocuted when I'm summoned from my shower, which happens almost every day. And why I use 3 different kinds of soap, one for my hands, one for my face & one for my body.

Why do I have nightmares about George Yates standing on

a ladder long ago in the square at Denison taking snapshots of Governor John Hammill? Sleep under an electric blanket for 2 winters without ever turning it on? Swear I'll cycle or ride a horse every morning, & do it only a few times a year?

I've come to enjoy swinging an axe more than swinging a midiron. If a duck drops at my feet in a duck blind, I won't believe my shot hit it unless mine was the only shot fired. I hate to write letters except after midnight of the night before I'm leaving on a long trip.

I'm still irked about books people borrowed 15 years ago & never returned, but can't remember whom I'm irked at. Sometimes when I reread a book I'm struck by passages completely other than the ones that impressed me the first time. A psychiatrist might say I'm not half as smart as I think I am.

At breakfast I'm always more cheerful if I've finished shaving & bathing before the phone rings. I pay my bills more promptly when I have very little money than when I have enough. I'd give up the cash value of all my insurance policies to be 6 feet tall.

My secret ambition: to clip off all my hair some day & grow a butch haircut. Sometimes I suspect my interest in art is just a boyish fondness for looking at pictures. One of my suppressed desires is a jacket in a small check pattern, what we used to call a gambler's suit. Let the psychoanalyst make what he can of that!

I wish we could dress as informally downtown as men do on the main streets of our villages. Once or twice a week I'd like a meal of crackers & milk & nothing else. I like crackers better'n cake, incidentally, so there must be a plebeian streak in me.

Good meat loaf tastes better to me than any steak, & I like it better cold than hot. My one-dish breakfast: an orange milkshake with a raw egg in it; but I prefer crisp bacon. I've got a strong poor-boy complex, & when I pay a $40 dinner check in NY I feel as if I'd been caught in adultery. (Also, it's page one news.)

We're all better aware of our peculiarities, & it's better to write 'em down, study 'em & face 'em. Do you hate to shave? Prefer old clothes? Quiver when confronted by an ultra-fashionable dame? Like to lie long & read in a warm tub? Put everything off to the last minute? Maybe you suffer from an "old Adam" complex & need psychoanalysis, preferably by the prettiest sympathetic woman you know.

Puff-puff in a nervous era

This is the Era of Nervousness, & you probably smoke because like most people you're nervous about something. Maybe you're nervous about sex; maybe about something more trivial. Actually, there's less to be nervous about than in the days of no penicillin, no tinned frankfurters, no frozen fruit juice!

Does smoking diminish your nervousness? I doubt it. Not if I'm a fair example. Today I'm less nervous than when I was smoking 2 packages a day a fortnight ago. Smokers tend to dramatize their little hourly crises. Then they light one to help 'em cope with a pretended, imaginary strain.

If you're an average smoker, you probably light around 8,000 a year, or the equivalent of 1 cigarette about a quarter of a mile long, or from here to the water tower or the Locust Street bridge or someplace. If you tried to smoke one that long all at once it'd be quite a chore; but little by little you manage it.

For me the tip-off came when I realized it was as much fun to throw a cigarette away or squash it out as it was to light one. It's a pleasure you can't enjoy, of course, unless you've lit one first. (You can, of course, cut a cigarette up into 6 pieces & stamp each one out separately or hurl it away!)

This time—I've quit 8 or 9 times now, maybe more, twice for a year at a time—my cigarette wheeze took about 10 days to disappear. I can think more clearly, & my memory must have improved by 50%. I can remember which drawer or folder I hid something in, on what floor I left my reading glasses, & my engagements 3 days ahead.

At just this moment, after 14 days of freedom, I happen to want a cigarette very badly. I'm sitting in the rear end of a DC-6, flying high above a bank of clouds, through the blue, woolly-bottomed inverted bowl of the skies. The men on each side of me are smoking, & each has offered me a cigarette twice.

So right this minute I want a few puffs, & if I weren't writing about swearing off I might be vulnerable. But if I can get over the rough spots like this, I solemnly intend never to smoke again. Yes, I know, a cigarette may help you act nonchalant in a pinch, but so would it help to play with a yo-yo as you cross the dance floor at our town's charity ball.

But a yo-yo isn't quite the answer. Who'll invent a sensible substitute, a reasonable facsimile of smoking without the smoke & the goop & the wheeze in the bronchial tubes? For a while I thought of a tobaccoless substitute, but I'm afraid that might be cruel to tobacco growers & their kept clowns & crooners & the rest.

Maybe a sort of a smoke-consuming cigarette-holder? Perhaps you could puff in & puff out, but the smoke wouldn't reach your end of the mouthpiece; none of it would enter your mouth or your throat. Some sort of bypass valve? Could it be so devised as to retain the fresh, sweet tobacco aroma of a newly opened package, unburnt?

I think our heavy smoking is partly responsible for our characteristic national jitters. It helps make us nervous about the Russians; it helps fill us with foreboding about our children & our work & our old age; it has something to do with sex problems & cancer & sleeplessness & indigestion, if my hunch is right.

Oh, not for everybody, perhaps; maybe there are a few cast-iron exceptions. I won't quote any of the deadly warnings I've reread to stiffen my anti-smoking vow. But since I first swore off smoking—& since I first wrote a column against smoking—I suspect the number of cigarettes Americans smoke annually has doubled or tripled. But today I've fought my way through my 15th cigaretteless day, & we're flying above the clouds, above Pennsylvania's peaks, & no itch for one.

If men die young, it's unfair to their widows

When we moved into this neighborhood, the b.w. counted 13 widows living in solitary splendor in houses around the block. But only 1 widower. All within a long mashie shot of our house. In a way it seemed funny then; our friends joked; but it no longer seems funny.

What do we men do wrong? Why can't we live as long as our women? Why are there so many widows & so few widowers?

Why do the ladies outlast us 8 or 10 years on the average, but often 20 to 30 years? Are we the weaklings some of the feminists in pants (like Ashley Montague) say we are?

It isn't fair to the ladies either. They may be secretly relieved for a little while when we're no longer around to stir up a selfish commotion. They may secretly enjoy having the bed or the bedroom or the house all to themselves awhile. But after a time they begin to miss us, even if they won't admit it. We're better than nothing, & few of our widows ever remarry.

My guess is that more men died early in this decade in their 40's & 50's from the ordinary modern strains of work, play or family life than we lost in the Korean war. They were carried out on a stretcher at high noon, their widows & friends were stunned. But nobody sounded an alarm; no bugles.

What do we do wrong that women do right? I've been bludgeoned into admitting that men don't work as hard as women; I concede that the b.w. works harder than I do. Then why is the masculine strain greater? I dislike the notion of the b.w. being a widow for 30 long lonely years.

Of course, the gentlemanly thing might be to go early & go quietly, while the wife is still youthful, charming & likely to remarry. But we men aren't often farsighted about such things. We have silly daydreams of living to be septuagenarians. And No. 2 might not last long either.

Any zany can see that housework is harder than sitting on a swivel chair with feet on a desk & being brilliant. Do men suffer more from worry or anxiety? Is the everlasting pressure on men more ruthless? Is the hot rivalry more bitter downtown? Do they take the daily scuffle for a livelihood too seriously?

Maybe there's a touch in me of masculine selfishness, but it strikes me that the world is taking this phenomenon of male mortality with a fairly complacent shrug. All we can do is keep our insurance payments up & our weight down. "Take it easy!" the doctor tells you. Exactly how? While the doctors in geriatrics & gerontology help patriarchs of 80 reach 90, who helps the man of 55 reach 70?

Recently another of the friends of my youth died prematurely, & I fell to brooding. He was a dynamic & brilliant man; he lived with zest & gusto; he crowded a good deal of living into his short life. But I feel if he'd used part of his brilliance to save himself, he'd have lived 25 years longer.

I'd like to see the Vital Statistics column keep a sort of running tabulation, a daily box score on deaths "from natural causes" below 60. (Like the boxscore on persons killed in auto accidents, which stays in our Great State around 600 a year.) Does something go wrong with the steering mechanism?

Maybe the family doctor could fill out a questionnaire about each death under 60: circumstance of work, tensions at home & downtown, unusual habits, smoking, & drinking, personal foibles & low boiling points, secret inner warfare?

What is the New Strain? The life expectancy is now 70 or better, so why these premature departures? Money? Rivalry? Poor diet? Bad temper? Too intense feeling on too many things? Too much perfectionism? Maybe the university women, the Junior League & the League of Women Voters should look into this, if they dislike widowhood.

I know Omar Khayyam wrote that nobody "into such aureate earth is turned, as buried once, men want dug up again." But maybe we're all taking this too philosophically. I think it's too simple to blame it on heart trouble, blood pressure, high tension. What causes these? And why can't men learn from women how to avoid them? Or must the ratio rise to 26 widows to 1 widower in our block?

※ ※ ※

Our youngest threatens to sleep in the back yard on alternate nights, with pup tent and oilstove, if we'll keep one window illuminated. As an ex-boy myself, I predict (a) we'll peek through another window every twenty minutes, and (b) he'll be indoors by eleven o'clock.

When I think of Ike and Mamie eying the grocery bill in the White House, I wonder if they still have that gallon tin of synthetic maple sirup the Roosevelts used to hide in their big storage pantry.

Senator Mucklethump has taken a strong position against furriners sneaking into this country disguised as immigrants, ready to do yard work and wash dishes. He favors an even stronger bill that would have excluded three of his own grandparents.

Several nervous matrons in our country-club set are tempted to cancel appointments with their psychiatrists, since they saw *The Fourposter* and discovered that happily married wives and husbands quarrel frequently, even in bed.

My prestige has gone up locally since I officiated as a linesman at the pro tennis matches. My fellow enthusiasts thought I'd be afraid to call a foot fault on Kramer. Well, I was.

I'm medium popular when I compliment my Lady Love on the exactitude of her three-minute eggs, the pungency of her coffee, praise the crispness of the bacon. But if I dare scrape a singed spot off the toast, I'm instantly in the doghouse again.

Our town's home-grown Edison aims to keep his promise to picnic outdoors among the mayor's unsprayed mosquitoes at least fifty times this summer. He merely erects a slender framework around the picnic table and drapes mosquito netting over it, as they do over beds in screenless Brazil.

I see that a male N.Y. society columnist has left Toscanini off his new list of "400" aristocrats but included Louis Armstrong. Is this on the assumption that Toscanini is a furrier and that Armstrong is a great musician?

PHARMACEUTICAL SUPPLIES

Mystery in the medicine cabinet

I took a frank look at our medicine cabinet yesterday. It was mildly appalling. Ordinarily I don't look at it too closely. But with the phone strike on, we might suddenly have to fall back on it, instead of on doctors & drug stores, if the dial system should get tangled up. And what a baffling clutter!

Usually I just mumble that it ought to be tidied up a bit. If I can't persuade somebody else to do it, I do it myself. I'm just an old martinet who wants to know what's in each bottle or box of pills, & what it'll cure.

Two weeks after you've used some medicine the bottle begins to look mysterious. It cost you $2.25, & there appears to be $1.60 worth left, but what for? All the cryptic label says is: "No. 265020. One as directed."

How often?

What for?

Which child took the dose, & what were the preliminary symptoms?

Once when I was waiting to have 3 prescriptions filled at one time, I asked the pharmacist if he or I could write something on each label to augment the cryptic data a bit. He looked at me as if I were trying to crash the inner sanctum.

If any druggist writes in & complains that I'm unreasonable, I'll reprint a column I once wrote in which I asserted flatly that the corner druggist is the No. 1 citizen of any neighborhood, & that the drug store is the rallying point of civilization.

Our medicine cabinet seems to contain liquids, pills & capsules for almost every ailment & orifice of the human body. Here are two kinds of thermometers, & there are powders to be applied "as needed," & here are suppositories apparently intended to relieve a child's internal blockade.

Here's a red liquid that smells awfully good. You could probably serve it as an after-dinner liqueur & no one would know the difference & probably someone would smack his lips & say, "This is great stuff!" And possibly it would do 'em more good than the meager thimbleful from the $9 bottle.

More than once I've vowed that every bottle & pillbox in our medicine chest must be labeled specifically, so we can discern its magic virtues at a glance. More than once I've waked up at 3 A.M. & haven't been positive which of two ruddy bottles to administer to our coughing youngest.

In all this I have a selfish interest, too. I'm the official medicine taster for the family. Whenever one of the children has shown an understandable reluctance to swallow a sticky spoonful, it has been my lot to swallow a small dram of it myself, smack my lips & proclaim how delicious it is.

It isn't always easy to get a doctor nowadays, & some of the neighborhood drug stores close at such unpharmaceutical hours as 5 (on Sunday!) or 8 o'clock. Remember when the cheery drugstore lights glowed till midnight?

In moments of skepticism or resignation I've thought that almost any mild ailment or distemper might be assuaged by reaching into the medicine cabinet, picking almost any non-poisonous bottle or box of pills at random, & swallowing a modest portion. But this method is not for those of little faith.

I suppose that some day, when we've come to understand better the magical & mystic properties of the sulfas & penicillin, we'll swallow a small dosage of these pills for certain fevers & infections as nonchalantly as we now swallow a pill for a headache.

Or as trustingly as a soldier nicked by an enemy projectile dusted his wound with some of his sulfa powder and swallowed the rest.

Here's a brown bottle with about 30 charming little pills, half red & half yellow. It says on the label to take one twice a day. But what for?

In a pinch phone your doctor immediately, of course, & (holy cornflakes!) don't make the mistake of trying to practice medicine without him. And don't imagine I'm pretending I know anything about the pills & fluids even in my own medicine cabinet much less yours. I'm just flabbergasted. But you'd better know what's in the bottle, or throw it away. And frugal as I am, I ask the b.w. to tape supplementary labels on them.

Is penicillin your dish?

Perhaps I ought to warn you that the "wonder drugs" may not be your dish. My scuffle with penicillin has taught me a lesson. One man's miracle drug may be another man's poison. Maybe the army doc was right the first time when he said, "Paint him with iodine & mark him duty."

Some of our best people are allergic to penicillin & the sulfas. Penicillin knocked out our town's most famed explorer for almost a month. It laid an eminent editor low in the hospital for almost a fortnight of discomfort & anguish. It burst out in hives all over a scion of one of our town's old families.

Exactly a month ago, an old tennis bruise at my ankle flared up with a temperature of 103. With the thermometer still in her hands, the b.w., who's quite a nurse, summoned our doctor. He frowned at the reddish spot & cut short my feverish greeting of semi-humorous apologies.

"Ever had any penicillin?" he inquired. "Sure!" I told him nonchalantly. "Bother you any?" he asked. "Nope!" said I. "Turn over," he said, "I'm going to let you have it. I don't want that inflammation to spread above the knee."

In 3 days he squirted 3 shots of penicillin into me, 1,000,000 units in each shot. "You should feel overprivileged," he said. "When we landed at Saipan I had a total of only 2,000,000 units of penicillin for a whole battalion."

He also gave me some penicillin pills to swallow between & after the shots. His attack on the infection was successful. In a week it had vanished. "Ah, those miracle drugs!" I murmured.

Ten days later I was walking on Locust Street when suddenly I noticed that my ankle seemed painfully sprained. What's more, I seemed to have 10 or 15 marbles on the bottoms of both my feet, just inside my skin. "Ouch!" I muttered, & began to limp.

I massaged 'em & soaked 'em & scowled at 'em. That night, 2 enormous bumps the size of golf balls appeared on my forehead. "Mosquito bites," I told myself. On the 3rd day the bumps on the soles of my feet subsided & I caught a plane to the GOP convention.

At dinner that evening with friends, 3 enormous bumps asserted themselves on the back of my neck. The marbles inside the bottom of my feet returned, redoubled. I limped around the Conrad Hilton & the convention hall. New bumps appeared around my midriff, front & rear.

I caught a train home. "The chiggers have certainly attacked me," I told the b.w. "Chiggers, eh?" she queried, & phoned the doctor. He looked at me and grinned. "You've got a reaction to the penicillin," he said. "You're allergic to it."

I'll say I was. New bumps popped out in my hair. Both big toes swelled up. Both my navel & my coccyx were inflamed. In turn, all my joints were swollen, ankles, knees, wrists & elbows, tender & painful. I sat in bed with my tiny typewriter on top an inverted bucket between my legs, trying to be gay & blithe. My fingertips hurt.

All sorts of alarming penicillin gossip drifted in. A chap at the state university had taken 6 months to get over his penicillin allergy. Others were covered with hives so tender they couldn't lie down comfortably. Some people were even allergic to aspirin.

This wonder drug was treating me more brutally than my original fever-infection. How I longed for the peace & quiet of my 103-degree temperature! I could picture the 3,000,000 moldy little penicillins racing through my veins, trying to fight their way out, from cranium to big toe.

Against this miracle drug on a rampage, my doctor mobilized other wonder drugs. First antihistamine & then cortisone, in hot pursuit through my arteries. Then a posse of terramycin with a battalion of ACTH. Then a wave of adrenalin, & some APC with codeine to soothe me.

I've learned this: you're not allergic to a wonder drug the 1st time you take it. But the 2nd time, watch out! There's a non-allergy penicillin coming up; be of good cheer.

After 3 weeks, I tried to hold my tennis racket. But there was still a tender lump in the palm of my hand.

* * *

Those gals in the League of Women Voters really get things done in our town instead of merely talking about 'em. They've not only wangled us a city manager (with negligible male help), but one of 'em actually has a room papered with New Yorker covers and road maps!

One of the fathers in our neighborhood is a pushover for the American legend that a man must monopolize his son's electric train. Our youngest is so captivated by his example that if I decline to erect his train in the garden or garage he treats me like a traitor to American boyhood.

By mid-vacation a certain mild apathy has set in among our youngsters; their diabolic ingenuity sags. It's now up to their more modern mothers to think up mischief for them so they can lead full, untrammeled lives.

At lunch our town's merchant biggies were mourning the downtown traffic jams and the hot competition from suburban stores with parking lots. Over their pie à la mode they discovered the traffic jams and parking shortage were augmented by their own cars, their staffs' and their wives'.

My master stroke as a grass-lawn expert came twelve years ago, when I built a concrete tennis court to cover half our back yard, faintly tinted green, 120' x 44'. Now I conspire darkly again: maybe concrete shuffleboard, horseshoe and badminton arenas in the bad spots; perhaps paddle tennis in front?

Even when we want to be big-hearted to each other, my Dream Woman and I manage to quarrel violently. I argue our next binge ought to be a clothes dryer; she insists on a power mower. So we're at swords' points (even if they're rubber swords).

"DR. MILLER" PRESCRIBES

How to cure a cold

I am momentarily between colds, & I owe it all to my careful reading of a series of learned articles that the common cold is incurable. At this moment I estimate there are 500,000 sniffling in the Great State because they read the wrong article.

In a movie theater I saw an attractive pair sneezing in each other's faces, kissing not too stealthily (no sneaks they!), rubbing cheeks with each other, breathing the same air less than 4 inches apart. Every time they sneezed or coughed, people looked daggers at 'em.

But did they look daggers at each other? If they did, it was while I was watching the little signs on Grace Kelly's face that she's dieting too strenuously. This fascinating research left me time enough to count a total of 17 kisses exchanged by the sneezers; I may have missed a few.

Tell the truth. When the hot blood was racing through your veins like champagne, did you ever pass up a kiss because you were sneezing a little? Did you look daggers at a girl just because she sneezed before, after or during a kiss? If you did, your blood must have flowed like lunch-counter ketchup.

My theory is that the common cold is a resistance disease. You catch it when your resistance is low. The way to build up resistance is to expose yourself to a girl who sneezes between kisses. Or the next best thing: Go to a movie where maybe 2 young hellions nearby will be kissing & sneezing. Some people are afraid they'll catch cold in crowds, at church or movies, or on necking parties. They miss a lot of kisses.

But that's no way to build up resistance; ask your own doctor. I think people who keep their houses all winter at 75 to 80 degrees & go to Florida catch more colds than people who keep their houses at 65 to 70 degrees & wear sweaters & shun Florida, & they have pinker cheeks & better complexions (like the Irish or the English)—at least their noses are pinker.

I may have this mixed up, but aren't summer colds caught in damp houses by people without dehumidifiers? People keep urging me to buy dehumidifiers, whether I need 'em or not, because they'll capture a gallon or 2 of water out of the air every day & that ain't hay. "I haven't had a cold all summer," they brag.

Then, too, aren't people susceptible to winter colds because the furnace heat in the house dries out the air? So you need a humidifier to keep the air moist? People are constantly urging me to buy a humidifier because it saturates the air with gallons of water. "I haven't had a cold all winter," they boast.

What I'd like to watch is a humidifier & a dehumidifier throbbing side by side, battling it out, & see which one wins. Or have 'em in adjacent rooms, winter & summer, & see who catches the most colds, the humidified or the dehumidified. My b.w. often keeps the bathtub filled just to humidify me.

I'm suspicious of a girl who says, "You'd better not kiss me, you'll catch my cold." It isn't her cold she doesn't want you to catch; she doesn't want you to catch her. If she loves you (or even *likes* you sufficiently) she'll gladly share her cold with you, long before you're married.

Lately I've happened to be under the influence of people who say, "For a cold, go to bed with a big pitcher of hot lemonade laced with rum." I take such advice skeptically. I've seen such colds linger on, week after week, until you're sick of the taste of lemons.

Why is the common cold so mysterious? They can operate on the heart, they can splice you a new eye, but they can't cure a cold. "It's a virus," they say, "so take it easy." I think the cold is often a psychosomatic disease brought on by non-filterable self-pity & a desire to stay in bed all day.

Did you ever see an Eskimo bare-headed in a blizzard, or with a runny nose in July? In short, did you ever see an Eskimo? The sensible thing to do is to *have* 6 colds a year, like the average man, some of 'em lasting 6 weeks each. This'll build up your resistance for the other half of the year when you're between colds.

Sex in 10 easy lessons

Maybe I can't write my sex column in time for this year's crop of bridegrooms & brides, but perhaps I can give 'em a few preliminary hints. I apologize for the delay; some day I'll master this delicate theme.

Meanwhile, they mustn't forget that God invented sex, too; it's nothing to be ashamed of. Blushes? Yes! Shame? No!

A man whose father-in-law is a famous millionaire told me that on the eve of his wedding he knew nothing about sex, incredibly, though he was a Princeton grad & of fashionable family. His own father & brother were traveling in Europe, so he asked his father-in-law for sex advice.

"I never," his fiancée's father said, "discuss sex!" Was a father-in-law ever crueler?

Even bridegrooms (& maybe a few brides) who think they know all about sex don't really know enough. I estimate that 85% of this spring's Young Enchanted haven't ever read a book on sex clear through. What a pity somebody doesn't give 'em a $7.50 copy of Van de Velde on sex for a wedding present, instead of trivial bric-a-brac.

My wedding gift to 'em is these 10 suggestions.

1. Get over your embarrassment about sex, if any. It must be discussed just as your house, travel, food, work, relatives, children & other facts of life must be discussed. The bluenoses are the only ones who don't want you to, & you owe them nothing.

2. Ask your father or mother first for advice on sex. Maybe they aren't the type, but ask 'em first. If Dad is too bashful, maybe he'll talk more easily & candidly by candlelight or in the dark, or outdoors under the stars.

3. If the idea of seeking sex enlightment from Mom or Dad embarrasses you or makes you laugh, try your preacher. Some churchmen, I understand, are now up to quite a practical & scientific little informal lecture. They may even lend you a good book.

4. Too homey or sentimental? Then ask your doctor or your doctor's nurse. Their advice may be worth more than any $5 prescription for a tummy ache. Maybe you'd better plan to consult 'em again after you've been married a year & run into problems.

5. All right, then, you think it'd be more fun to ask your dearest "sophisticated" friends? So go ahead & ask 'em! But remember, 49 times out of 50 they're strictly amateur; even if they're hussies or blacksheep or roués; & their problems aren't necessarily your problems, nor vice versa. But they'll tell you a lot.

6. So you think sex finesse comes instinctively, eh, or after years of experiment by trial & error & all that rot? Ho, hum; the human race survives, yes. But so do tension, jealousy, frustration, resentment, unhappiness, neurosis & divorce. One couple's sex life differs from another's as much as their faces & personalities differ.

7. Cut loose from the Victorian notion that sex is wicked; or sacred in the solemn, pompous sense; or hush-hush; or a monster; or a mystical labyrinth. You didn't dream it up, nor did the 1,000 naughtiest people you ever met. It's complex evolution & it's still evolving. (Even the Russians don't claim they invented sex!)

8. Any lawyer, doctor or psychologist can explain in 10 or 15 minutes the numerous advantages of chastity & fidelity. In spite of the more lurid phases of Kinsey's discoveries, most of the people are well behaved most of the time. Especially the better people.

9. Take along on your honeymoon a couple of the better books on sex; there are several good ones that cost only 25 or 35 cents. Maybe that's silly; you probably won't have time left to read 'em. Better read them *before* you get married.

10. You newlyweds ought to discuss sex frankly & without embarrassment. A little discussion now may prevent distress & cross-purposes later. Maybe you're emancipated enough to read those books aloud. It's no sin, & it's no sin for me to suggest it. Sex snarls cause half the divorces.

Can the Golden Rule apply to the sex life of young married people? All the experts in the 9 or 10 books I've read agree that it had better apply (or else!): "Do as you would be done by if you were your mate." Once you solve this delicate & complex relationship (who knows) you may live happily forever after.

Maybe you need trifocals

You'll probably be wearing glasses by the time you're 45 if not sooner or already. The chances are almost 2 to 1 you will. I hated it when I had to put 'em on for reading & so will you. But you'll adapt!

The human eye was designed by the Master Oculist to focus at 20 feet or more, ere civilization overtook us, as when trying to spear a rabbit for supper. It can't stand the strain forever of reading at 20 inches or less. So rather than hold the phone book out at arm's length, better get some specs.

But promise me one thing. That you won't wear 'em when you sit for your picture. Why people do puzzles me. They wouldn't pose holding an ear trumpet at their ear, would they? Yet some charming & intelligent people feel nude in a portrait without their bifocals.

Corny jokes about bifocals deter many a timid soul from wearing glasses long after she needs 'em. Never was there a duller or flimsier gag, because people with bifocals often have better natural vision than people with monofocals.

Actually, what most people need in their 40's is glasses to help 'em focus for close-up work; their distant vision often isn't impaired. So they start with plain reading glasses.

Then they discover that when they try to look farther away than 20 inches through their reading glasses, they can't see clearly, any more than they could through a magnifying glass. Many a keen-eyed exec can't see a pretty stenographer across the room.

So he braves the gags about bifocals & finally buys a pair. A bifocal usually has the small magnifying segment for reading in the bottom of each lens, with clearer glass above for more distant vision; sometimes almost plain glass. (People used to achieve the same result by wearing their specs on the tip of their nose, & thus won a reputation as quaint, lovable characters.)

I'm amazed at the number of attractive women who're so nearsighted that they can't recognize a friend clearly on the street without their glasses, though they can read without 'em. Some of 'em try expensive contact lenses, but wearing 'em is a career by itself.

Many a man who can't look up a number comfortably in the phone book without his glasses never wears any for shooting, golf or tennis. If you stumble along without 'em when you need 'em, though, you're apt to get crotchety, like a deaf man who suspects everybody's mumbling.

Some people avoid bifocals by wearing crescent-shaped reading glasses, with no glass at all in the upper part. Those look almost as affected as lorgnettes or monocles, which really aren't affected at all, but merely convenient or fashionable forms of specs.

We've had a plague of overly ornate glasses since the war, pink & red & green, studded with rhinestones, filigreed, carved & sloe-eyed. They make women look queer. I think no glass is more comfortable (or more becoming) than a plain pair of substantial brown tortoise glasses.

When I was a boy I once tried to wear a pair of 'em with plain glass, in a valiant attempt to look intellectual. But I gave it up. They have a more important virtue: when you drop 'em, the resilient frame prevents 'em from breaking.

When I began to wear glasses I got kidded a lot, around the house, because I was always mislaying 'em. So I've gradually scattered 7 pairs strategically around home & office, on my four desks. Mislaid ones always show up in the pocket of another coat. But there should be tiny name & address tags to help you recover lost glasses. (I don't think the specs tycoons go for that idea much.)

If I go a day or two without reading or writing, I find I can read comfortably without glasses. But after 8 or 10 hours at desk or typewriter or the printed page I need 'em again. All I need is monofocal reading glasses, yet I'm happiest in my new trifocals at an art gallery—for (1) catalog, (2) pictures on the wall, & (3) friends in the distance.

I'm amused by naive darlings who pick up somebody's reading glasses, look across the room, & exclaim, "Oh, I can't see anything through 'em!" "Oh, I'm so young!" Neither can the man they're made for, beyond reading range. (Same effect as a magnifying glass.) I'm surprised at how many people in their 40's can use each other's glasses to read a juicy passage.

※ ※ ※

"Some of the wives in our town," muses Peter Comfort, massaging a blighted area on his lawn, "can't see anything funny about men unless they happen to be talking about their own husbands."

So far I've still been unable to negotiate a compromise with my wife about which tune we'll wake up to—my Lombardo swing version of "Tales from the Vienna Woods" or her "Meet Mr. Callahan." The machine's nearer her bed, so we're waked by Mr. Callahan.

I'm better able to understand the kind of music collegians play on their phonographs till 3 A.M. since Junior explained to me that a tolerably good musician may be hot, but if he's really hot he's cool.

As a bachelor I used to think there were only two sides to any question. My education in logic is more complete now: we've five in our family and every question has five sides. (If my opinion may be counted as one.)

MEDICAL BRIC-A-BRAC

Mecca for the middle-aged

Recently I flew to the Mayo Clinic at Rochester to visit a friend who'd flown more than 1,000 miles for an operation. Some of the world's finest surgeons & hospitals operate within an hour or 2 of his home in the East. But he felt safer at Mayo's.

    Doctors in our town make a little face, what the French call a moue, when you mention the allurements & marvels of Mayo. What has Rochester got that our own hospitals, doctors, interoffice "clinics" haven't got? But why argue with superstitious & moonstruck invalids or hypochondriacs? Or people with money?

A trip to Mayo's, a few decades ago, began to be a reward to Ma for a well-spent life, maybe after 6 grandchildren, a fur coat, a big car & a trip to New York or California or Europe. She wasn't feeling as chipper as she used to; maybe the Mayos could wave a magic wand & restore her youth.

The Rochester routine, the Mayo tradition remind some of us of pilgrimages the natives make in Central Europe to visit a famous wise man, neither saint nor surgeon, but a whiff of each, in a village often 100 miles away. He'll listen to their troubles, rub their sores with oil, & they'll go home (they devoutly hope) maybe healed & whole. The Mayo patient's faith is like that.

But the Mayo Clinic, of course, does far more. I'm not an expert on exactly what it does. I only know that doctors in our town who've been exposed to it speak of it as an Arab speaks of Mecca. My friend, languid on his hospital cot, able to pay for the best in the world, had no doubt that he was getting it.

But I for the moment was interested in the town, as I left him to rest after our first half-hour visit. Rochester is more like a resort town than a medical center. It has the glitter & perfume of affluence. More men with fur hats, fur collars, fur-lined coats than I'd ever seen in such a small town; more marble, tile, chromium, aluminum.

I strolled down the opulent main street, past the liquor stores & the souvenir stores, & popped into a famous cafeteria for some coffee. On the wall was a sign I admired with a grimace: "Of course we'd like to hear all about your fascinating operation. But not while we're eating, please!"

To my delight, I discovered that some of the bigger hospitals, the Zumbro, Kahler & Damon hotels & restaurants are connected by shiny white-tiled subway tunnels with the Mayo clinic buildings. I wandered through them & in a jiffy began to run into friends from back home: some proud, some furtive, caught in the act.

I wandered through the marble halls of the clinic (7 kinds of marble, from Africa, Europe & Pennsylvania). On each floor was a large waiting room, each with 5 times as many seats as our Rock Island depot. Patients & their friends waited to be called, or for reports from diagnostician or surgery.

This is the heart of Rochester. But the town itself reminds

you more of Saratoga or Hot Springs or Reno or Long Beach. It has the "biggest souvenir store in the world," & 6 lighted horseshoe courts as well as 5 concrete tennis courts, & a 5-cent bus line & 4 airlines, an incredible number of churches, & more bars than churches.

When I was a cub reporter in DM I once interviewed Charles Mayo, & later when I was a New York journalist in a $125 suit I interviewed his brother William. I can't remember what William told me, but Charles told me that women who smoke & drink lose their good looks sooner. It made a sensation & I was quoted in *Reader's Digest*.

The air was nippy, so I dropped into a café for a Tom & Jerry. I espied an item in the local gazette: "Local Young Man Makes Carleton Frosh." The young man was David Mayo of the Mayo clan, 4th generation. No Yale or Princeton for him; he was at Carleton, a nearby small-town college only a few miles away.

Gosh, I haven't lifted even 2 of Rochester's 7 veils; about the Bingo & the Alcoholics Anonymous & the 95-year-old Hubbell House where you drive quite a few miles for a $3 fish dinner. And I haven't told you of my friend's fascinating operation. Maybe he could have done as well at Massachusetts General or Johns Hopkins or NY's Doctors Hospital. And maybe I'll give Rochester another whirl later. Tonight, shall we bowl? Or shall we study faces in the lobby & guess who'll die next?

Planned parenthood preferred

When I was 16 I won an essay contest run by a DM afternoon paper. The assigned topic was "The Most Important Thing in the World" (which was also, by a coincidence, the title of a movie then due in town). As a juvenile disciple of H. G. Wells & Bernard Shaw, I chose "birth control."

By an even more historic coincidence I married years later a lovely brunette who also thinks birth control is important. She did more than write essays; she raised money, became Iowa president of Planned, & eventually a member of the national board, &

permits me to go to conventions with her, & even help defray her expenses.

Since I was 16 I've traveled a lot, & my enthusiasm for birth control is one enthusiasm travel has not quenched. I've seen a lot of babies who weren't eating well. Scientists keep talking about nourishing pills & synthetic foods & making ham & eggs out of thin air. But famines still kill millions, & more millions are always hungry, from birth till death, millions who didn't ask to be born.

I know that many object to birth control; & why not? It's a free country. They may even be right, though I don't happen to think so. But when hungry people keep the world in turmoil & drag our sons off to die on muddy battlefields far away, we can't kowtow to opinions. A world which can use atom bombs can use birth control.

Will synthetic foods or "miracle farming" save us from the bared fangs of overpopulation? I doubt it. Our stomachs got set in their ways a billion years before the chemists came along. We can't go back to nibbling seaweed; even the fish don't like it. Shall we be patient & wait for the chemists? If I were dying of hunger I'd resent such patience in the well-fed.

I receive bitter snarling letters when I mention birth control. For every sweet & lovable soul who tries to reason with me, pitying my proneness to error, 10 letters boil with anger & intimidation. Maybe the topmost anti-birth-control leaders have begun to examine the hope mankind reposes in birth control; but their devoted lesser followers are still adamant.

If by a miracle of chemistry or agronomy we could make edible the grass, the weeds & the leaves, & if there were enough weeds & leaves & grass to feed the limitless hordes in China, India & Japan, then birth control would quickly become less important. Though free people would still be wise to space & control the arrival of their babies, if only to spare their women.

Every act of intelligence contravenes & harnesses "nature": cooking, building a roof; air-conditioning or inventing TV; weeding a cornfield or writing a love-letter; praying, or breeding better sheep. I believe the Almighty wants us to use our brains to improve our lives & the lives of our children. And to help our suffering brothers—& sisters—across the seas.

Luckily, birth control is now an exportable surplus. As I

urged the b.w. 15 years ago, she & her clear-eyed associates have adopted the policy that India needs it more than Iowa. Americans of every sect & denomination practice birth control; nowhere under the Stars & Stripes is it a secret. (And our American people can mostly afford all the babies they want. Maybe we should have more.)

I was ashamed at our town's neglect of Dr. Ab Stone, the serene & inspired birth-control expert. As I listened to him tell quietly about his expert advice to the Indian government & Japanese government (no longer blocked by a timid American army of occupation), I thought: "This man is doing more singlehanded to bring on a peaceful brave new world than any other one man alive."

Hear this, neighbors: The hungry people are peeping over our frontiers, over our fences, into our pantries. How many unlimited billions can this limited world support? While you & I ate our last 25 turkey dinners, 100 million have died in agony from hunger in Asia's villages & streets.

I prophesy solemnly that unless we help the unenlightened control the onslaught of unfeedable babies, this desperate overpopulation will march against us—or against our children.

I wish I could find that essay for which the DM *Capital* awarded me $10 long ago when I was in high school. Maybe I was more eloquent then.

Into the valley of the shadow—I take our young one to the dentist

I never realized how dangerous it was to have our 10-year-old's tooth pulled till I heard of a friend's ghastly ordeal with *his* child's tonsils. That had been as ticklish as any skull or heart surgery, to hear her tell it.

So I didn't undertake my mission lightly. It's still a nightmare. I could have let the b.w. escort the young one to the dentist's. But I decided it was a man's job. "You'll have to skip your breakfast, Son," I said. He agreed instantly & said, "You can't have any either!"

"Just so you buy me breakfast afterwards at the cafeteria!" he stipulated. At such a moment I could deny him nothing. "Two breakfasts!" I exclaimed impetuously. Later I was sorry. But at the moment I was thinking of a friend who had died of an embolism after an operation.

Just like a man, trying to delay the crisis, I stopped at the barber & got him a butch haircut. It made him look oh, so young & vulnerable. Like a profile of a young emperor on an old Roman coin, I thought. "Do I get some gas?" he teased. "I want some gas!" With red hair clipped, his freckles loomed up brighter.

At the dentist's a pert girl in white challenged my contention that we had an appointment. "Not 9:30 Tuesday!" she said. "It's down here 9:30 A.M. next Saturday." I looked around. It seemed a small anteroom, crowded, & hardly equipped for a 4-day visit.

"But maybe we can squeeze him in!" she said brightly & cheerily. I dug for a diverting magazine. Why are lights so difficult in doctors' waiting rooms? Maybe this'll mean a reprieve of several hours! Quentin behaved with the unconvincing gayety of a B-17 bombardier off for Berlin.

Before I could finish one page of an obsolete magazine article the Girl in White ushered Quentin into the doctor's inner sanctum. The sweat was warm along my backbone. I squeezed in, too. Nobody was going to keep me from my son's side in this hour of his supreme ordeal! This was just as rough as adenoids, & nobody could tell me different!

He was full of beans. He bounced up & down in the elaborate chair. "It won't hurt!" said the dentist. "Hurt?" he exclaimed. "I love it!" They took a half-nelson on him & began to pump the gas. My heart went into slow motion. I needed gas, too. (But I wouldn't order any for myself without knowing what it cost.)

That bouncing, pneumatic, eupeptic little boy began to droop. His eyelids closed. His head fell back against the headrest. His words faded off like a phonograph record running down. My heart bent toward him in compassion. How pale his skin, how brilliant the freckles!

No time to be lost! The doctor went after him with a pair of high-polished pliers. Doc gently gripped the little ivory, pulled it out effortlessly, a tiny rootless thing. (An incongruous thought occurred to me: I could have yanked that over-ripe baby-tooth myself with long-nosed pliers.)

Animation began quickly to flow back into his arms & legs; they began to twist & wriggle. "Where's the 15 cents you promised me for the tooth, Dad?" were his first words. "I want some more teeth pulled! When do I get some breakfast?"

"You'd better have some lunch, too, Son," I said at the cafeteria. So he added a few midday items till he reached a cool $1.47.

In my side pocket was the tooth, with his 2 dimes. I now have one or more teeth from each member of our family. Some day I'll have 'em made into cuff-links.

One of his desserts was lemon meringue pie. His meringue collided with my butter-dish. I reached for some butter & got meringue on my sleeve. I wiped it with my napkin & began to act normal again. When I used my napkin, it got on my vest & lapel. . . . I reached into my coat pocket & got more meringue on my coat. Back to reality. When I reached for my handkerchief, meringue stuck to my pants. A newly cleaned suit. My father-love began to fade. I got him back to school in time, I hope, for his arithmetic class, still a little shaken.

* * *

What unafraid America really demands: a contraption to whisk food and dishes from tin can and cupboard to stove to dinette nook to dishwasher to cupboard and garbage grinder automatically. Which Edison-Goldberg will save our dream girls from skillet melancholia?

We've hung John Sharp's exquisite painting of exotic undersea life over our mantel, and our neighbor with three porches is puzzled by the clusters of starfish, sea anemones and sea horses. Nor can we understand his love for his sepia prints of the Parthenon and a lady taking a nap at Pompeii, either.

At summer's end, it's no wonder a smart schoolboy is glad to swap his testy dad and mom (worn to a frazzle) for a fresh, well-rested teacher, maybe a nondisciplinarian in a superprogressive classroom full of personality kids!

"I got snubbed," reports Peter Comfort, eying a sprayed weed for signs of wilting, "for needling Betty about her heavy outside schedule. 'Running for Congress?' I asked. 'Do you expect me,' she retorted, 'to waste all my time on you?'"

FOR MEN ONLY [V]

When Junior uses what he's learned from Darwin to prove the Russians may revolt against the Politburo . . . or our daughter plays on the phonograph my five favorite tearful records, which she dislikes but which she knows make me feel cheerful . . . and Quentin at every meal for a week offers to use his summer-camp money to finance a family motor-trip vacation . . . or my wife pats me gently on the cheek as she slides through my den on her way to scratch in her garden . . . then I quit mumbling to myself and concede that I'd probably have had no better treatment as a bachelor than I get as a husband.

6

Sports illuminated

FIELD & STREAM

Daddy goes a-hunting

Thoughts the day before: I wish I'd kept my vow to practice shooting clay pigeons all summer. . . . Wouldn't I wow 'em! Three shots, 3 ducks. You certainly get ribbed if you miss too many. Not right away, but later.

Well, you can get by for a year on 1 or 2 lucky shots, if you keep mentioning 'em casually. Sometimes the birds fly right into it. Shucks, isn't every American a natural marksman?

Where are those wading boots of mine? Last time I saw 'em was when the kids filled 'em with water to see if they were really waterproof. If I can't hit any ducks, I can at least wade out good-naturedly after the ones the other men shoot.

Never saw my dream girl so enthusiastic about my going hunting. She's hankering for a taste of wild duck. No woman ever takes much stock in the explanation "the ducks just weren't flying."

Wonder if I still remember how to put that gun together? It's been a whole year & it always was tricky the way the bolt got stuck. Maybe I'd better practice putting it together & taking it apart, so in the blind I can do it casually, like a veteran hunter.

It'll certainly impress the kids if I come home with a pile of ducks—for about 5 minutes. Daughter will be sure to observe that they're such handsome creatures & it's a shame to shoot 'em. . . . She'll eat her share, though.

I must remember to lead the ducks, to aim ahead of 'em; all

the hunters are agreed on that. Unless they're flying sideways or backwards. Let's see, a duck flies up to 60 miles an hour, so while I'm making up my mind to pull the trigger, a duck can fly a quarter of a mile; that seems a long way to lead 'em.

Guess I'll lead the first duck about 6 feet & then maybe I'll hit the 2nd or 3rd duck. Shucks, *how* I wish I'd done a little shooting with the old hand trap. Maybe I'd better just shoot by instinct. Atta-ole-instinct.

Where on earth is my hunting cap? If it's still where I put it, then I've done Junior an injustice. With 200,000 hunters in Iowa, I can't possibly be the worst shot. My last shooting was with a carbine. But then you don't have to bring home what you missed with a carbine.

Let's see—woolen undershirt, wool army shirt, shell vest & hunting jacket—that oughta keep me warm enough. Probably be roasted; you're always either too warm or too cold. Can I wear those fleece-lined moccasins inside my boots? Hope I don't have to chase those ducks far.

It seems silly to take along 200 shells for 5 or 10 ducks. Might have to lay a barrage, though. Wish I'd put a rubber recoil pad on my gun, as I decided to 15 years ago. Mustn't forget my duck stamp, either; the kids'll like it for their collection. Gee whiz, I wish I'd done some trap shooting.

Well, this is certainly the de luxe way to go hunting, in a station wagon with bed & board. We weren't exactly underprivileged on that big barge on the Mississippi, either. Or on the gigantic hunting bus. Wonder if we'll ever go lion hunting in Africa. (Probably in a covert made of glass brick.)

But right now the problem is ducks, & how am I going to tell a teal from a mallard on a foggy dawn with 'em flying in curlycues? Oughta study my recognition charts. Gosh, have I still got that wooden plug in the magazine of my pump gun? Hunting isn't as simple as it used to be in Daniel Boone's day, is it? If you didn't shoot anything you just didn't eat. Maybe I can still get out for a few minutes with the hand trap & some clay pigeons.

Rendezvous with a duck

Rumors of my prowess as a hunter seem to spread like wildfire. Probably they're responsible for my flock of invitations to hunt ducks, pheasants & quail all over Iowa & surrounding states. Shucks, men, I learned to shoot out of a book. My big secret? Not to shoot when anybody's looking.

Old Chinese proverb: If you wish to be happy for an hour, get intoxicated. If you wish to be happy for 3 days, get married. If you wish to be happy for 8 days, kill your pig & eat it. If you wish to be happy forever, learn to hunt & fish.

Some book lore: With a good 12-gauge shotgun (full choke) & long-range shells you can kill ducks up to 60 yards away. . . . Or from Sears-Roebuck's Walnut Street door to the Montgomery-Ward alley. . . . But large ducks & geese always seem closer than they are.

Here's what loses you more ducks & pheasants (& especially quail) than anything else: failure to make up your mind promptly enough to take a shot. Two seconds (often only one!) make all the difference in the world. Simplest & cheapest way to improve your marksmanship. Raise & aim your gun 100 times at & 24 feet past an imaginary live target.

You lead your target by 24 feet (shoot 24 feet ahead of it) in "snap shooting." That allows 18 feet of movement (in 1/5 second) by the target while you move your gun & pull your trigger, & 6 feet more while your pellets fly to their rendezvous with the pheasant. Lazy as I am, I've been told to carry the heaviest gun I can handle comfortably.

For cold weather hunting, don't bundle up in tight, stiff, heavy "armor," like tin plate. Far better, wear 2 suits of light woolen underwear (I know a DM man who wears 3) & wool outside, too, or waterproofs in rain or snow. . . . Never let a fowl see the glint of your specs or the whites of your eyes.

At 40 yards your shotgun with full choke will fill a 30-inch circle so full of pellets that no bird can escape through 'em. An improved barrel without choke fills a 30-inch circle at 20 yards. Don't throw your gun away or buy a new one if you're missing; it's probably not your gun's fault.

Sometimes a bird flies straight across in front of you at 60 mph, or 88 feet per second. Then you'd better shoot—if you can get the shot off in 2 seconds—at a point 200 feet from where you first saw it. But by that time it's probably out of range; you must shoot in 1 second or less.

All these little tidbits convince me that I'll probably never hit another duck or pheasant as long as I live. It sounds almost mathematically impossible. It takes me not 2 seconds, but 2 minutes to choose 1 of the 3 ways to shoot—whether to (1) "point out," or (2) "swing past," or (3) snap shoot. . . .

After I'd spent years (probably several minutes each year) learning to master a slow trigger squeeze, I discovered that this is only for pistol or rifle, but not for shotgun shooting. Then I had to learn to "slap" the trigger fast & sharp—but without shaking the gun.

Around Chariton they say a quail in the open always makes for the nearest woods. So flush 'em *toward* the woods. Try to arrange things so the duck'll strut his stuff in *front* of you. Aiming a golf club at a picture on the wall is good practice, too. If you're a one-eyed shooter, begin to use both eyes!

I can say *that* again (it's been said to me 100 times): shoot with both eyes open. All you must control simultaneously to be a good wildfowl shot is 2 feet, 2 legs, 2 hips, 2 knees, 2 shoulders, 2 arms, 2 hands, 1 head & 2 eyes, or 17 items, so you see it's very simple & quite impossible to hit a flying elephant at 20 feet.

Never let the urgent whir of wings stampede you into an unaimed shot. . . . Proper gun fit (say the finicky) involves your facial contours, especially of your jaw & cheek bones. Keep your gun on the shoulder nearest your master eye. Does your wife admire & even drool over you when you bring home a full bag of wildfowl? Well, she should!

Miracle for duck hunters

When the talk turns to the "fabulous" de-luxe duck hunting camps, where you sit in steam-heated blinds on a semi-submerged portico with hot & cold running butlers, & the ducks are lured with baits of floating corn to the muzzles of the millionaires' $1,100 shotguns, I like to think of our fabulous hunting pond 20 miles northeast of DM.

One of our little group leased the exclusive hunting rights to this pond sight unseen for 5 boxes of shells. "It ain't much," the farmer said, "but you'll see some ducks."

He referred to it also as a lake, slough & marsh.

On the day before the hunting season began, we went up for a look at our pond. It had disappeared. In fact, it had quite dried up. The bed of a brook, or rill, about 11 inches wide, that led to it & onward, was also dry. We congratulated ironically the explorer who had found this game preserve for us, so cozy & nearby.

Luckily, one of our hunters was a sort of 4th generation Dan'l Boone, high & dry in an urban niche & partly citified, but still close to nature. "All this needs is a little rain," he said, squinting at the lay & slant & roll of the land.

He squatted down & eyed the low caked sump of what might once have been a pond. With his toes he kicked a few twigs into what might have been the main outlet. These he braced & weighted down with some rocks.

"Better throw a little earth on this dam," he said casually, & we quickly caught on. He found 2 or 3 other possible outlets, & we constructed more dams, each a foot or 2 across & a few inches high. We did this skeptically, because it took only a few minutes.

(Once I was accidentally invited to shoot at a hoity-toity club on Delaware Bay, where the shooting was virtually done from hammocks. There were men to load your guns & serve hot coffee, & the more rugged members roughed it in blinds made of large bathtubs with only radiant heat. You found more ducks than you shot, wrapped in cheese-cloth in your car.)

Next day 4 A.M. came early, & we seemed like a little coterie of zanies in the murky pre-dawn rain. "I never met a duck worth an hour's sleep," one of us muttered over our coffee at the truckers' haven on the east 14th Street road.

Well, sir, we couldn't believe our eyes. Where there had been gray caked seamy mud the day before, the busy little rill was feeding a flood penned up by our little dams. About an acre was covered over with water to a depth of 8 to 15 inches.

(Some DM hunters with good Chicago connections tell of duck blinds on the Illinois River which must be "fabulous," since a membership costs $5,000, give or take a few thousand. You sit in a luxurious underground room behind a camouflaged plate glass window, & the ducks are lured to sport & destruction with sinister gifts of rice & millet.)

We were still gazing at the miracle of the pond when our Dan'l Boone (he played the saxophone, danced like Vernon Castle, & had more phone numbers than any other man in town) hoarsely whispered, "Ducks!" We crouched in the dry reeds. As the ducks hovered, inquisitive & skeptical, poised & floating in the air, eager to light somewhere, our guns roared into the dawn.

(I suppose most of the stories about de-luxe duck camps, luxurious blinds & waterproof attendants are so much hogwash. My observation has been that a millionaire likes to rough it a little on a hunting trip, too.)

We got 7 ducks that morning for the 5 of us, & felt well rewarded. I've been in good blinds 200 miles away on the Missouri, where we waded half a mile & the ducks flew intermittently all day, & we shot plenty; probably these are the best duck sloughs within a night's drive from DM. But I've never felt more like a duck hunter than at the little pond we dammed up, 20 miles northeast of DM.

Day of an Iowa nimrod

Early stirrings under great piles of bedding, by huntsmen still dreaming. Shouts from the inveterate early riser: "It's 5 o'clock!" Leo Plumb, the veteran Iowa hunting guide, in a sleeping bag under 12 inches of blankets & quilts.

Yells for Henry, the gifted cook, who has been up almost an hour. The moon still is high & bright, & the stars reflect brilliantly in the dark river. Early morning rural hilarity on the radio. Thunderous coughs & heroic stretching of stiff muscles. Stiff movements as the hunters don 7 or 8 layers of clothes. I feel like a tenderfoot.

The last lazy sleeper lumbers downstairs as the bacon & eggs hit the long table. Learned speculations about the weather & optimistic prophesies. Thin ice on the gray Mississippi—favorite highway-flyway for southbound ducks.

The swifter eaters take their guns off the rack for a last drop of oil. The cigarette with the third cup of coffee. Pulling on of the rubber hip boots over fleece-lined moccasins & 3 pairs of socks.

Scrutiny of dark sky & water from the porch end of the camp barge. Assembling of assorted decoys & futile yearning for more. "We could use 500 decoys." The motor-boat coughs, too, but finally starts. The sky beyond the low dark Illinois shore is pinker.

Hunting legally begins this morning at 6:57. But all the hunters want to be ready in their blinds then. The hull of the shallow quarter-boat crunches against the half-inch film of ice frozen on the river overnight. Duck hunting is a somber, ritualistic pleasure, a hangover from our primitive forebears.

Now the first flights of ducks are visible high against the blue-green sky & the rosy-fingered dawn. Like wisps of lace, as Bob Colflesh puts it. Here is No. 1 blind. The hunters load their guns. Out near the shore go the new decoys. The overnight decoys are white with frost & must be splashed to restore their deceptiveness.

You never saw so many ducks. There must be a million in the air, over the river, over both banks, over Turkey Island. We add more branches, weeds & marsh grass to the blind for concealment. But we still are busy with these chores when the first curious ducks fly over our decoys. A fusillade & 3 ducks fall.

High overhead is a precise V-formation of geese, a magnificent spectacle, each goose a cross against the heavens, neck far outthrust. "We certainly got you up betimes this morning," gibes Ed Hicklin. Our experts are sounding their duck calls.

Barely room to turn without jostling. Or knocking down some cover. The guide is retrieving the ducks in his boat, twisting the necks of the cripples, biting one neck in pantomime. Gun shots echo across the river. They explode near my ear.

The moon still is high but pale against the sun. Now the sky is filled with triangles & columns of ducks, like an unreasoning force of nature. Their wheeling flight is like a ritual. Several hunters are smoking. What's become of the old myth that hunters must chew? This sport is the Anglo-Saxon substitute for bull-fighting.

In each blind it's assumed that the fellows down the river are getting better shooting. The motor boat is cutting lanes & channels through the thin ice for the ducks to land. A few gullible ducks curve down in narrowing ovals. Their more suspicious comrades in the same flock wheel away, subtly, safely.

Now & again, a lone duck looking for company. Occasionally, a pair or a quartet. Now cripples are hiding under the overhang of the banks. In the willows & rushes. The locals shoot like automatons, schooled since childhood in the river. Hunters from the city fight their guns a little. The smell of powder as the bag increases. The contentment of hunters who enjoy merely crouching in the blind. The restiveness of those who yearn for more game. This scene is not gay; it is grim & fundamental. I feel less like a tenderfoot.

A fish called "Solitude"

On your way to your secret rendezvous with the fish, you might stop & buy a few packages of frozen halibut. Of course, if your wife's a born zoologist or ichthyologist, she might be suspicious. Maybe you need fish with tails. But most women nowadays assume that modern fish come without head, tail or intestines.

I figure that one 2-pound catfish caught in the DM river anywhere between the Camp Dodge rifle range & the power plant downstream is equal to 10 northern pike (3 pounders) which jump into your boat up in Canada. Of course, people won't listen to you quite so long about local fish, but think of the money you save.

With most fishing trips the trouble is there's always some zany along who worries about the fishing. If you go 15 minutes without a nibble, he emotes in high tragedy; & if you're left the only man who hasn't caught a fish, he wants to make a federal case out of it, & focuses too much attention on you when you'd rather suffer in silence.

Most of the sensible fishermen you see on the riverbank beyond Euclid Avenue don't seem to be fish-frantic. They just want to sit there far from city pavement, 4 walled brick buildings & human nuisances, revert to nature & think, or just sit, in a coma.

The last 6 times I've been in Paris I've always stopped to chat with a chap who fishes constantly under the Pont de l'Alma. He tells me frankly (& without melodrama) that he's never caught a fish. He isn't very hopeful that he ever will. But he likes to sit there under the old bridge on the embankment & watch the water & the barges flow by.

Some fishermen like to mix their fishing with other activities. I know a trio of fishermen who load a small icebox into their rowboat, chug out a ways, drop their lines, & don't pay much attention to their hooks until hours later when the last can of beer has sunk below the ripples. The legal limit: one beer per fish.

I know a fisherman or two who like to fish & read. Some of the more zealous fishermen regard this as sacrilege. They think the man with the rod should watch wind, sun, waves, sand, stars & try to out-think the fish. But if you can read a whole book while catching one fish, you may be ahead of the guy who catches 2 fish & no books.

When I was still a small boy I knew enough, before I lay down on the river bank to daydream & look up at the sky through the leaves, to tie my line to my toe. It seldom made any difference, but it seemed a sensible precaution. Once I almost caught a fish that way. I know a gal who paints while she fishes.

What with our brave new world, this chromium-plated civilization, some men—especially city men—might go crazy if they couldn't get off to the solitudes occasionally. Fishing is an approved excuse. The real reason: to get away from civilization long enough & often enough to preserve sanity.

Since the days I seined for minnows in the DM river I've fished off yachts in the Gulf Stream; off Monte Carlo & Lima, Peru; off Montauk Point & in Lake Saganaga up on the border. I've hooked a sailfish & a tuna & shark, caught barracuda & fish that didn't even look like fish; yet I've never had a greater thrill than when I captured a turtle in the Raccoon.

But often I've been the only man aboard fishless after 2 or 3 hours. That's happened off Bailey Island, Maine; off Rehoboth Beach, Delaware; & on the White River, in Arkansas. One time 3 grandmothers & 2 tots under 5 had caught fish, & I hadn't. (But I ate more fish than they did.)

Isn't it odd that so many expert fishermen don't eat fish? Once we had fishing champs on both sides of our cottage at Okoboji who almost always caught their limit & never ate any. Boy, did they keep us supplied! It got to be a chore to clean 'em, & I threw out broad hints that the guy who caught 'em should clean 'em maybe.

The b.w. never gets hungrier for a thick juicy steak than when we have an icebox filled with fish. But, shucks, the sun is low in the west, & by now those frozen sea perch you bought in the first paragraph are thawed & you can take 'em home to your b.w. & she'll think you're wonderful to catch those fish, & especially to get 'em cleaned.

❋ ❋ ❋

I detect the dawn of teen-age love among the ex-brats around our block: they now borrow our old two-seater bike to take their dream chicks for a ride around the block.

One small reason why I carry my hat or go hatless is that I'm tired of getting it knocked off every time I get into or out of a modern designer's dream low-roof automobile.

Some of our town's families share old inherited family cottages up at the lake. The hidden strains among even the most amiable brothers and sisters and cousins seem so great that they're almost unanimously convinced communism can't succeed.

Around the canasta tables there's a rumor that one of our town's sprightlier matrons has called off a budding romance. She explains that it interferes too much with her sacred nightly ritual at her boudoir cosmetics lab.

ARE YOU A MAN OR A SPECTATOR SPORT?

Sport keeps me young

This cluttered life, this unmitigated pace, is leaving too many young widows. How can modern man survive this frenzied world without some outdoor activity or sport? Unselfish gallantry spurs us on to live longer, to escort 'em, to support 'em as lavishly as we can.

Any duffer (if I can you can) can participate in these 12 outdoor sports:

1. *Golf:* A healthful brand of walking & swinging a fly swatter. Who cares about the score? You stop counting at 99, or at 6 for any one hole. The important thing is to walk amid landscapes on the wonderful turf. The worse duffer you are, the more exercise you get.

2. *Walking:* Almost as good as golf, especially if you carry a stick & swing at things on the path, or kick at pebbles. If a man walks 3 miles a day, or at least 5 miles 3 times a week, his physique will remain in the pink, like a leopard's on the prowl.

3. *Horseshoes:* Poor man's polo. I'm told the townspeople in this Great State now pitch more horseshoes than our cousins in the great open spaces around us. And what has polo got that

horseshoes haven't got? Plenty. But it's hard to get good polo ponies nowadays.

4. *Shuffleboard*: Patriarch's polo. Every village in this super-Texas of ours ought to have a concrete tennis court surrounded by 2 or 4 shuffleboard courts. Then young & old could keep an eye on each other. Fun, sociability & exercise.

5. *Worky-Up*: This includes playing catch, shagging flies, pitching to the neighborhood Babe Ruths. In 20 minutes of chasing flies you get more exercise than in 40 minutes of tennis. Or hit grounders & flies to the young. You sweat.

6. *Kicking FB*: You can kick until your toe hurts or you discover your punts average only 27 yards. Then you can pass till your arm hurts. The last time our crowd of sportsmen played touch football, 3 wound up on crutches & 1 in the hospital.

7. *Hoop Toss*: At first glance, shooting baskets, tossing a big ball through a horizontal hoop, seems a strange pursuit for grown men. But it's more fun than you think, & exercise, too. I shoot till I loop 10 shots in from the 22-foot line, & sometimes that keeps me outdoors a long time, even in winter.

8. *Tots & Dogs*: If you take a dog or a child (or both!) out for a constitutional, that isn't merely walking; it's guarding an unreconciled hostage. Ours used to run into every driveway & across every lawn when I took 'em out; both kids & dogs. (I'd rather adopt a pet child than buy an expensive temperamental dog.)

9. *Fishing*: Millions prefer this, because it combines exercise with plenty of sitting. Avoid it, though, if you or your companion is bitterly eager to catch a fish. Just sitting on a bank pretending to fish is a reasonable facsimile, especially if you have to walk a long way from the car. Hip-booting through a trout stream is tops.

10. *Rowing*: This is the best all-round exercise, especially without an outboard motor. Tests every muscle, including your rump; almost as good as snow-shoveling. Gets you away from people, too, if you row alone.

11. *Horses*: I used to ride a lot, until my friends' horses ate 'em out of house & home. I even hired horses at $2 an hour, or a half hour that sometimes seemed like an hour. Don't get the silly idea that the horse gets all the exercise.

12. *Hunting*: Do I mean deer or pheasant stalking, or do I mean sitting in a duck blind? In the right mood, shooting from a duck blind can (like sailfishing) be the 2nd most blissful experience on earth, even if you only see your quarry & never shoot or land one.

Whichever of these you try, or any combination of the dozen kinds, try to be an outdoor sportsman at least 3 times a week for 2 hours each time. You'll be surprised how long your ulcers & high blood pressure will remain latent. But don't overdo; take a breather.

Shoot 20 baskets before dinner

When I saw an athlete quoted in favor of more sports for Americans, I hoped for a moment he meant more exercise for pot-bellied Americans with out-thrust rear-ends. "Ah," I hissed, "cleverer than I thought, this squat, pugnacious, beetle-browed outfielder."

I'm afraid, though, that all he has in mind is more spectator sports. The flabby American sitting on his broad posterior yelling for the coach's or the pitcher's or the umpire's blood. Exercise? Limited strictly to carrying his wife's blankets, galoshes & thermos bottle up to the 69th row. Or to waving for a hot dog.

But I'm not going to let you down. What *you* need is exercise. The American jitters is partly due to lack of it. Here are 10 kinds of exercise you can take without a $150 set of golf clubs or a Wakonda or Grand View membership or a $15 tennis racket, & without even being recruited, subsidized, bruised, overtrained, & corrupted.

1. Calisthenics under your wife's eagle eye every morning before breakfast. This'll humiliate & frustrate you & you'll collide with furniture, but it's good for your wife's ego.

2. Chores around the house can give you plenty of exercise, provided (a) you obey all your wife's demands for washing the windows on the outside & (b) disarrange your schedule so you must keep running back & forth between attic & basement.

3. Walk downtown, 3 times a week at first; then every day,

if you're a sluggish office worker. You'll help solve the traffic & parking problems & probably live 10 or 15 years longer & save a lot of money on fender repairs.

4. With a heavy shotgun, do these 3 exercises: (a) knee-bend squat, thrusting gun forward as you go down & upward & back of your head as you come up; (b) revolve gun in front of you in a vertical plane, in both directions bending left & right; & (c) revolve gun overhead in horizontal plane in both directions twisting 180 degrees left & right. (This is the best.)

5. In the living room after dinner (wait 20 minutes) do 10 somersaults, chin yourself 5 times & do 5 push-ups from the floor, then roll over exhausted. This will either give you all the exercise you need or bring on angina pectoris.

6. Get down on your knees after dinner & put on the boxing gloves with your small son. Let him hit you as hard as he wants to, but be careful to miss him with your round-house swipes. Just holding up the 8-ounce gloves will be almost all you need.

7. Pretend to buy the kids a basketball ring for Xmas—and then use it yourself. Make yourself throw 20 baskets from the foul line before breakfast & dinner, & after dinner if there's a full moon. If your wife gets comical about it, make her do it, too.

8. Rearrange the furniture 3 times a week. Take turns with your wife. On evenings when it's your turn, you can get double the exercise by restoring it immediately to where it was. On her nights you move it only once—where she tells you. Next night you change it your way.

9. I've thought of a bright idea—fairly bright, that is: At all football, basketball, baseball, wrestling & boxing matches, make it obligatory by law to put all spectators through 30 minutes of physical culture. Penalize the home team if they refuse.

10. You've undoubtedly thought of this one yourself: "I get my exercise acting as pallbearer at the funerals of my friends, who take too much exercise." Most of DM's fat men wisecrack whenever they catch anybody exercising.

Of course, you can get all the exercise you need hunting, chopping wood, washing your car or rowing. (Even fishing may be classed as physical exercise, by courtesy.) But with mallards available by mail C.O.D., & gas furnaces & artificial fireplaces, & weather too cold for driveway car-washing, & outboard motors with self-starters—why, better put yourself in your wife's hands. She'll make you puff & pant.

* * *

How sporting of the Democrats, not to reveal the most vulnerable skeleton in Ike's closet, even in the fury of the campaign: that he never plays bridge with his wife.

Among my favorite summer flowers are the married-daughters-in-exile who return from far-away, maybe with a dimpled cherub or two. They remain long enough to "liberate" a few portable heirlooms, and maybe to wangle some dental work at Dad's expense.

Junior is angling delicately for a jalopy on the campus when he's a senior. "Most" of the boys have 'em, he argues; but none of 'em do any chores in exchange, or make any promises or take any pledges. I guess I'm just a medieval father; we used to swear off till twenty-one for a gold watch.

Maybe the magnolia tree and birdbath are the smartest presents I ever gave my royal consort. She can't hide, misplace or lose 'em; they're always visible from the west windows; and the $28 tree has already burst forth in two blossoms.

"Perhaps the gals actually like it when a pretty woman's hair goes gray," muses Betty Comfort, moving her new yellow lawn couch so it's visible from the street. "They're edgy if she dyes it, and when she lets it go gray again, they almost smother her with flattery."

Our luncheon club's idealist brought up world government at the big round table again last week. Same blank wall; the superpatriots oppose it as heartily as Moscow does. He reached the same solution: pie à la mode with two dippers of ice cream.

On this summer's vacation trip I really got stubborn when I ordered canned soup and they offered me "homemade soup" so magnanimously at the roadside lunch counters. I simply insisted on canned soup, despite the American legend that bad "homemade" soup is better than good canned soup.

TENNIS, ANYONE?

Don't throw your tennis racket away

Our neighborhood bantamweights, 5 or 6 of 'em, have begun to take tennis lessons; miniature athletes from 8 to 13. Before our 1952 crop of Kramers & Gussie Morans in DM & all over Iowa gets into bad habits, I want to ease a few opinions about tennis off my chest; it's the greatest of all games.

1. Tennis is a more difficult game than golf. In tennis, you hit a moving ball while in motion yourself; in golf, your ball is standing still when you hit it & so are you. Almost any tennis player can, if he concentrates on it, become a tolerable golfer; it's an open question how many golfers could do much at tennis. In golf you never have to hurry.

2. Courtesy is the first rule of tennis; it's a gentleman's game. You call all close line shots in favor of your opponent. If there's a referee, the only excuse for you to argue with him is to question a decision in your favor. It's the only game where losers leap over a net to congratulate winners, if they can beat the winner to the leap.

3. A dub at tennis has more fun than a dub at golf. Some stout fellahs argue that it's a pleasure to shoot a 105, & in a way it is; I ought to know; but they don't act happy when they shoot an 8 on No. 18. At best, it's bittersweet. At tennis, a dub doesn't feel too ulcerous when he's been beaten 6-1, 6-2 by another dub.

4. About one-fifth of the cost of a tennis court goes into the

"alleys," & at doubles it's a shame not to use 'em. The thrill of a passing shot down an alley is like the thrill of a 150-yard approach shot dead to the pin. Why waste all that tennis alley space?

5. I've never known a tennis player who was all bad; most of 'em have charm, flexibility & aplomb; they are customarily alert, clean-cut, modern, well-poised & urbane. One way to improve any town from Sibley to Keosauqua or Waukon to Sidney is to indoctrinate 50 or 100 youngsters with tennis. It takes not 40 acres but 120 by 60 feet.

6. Placement is far more important than cannonball speed. Tennis is a game of accuracy & steadiness; in that respect it's like golf. Youngsters want to murder the ball, hit home runs, but they get over it. Watch your opponents & hit 'em (as in baseball) where they ain't.

7. Keep your shots deep. You can't win consistently unless you hit most of your shots to the rear half of your opponents' backcourt. If you barely get 'em over the net they'll rifle 'em back past your partner's ears or at his feet & he won't like you—though he may try to conceal it.

8. Tennis is one game which males & females can play together without feminine squeals of dismay. Mixed doubles is a pleasant game for teen-agers & for patriarchs, & the in-betweens, too. DM's matrons who play tennis are the youngest in town for their years. (But an occasional game of all-masculine doubles is a welcome change.)

9. In our town we have a college president, a general & 2 bank presidents who play tennis or threaten to play, & one of 'em swings a doughty racket. But a blond left-handed taxi driver once held the US singles title. Either type can unkink his muscles in an hour of tennis, but a golf foursome requires all afternoon. One of the best moments in tennis: when you sit down to rest.

10. Anybody who keeps his eye on the ball can become a Demon Net Player. If he returns 3 shots successfully up front for every 2 he fluffs, he's doing okay. You can win a close 6-4 set with 24 points to your opponent's 20; or you can win a 6-0 set with a point score like 30 to 18.

11. You don't need to rifle your serve like Trabert or Seixas to make your serve troublesome to return. If you place 'em delicately & accurately in the corners, or near the outside line, or deep,

or to the receiver's backhand, or mix 'em up, his returns aren't likely to imperil your partner's face up at the net.

12. Week-end players develop a secret stubbornness, a super-competitive will-to-win which is one of the funniest things in tennis, reminiscent of a golfer who tries to murder his drives or takes an eon to line up his putts.

It's far better to keep the ball in play & watch for your chance than to try to kill every shot. All in all, a player's traits & foibles are as visible in tennis as in bridge or poker. Often he's enjoying the game even if his face is dour & agonized.

※ ※ ※

Proof of a happy home life: if you can persuade your wife to select some tender valentines filled with nostalgia to send to your old flames on the 14th. (Better look at 'em yourself first, though!)

My theory that it's better to write my Dream Girl a tactful note on delicate household differences than to argue orally is breaking down. I write her a note worthy of a Talleyrand and she writes me back a scorcher.

Some of our town's most sophisticated people go to Aspen to ski instead of to Florida to sunbathe, maybe to kid their neighbors into thinking they're still under forty and just slopping over with vim and vigor.

I'm a trifle embarrassed when I try to parade George Washington and Abe Lincoln before my two sons as illustrious models to emulate. They see readily enough how noble G.W. and Honest Abe were. But they also see too clearly how little their dad resembles either one.

My crusade to learn five words of Spanish at breakfast and read four lines of poetry at dinner is running into obstacles: eggshells are tossed at me before I can say *"usted,"* and bread crumbs thrown before I utter a whole line of iambic pentameter.

I've wagered the janitor at our office building $2 that he could air-cool every room all summer on what he wastes overheating the building all winter.

The social-science researchers at our bridge table conclude that most husband-wife quarrels begin before breakfast. Our findings: begin the day with music, a shower & hot coffee, and a wordless kiss after the ham and eggs.

At last some of us rebellious fathers begin to understand one phase of "progressive education": it trains our little geniuses to read the lurid comic books instead of *Ivanhoe*.

One of our town's animated young matrons sent me a post card from Europe that squeaks, and until I answer it, every time I hug my Dream Girl it makes a noise like a cat miaowing. "Either answer it," she says, "or take it out of your breast pocket."

DID I EVER TELL YOU WHEN I...?

When a team catches fire

I can testify that basketball is a game where a mediocre team can catch fire & play like heroes miles & dreams beyond its ordinary prowess. With an almost spiritual force & divine will-to-win. I once played on such a team. Even as I tell it, it seems incredible.
  We were as sorry a tail-end team in our league as you ever saw. Nary a 6-footer in our lineup. Our center was only 5 foot 9 & on evenings when he dated that redhead at the phone company I

had to play center! Our subs forsook us, & often we trotted out on the floor for practice with only 5 men.

When we lost a man on personal fouls, we'd finish the game with 4 players. Often in our fury we played better that way. Once we finished with 3 players, & gained on our opponents. We were scrappy, but we admitted wryly in the locker room that a good big man is better than a good little man. We faced it squarely, but with agony.

Sometimes in desperation we played rough. It was our only strategy to reach or intercept the ball against 6-footers. There were moments when there were more athletes sprawled on the floor than standing erect on their feet. Or maybe our boys were standing on *their* feet; on our opponents' feet, that is.

We won a few games; not enough to bolster our pride. . . . Our lack of height was a bitter taste in our mouths. We had to jump for the ball at the center of the court after every point in those days, & often we jumped also against taller men after struggling for the ball in the fierce man-to-man guarding.

So height mattered enormously, maybe almost as much as it does today. At each jump ball the taller man could generally launch a rehearsed attack by tipping the ball forward or backward or sideways to a key player. We seldom got the tip aimed our way without jujitsu or skulduggery.

I remember vividly the day our team caught fire. We were playing the league leaders. Their captain was a handsome, stalwart athlete 6 feet 4 inches tall; he'd been captain of the Purdue team the year before. He had tall teammates, too; we would have traded our 5 foot 9 center *plus* his redhead for one of his 6-footers.

Suddenly their opulent height, their arrogant superiority became too much to endure. Their tall captain smothered one of our forwards trying to shoot a short one, & our man virtually climbed up the big boy's chest & dropped one in. We began to travel the court like lightning on steel muscles; our lungs were like bellows.

We spun & dodged & dribbled. We threw the ball like a forward pass the length of the court to a loose forward, faking just enough to catch his adhesive guard on the wrong foot. Our game was far from exquisite, but everything worked. We couldn't miss. Their attempts to stop us seemed puny. Too short, were we? We'd show 'em.

Word flashed around that the tail-enders were walloping the leaders, & electricity filled the air. The gym crowded up. We were unaware of exertion. We ducked & squirmed & dribbled like ballet dancers. We feinted like all-Americans showing off.

The pay-off came at the rebounds. Suddenly we found ourselves seemingly able to leap 4 feet straight in the air. We didn't merely snatch most of the rebounds; we got *all* of 'em, whether off their backboard or ours. We raced downcourt in a quick break despite height & bodyblocks.

I remember there was a fierce exultation in our chests. We knew we'd win, we knew we could not be beaten. Suddenly we were transformed into a quintet of small, atomic, radioactive Murray Weirs, leaping high & pivoting in midair as if standing on stairs, as if standing on the stars.

Too short, eh? Not too short when you can charge like bulls, leap like kangaroos, fly like eagles.

Well, we won 8 straight games, after winning only 2 of the first 6. We were invincible. Somehow height didn't matter any more; we defeated height with pugnacity; spiritually we were 7 feet tall. Maybe you couldn't do that in the gentler basketball of 1955.... But I can understand today what's happened where a team suddenly catches fire: They've swallowed a swirling potion of bittersweet stardust.

How did Connie Mack overlook me?

My greatest ambition & dream as a small boy was to make a triple play unassisted. Whenever there were 2 or 3 opponents on base, on at least 1st & 2nd, I could feel prickles on the back of my neck. Here was my big chance! (Some big-leaguer had made one the year I was 9 or 10 & been quickly forgotten. But that didn't deter me.)

I could see it all: The linedrive to me at shortstop, a leaping one-handed catch. My nonchalant toe touches the bag for the 2nd out. With easy grace & speed I overtake the panicky runner from 1st, as he tries to double back. I trot in across the diamond, modestly. Three down!

No doubt the small boys who now play ball in my back yard and the street also dream of triple plays. They seem to make up their rules as they go along, & the loudest wins most of the arguments. So if he wants an unassisted triple play badly enough he can probably cut himself one.

Today I'd gladly settle for a 2-man triple play, Miller to Musial. I'd get 2 put-outs & an assist, & Musial could run down the 3rd put-out. Or I'd even toss the ball Miller to Boudreau & let *him* get credit for the last 2 put-outs. I'm bigger-hearted than I was, & I don't like to run people down. Let Neal Ball & Wambsganss have the glory!

You won't believe this, but the British love cricket as much as we love baseball. They begin to keep records of their batting & fielding & pitching from the age of 8, & at 60 they pore over the written boxscore of every game they played all of their lives, all preserved in shipshape notebooks.

This would be impossible with our earlier worky-up or one-old-cat, what with the chaotic state of the rules. What one-old-cat needs is a czar, like Kenesaw Mountain Landis or Happy Chandler, to lay down the law. He could create rules for 2-man, 3-man, 4-man worky-up, & so on, with special rules for games in which girls intrude.

Then a boy would know exactly where he stood. As things are now, the biggest boy or the noisiest boy can remain at bat all day, hogging the thrill of clouting the pill, & forcing the smaller, quieter boys to chase the ball over fences, down sewers & across the creek into the timberland.

At some de-luxe golf courses it costs you $6 or $8 or $10 to play a round of golf, what with caddies & greens fees & lost balls & tips—especially if you have to rent a bagful of clubs at a faraway links. Frankly, I'd rather pay that much money to play shortstop (or preferably 2nd base now; you don't have to throw so far) in a full 9-inning game.

It's too bad we virile, keen-eyed younger fathers, in the pink of condition, don't gather occasionally for a bit of baseball. One sideshow I never pass up at fairs, circuses & amusement parks is the batting cage, where for a dime they let you hit 9 lobbed balls as hard as you can at a canvas a few feet away.

Since we can't play baseball after we grow up (I'm puzzled to this day why McGraw & Connie Mack ever overlooked me) we *can* go out to the ball game & dream, can't we? We sit there & try to estimate how much punch it might take to drive the ball over the short rightfield fence. Looks easy. Longer'n it looks?

I like night baseball as it's staged in our new ball park. It's a gay, brilliant scene. Everybody seems an intimate ringsider; the whole landscape has a brighter-than-dreamlike quality. But much as I like to *watch* a game, I wish the manager would invite me out to shag flies some noon when his boys are practicing.

And occasionally I'd like to see a daylight game played in dazzling sunshine. A 2 o'clock game, like the games of our youth. But we fathers in our neighborhood are looking for a reasonable man with a bulldozer or dragline to level off a stretch of our pasture big enough for a ball-diamond for the kids. And maybe for their fathers, too. We like to watch, but we'd still prefer to play.

* * *

"Why are all us girls so crazy to take off a few more pounds," demands Betty Comfort, twisting her hips like a corkscrew, "when a few extra pounds in strategic curves have done so much for Marilyn Monroe?"

As soon as we can all agree on the color of the tile, we aim to lift the face of our dignified old bathroom. From the lively difference of opinion you'd think it was an old family shrine.

"For a gold watch you could coax a boy to swear off liquor and tobacco till twenty-one when I was in high school," muses Peter Comfort, knocking icicles off his eaves trough with a rake. "Now you must promise your son a convertible plus gasoline money."

Lately our town's husbands and wives have found a new cuss word to throw at each other: "Perfectionist!" they hiss. If it's a sin to be a perfectionist, I'll gamble it's a forgivable sin; not all perfectionists go to hell; except maybe here on earth.

When I drive across the Republic's vast open spaces and see gobs of surplus real estate everywhere, I marvel how the go-getters manage to wheedle and squeeze so many families into life on a 50-foot lot.

At our club's big round luncheon table we're inclined to agree that while Art Godfrey may or may not be "humbler" than Julius La Rosa, we'd much rather hear Julius sing.

My favorite father-in-law growls that too many of America's best minds are concentrated on selling us too many marginal thingumbobs of chromium and plastic. "What they ought to sell," he vows, "is more new houses each complete with $4,000 of essential equipment, all on one and the same mortgage."

BULLFIGHT

Bezbul fan at a bullfight

With animation & vigor the brave bull gallops in. He doesn't suspect what's ahead of him. He has no inkling. El Presidente is in his box today, in his dark Sunday suit, surrounded by his generals & colonels in their tight khaki uniforms. All the toreadors are on their mettle. How bravely they strut their stuff, *con gusto*.

This is my first serious bullfight. The old circular stadium of concrete & brown wood is partially filled, like an average crowd at a DM ball game. I am lucky to have as my guide the loveliest of Pan American's air hostesses, a Swedish girl based in Peru with an American airline.

She esteems the bullfight far above that tame American pastime, baseball (bezbul), & I can understand they are of a different voltage. She prefers also this well-aged stadium to the new one across Lima town. Now all the toreadors parade, with sinuous grace & high knee action, in gilt & bright colors, with the picadors mounted on old expendable horseflesh.

In the rear shuffle the attendants in yellow jerseys & red berets, like camp-followers, around the dray horses which will in 20 minutes drag out the ultimate & inevitable victim. Our seats are about $5.50 each, like an orchestra seat in a Broadway play, & ten times the drama.

Now begins the first stage of the fatiguing of the bull. The doughty banderilleros wave their cerise & yellow cloaks to goad him. When he charges them too intimately, they leap nimbly over the solid board barrier, or find shelter behind one of the six redoubts.

In the 5 or 6 languages she speaks so liltingly, my guide, Senorita Ingrid Seth, explains the fine points. Matador Luis Castro (El Soldado) is unhappy, having a bad time today. Everything he does turns out wrong. He can't even jab the banderillos (darts) properly along the bull's spine. . . . My Swedish guide's English is rather better than that of the average Vassar grad's.

Behind this violent & unequal contest even a thick-headed gringo detects quickly a mystical link with the dawn of our race, a compendium of the long struggle between Man and bestial bull-headed Nature. Senorita Ingrid shudders a little as the blood spills over the bull's flank from the picador's lance. Keep your mind on the bullfight, Americano. The bull's horns are under the horse.

I pinch myself: this is only a day's flight from 8th & Locust or the Country Club golf links in DM, as Pan American's clippers fly. Now the cloaks have been waved, the lacy pink & blue darts implanted, the heavy lances thrust into the baffled creatures, the trumpets of mercy restrain the picadors, & 4 times the matadors have thrust downward their swords victoriously to the jugular & the heart.

Yet the impatient Latinos, the aficionados, have found it dull; death has come to the tired bulls without elegance, without the true curve of inspiration. But in the 5th bout the aficionados see what they came to see. The matador Raul Rovira turns too slowly, the bull too quickly; this hero with a clown's face is tossed, gored, trampled, his satin breeches slit up one thigh.

Bleeding, he waves his rescuers away, retrieves his sword from the dust, limps into attack again beside his crimson cape, & like Cyrano thrusts home while the music plays. He is awarded the supreme accolade, the bull's tail & ears; he limps around the ring twice in triumph.

But the true elegance comes in the 6th & last bout. Young Jesus Cordoba from Mexico is the matador of the day. He taunts & flabbergasts his 2nd bull with exquisite *delicatesse*. He is grace & valor incarnate. He, too, wins the tail & ears but with fluid & aristocratic aplomb; his silk & velvet breeches are intact.

My feeling about the bullfight is mingled, but this afternoon's spectacle alone has been worth the long flight. Senorita Ingrid thinks the trumpets of compassion waited too long for the blood to flow. . . . This is not an Americano's favorite dish; but our prizefight crowds can scarcely toss the first stone. They drag the last bull away through the dust in the late sunshine & the long shadows.

✳ ✳ ✳

After watching seven summer weddings, my Lady Love and I agree that, swathed as she is in veils and finery, no bride need fear the loveliest lineup of bridesmaids ever assembled; especially with her back to the church.

Our club cynic took a swig of buttermilk at the round table and argued it isn't the child who displaced Pa as the central figure in the family; it's Ma, an accomplished power politician skilled in using the child as decoy. (We threw the noon edition at him!)

So far as I can discern, the primitives who oppose four-lane highways are the illegitimate stepchildren of grim pioneers who thought the automobile was a transitory contraption invented by Satan to scare horses.

So far I haven't yet persuaded my Lady of Sheer Delight that she can bake a potato in a pressure cooker in ten or fifteen minutes. She suspects this is merely my cunning attempt to perpetrate an atomic-bomb explosion in our own house.

FOR MEN ONLY [VI]

When Junior gives me a candidly adverse comment on one of my borderline neckties . . . or our daughter's revealed as a thrifty soul with a cherished savings nest egg . . . and our youngest goads me to finish my stint early so I needn't work so late at night . . . and my Princess of Sheer Delight adopts my suggestion and returns a dizzy dress . . . then I meditate with a secret inner glow on my position of influence in my own family, where it's really a triumph.

* 7 *
Personal & otherwise

PERSONAL

Big moments in your life

Your first picture with a big string of little fish or one big fish. Your first glimpse of "dogdom's aristocracy" at a dog show. The first time your lighter worked the first time for a lady's cigarette. (Life is full of unforgettable firsts.)

The first time a girl beat you at ping-pong. Your first ringside seat at a big prizefight half a block from the ring. Your first snowman admired by your firstborn. The first time you heard the dawn chorus of bird songs, fortissimo.

Your first ringside seat at a cabaret floorshow with the talent within pinching range. Your first ride in a car with the top down. The first time you ever tossed a nickel to an organ-grinder's monkey. Your first May basket from the opposite sex.

Your first realization that people don't go to the races just to see the horses run. Your first plunge into a railroad tunnel. The first time you carried your golf clubs to the links on the 6 A.M. trolley filled with workmen. (What variety the world offers if you aren't too blasé!)

Your first glimpse of an oriental woman with a jewel in her nose. Your first close-up of newly hatched birds in a nest. The wedding of your first friend to marry. Your first peep at a shark in an aquarium.

Your first nervous approach to a uniformed doorman. The first time you ducked the boom (or is it spar?) on a sailboat. The first time you watched the nobles of the Mystic Shrine march in a parade. (You are the sum total of all the experiences you can remember.)

The first time you saw someone sunbathing in the nude on a faraway New York rooftop. Your first glimpse of Manhattan's shabby flats' interiors from the Elevated. Your first ride in a rumble seat. The first time you holed out an approach shot at golf.

Your first dance on an excursion steamer. Your first glimpse of a tall silk hat in a theater foyer between acts. The first time you saw a companion handle a gun carelessly on a hunting trip. Your first shocked glimpse of a whole roast pig.

The first time you saw the victorious rooters tear down the goal-posts. The first time you ever suspected the artist who painted that picture might be kidding or coo-coo. The first time you ever saw a Salvation Army lass collect dimes in a bar.

Your first trayful of Christmas cards. The first time you ever caught a butterfly. Your first view of a row of colored beach parasols. Your first puzzlement at seeing a fat soprano wooed as an operatic heroine. (What marvelous adventures you can look forward to!)

Your first sight of a mummy. Your first gazing at a faraway foreign shoreline. Your first sight in the flesh of a great baseball star. The first time you saw the beam of a 60-inch searchlight on the midnight sky.

The first time you ever moved into a new house. Your first New Year's kiss at midnight. Your first discernment of the lovely patterns of snowflakes. Your first realization that it's no disgrace to fall on your fanny at the skating pond.

Those giant flowers at your first flower show, & your first conception of breeding. Your first good report card & your dad's pride. Your first letter from a girl who had you dizzy. First encounter with a menu in French.

The first time you voted. Your first valentine to your first girl. Your first meal at an outdoor restaurant. The first time you ever shot a creature. The first time you ever got too much sunburn all at once. The first time your dad decided not to spank you.

If you jotted down all *your* big or memorable moments you could write a book. . . . Nobody's life is really dull.

—AND OTHERWISE

Maybe I can be a better man next year

If you want suggestions for your own New Year resolutions, ask your friends. They won't mention your *faults*, but they *will* tell you what to resolve to make yourself a better man. I've asked 20 DM friends for suggestions, unbeknownst to them, in a subtle, disguised way, & these 32 resolutions are the result.

So I resolve:

1. At a party, to look cheerful and make it a point to chat with everybody. 2. Not to expect people to be so all-fired neat, just because I have a mania for tidiness. 3. Don't sneer at yourself; leave that to others.

Still talking to myself:

4. Read more books & fewer book reviews. 5. Tackle your harder tasks first, leave the easier ones till last. 6. When you feel constraint growing up between you & certain friends, spend more time with 'em. 7. Don't be backward to praise people for what you admire about 'em.

Buck up, man, and:

8. Cultivate homely people; they're usually more interesting than the cover girls & boys. 9. Speak deliberately; make your point precisely or wait till you can. 10. Don't jump at the verdict that certain rich people are arrogant or snobbish; maybe they're just defensive or befuddled.

Examine your foibles, son:

11. When an argument stretches out, smile & change the subject. 12. Don't fancy yourself as a supreme court on others'

quirks. 13. Why scorn the prejudices of ordinary people? They're the majority.

And I further resolve:

14. To read a good poem a day; poetry is mankind's supreme thought, & it's silly to leave poetry exclusively to the young. 15. To accept a few enemies willingly; any man worth his salt has plenty. 16. To remember that man is merely one of the lesser phenomena on one of the minor planets.

All through the year I'll:

17. Treat every man as if he were a governor till he turns out to be unfit for a dog-catcher. 18. Restrain that impulse to preach to my children excessively. 19. Never eat more than 700 calories at a meal.

Even if it hurts:

20. I'll end a trivial dispute with "maybe you're right." 21. I'll definitely but quietly contradict even an important personage's intolerant, stupid or baseless assertion. 22. I'll never ruffle anyone's sensitive feelings publicly or in print unless it seems vital in the public interest.

And I also resolve:

23. Not to expect teen-agers to be as mellow as patriarchs. 24. To let others get a shade the better of a bargain rather than to seem to get the better end of it myself. 25. To accept a certain amount of imperfection in things I buy, without too much fuss, in an imperfect world.

On & after January 1:

26. I'll remind intelligent people once a week that world government is the inevitable goal of mankind. 27. Make no effort to control those near & dear to me unduly. 28. Remain unruffled in the presence of beautiful women, who are human too, even if slightly divine.

And when in doubt:

29. I'll assume that even the most unpalatable criticism may have a nucleus of truth. 30. Accept other people's personalities as part of all natural phenomena. 31. Explore the middle ground between my own extreme views & those of others. 32. Remember others are shy & reserved, too.

Some of my friends will recognize that these resolves deal only with my milder faults, & may wonder why I didn't consult them for more sweeping amendments to my character. Well, I don't advise anybody to disclose their grimmer faults publicly. But also I have a secret list, & I'm working with that one, too. And a happy New Year to you, chums, even if you're perfect.

10 hour pilot

Much to my surprise, I learned to fly in 4 weeks. I was a reporter, & it was a newspaper assignment, like any other. Mike Cowles asked me if I'd like to learn to fly & write a series of 4 articles about it. "Sure," I said. "When's my first lesson?" (Chance to be a hero, eh, right in front of my girl!)

He wanted an article each Sunday for 4 straight Sundays. It never entered my head that I might not solo in time for the 4th Sunday article, all about my first solo flight, after 19 or 20 half-hour lessons, 5 a week. I was an aviator only on weekdays.

This was the golden autumn of my courtship, a jeweled season of destiny, studded with sapphire skies. Each day my future b.w. drove me to the airport in her new roadster, or I drove her out in my old one.

I practiced takeoffs & landings, over & over & over, taxiing across the rough, unpaved field, bumpety-bump. It was a sturdy square-shouldered Waco biplane of wire & canvas, & the wires sang as I glided, slanting down into the wind, trying to touch both wheels to earth at once.

We flew inside a triangle cornered by Crawford's road-house on Highway 6 (where you could eat all the chicken you wanted for $1.50), the girls' training school at Mitchellville, & the old mineral springs hotel at Colfax. We flew in circles & squares & figure-eights, with that turquoise roadster often in the corner of my eye.

I soon learned to turn her in a tight bank with my left wing tips pointed almost straight earthward. The figure-eights were the most fun. But it bothered me when my instructor said, "You skidded on that turn," or, "Don't you feel that air eddying up, 5 or 6 feet off the ground?"

To be truthful, I didn't. The instructor wanted me to make tiny adjustments with stick & foot rudder a fifth of a second before our wheels kissed the yellow grass. "Feel that air current? Feel it in the seat of your pants?" I tried valiantly to make the seat of my pants more sensitive.

Far below shone yellow the rectangular fields in the autumn sun, & far away the city's towers, westward in the haze. He taught me to cross the controls for a spin, & to jerk the stick back into my lap for a loop. Then for a moment I'd forget my audience of one.

How the world spun & whirled! The earth seemed overhead & the sky far below, & the turquoise roadster was up where the sun should be. Once I caught myself climbing unintentionally above 4,000 feet, trying to escape the menace of inhospitable rocks & clay.

At my 16th lesson, on a Monday, I asked my instructor when I'd solo: "I want plenty of time to write my 4th story." "You aren't ready to solo," he replied. "I don't give a damn about your 4th story. What I'm worried about is your neck." "I've got a deadline," I said stubbornly.

So we concentrated on landings, with one takeoff for each landing. Any oaf can take her off; the pay-off is the landing. Especially on your first solo!

How I bounced that plane as I landed too sharply. The pressure was on. Once I bounced 40 feet high past the b.w. in the turquoise roadster

Would I ever solo? Those damnable air currents, imperceptible to the seat of my pants! That cushion of air, that vacuum! I landed & automatically began to taxi back across the field to take her off again.

"Hold 'er!" called the instructor into my earphones. He climbed out. "Take her off," he waved. "She's yours."

So on my 18th lesson, in my 9th hour of flight, I finally soloed. This story had to be a masterpiece (I must look it up some day) but above all it must meet a deadline.

They have little planes with such inherent stability today, you can step into 'em & solo on your first lesson. That's the kind I wish I'd had, then & now.

Try to mention your European trip!

I've tried manfully to tell people (as an explorer's duty) all about my trip to Europe, but everything I mention reminds 'em of something else, & so I've been interrupted quite a lot. Every time I mention Ankara, it reminds 'em of suburban Ankeny, & if I allude to Paris & the racy show at the Casino de Paris, they tell me about Grampa's visit to French Lick, Indiana.

"I hear you had a talk at his h.q. with Ike?" this lovely brunette with the soulful, intelligent eyes said questioningly, at a party.

"Sure thing," I said eagerly, "he told me we can stop—"

"That reminds me of Ike Armstrong," she cut in hastily. "Do you remember the name of the pretty Drake girl he married?"

I angled over to a guy who looked like a good listener.

"One evening I was listening to the Athens symphony orchestra, in the ancient amphitheater of Herod Latinus," I began lightly, "when a kitty-cat began to prowl among the musicians and—"

"Yeah," he said, "same thing always happens at the Iowa-Iowa State football game. Dog. Everybody laughs."

So I joined a group chatting about Coe's chances of licking Morningside.

"Our ambassador in Ankara told me confidentially—" I began.

"Sure enough?" he parried, agog. "My wife's niece up in Ankeny—did you say Ankeny?—tells her there are 9 more Fontana boys growing up who'll be basketball champs some day."

I sidled up to a bevy of matrons who were chatting about whose car was parked in front of whose house at 10 A.M.

"Did you see any mosques over there?" one of 'em asked politely.

"Did I ever!" I exclaimed. "A great big blue one, with towers & bumps & sharp points—"

"Mosques remind me," said the blonde, "I can sleep later in the morning if I wear an eye mask."

At lunch downtown I demurely dropped another name.

"One evening I was on the McCloys' terrace at Bad Homburg," I began. "He was saying the Russians—"

"I know a fellah named McCloskey at Hot Springs, Arkansas," said the man on my right. "He never wore a homburg hat, though."

A man stopped me on Locust Street & said, "Hear you've been in Yugoslavia!"

"Yep," I said nonchalantly. "I made a special study of Yugoslavia. Took me several hours."

"Well," he said, "tell me all about it. Do they have slaves in Yugoslavia?"

"I'll tell you," I said, "one day I was lunching in Belgrade—"

"Sure, sure, Belgrade," he said. "Some of my wife's people live up in Belmond, Iowa."

In the elevator at the Equitable, a chap on the 10th floor asked me if Ike's going to run. "Did he give you any clue?"

"I'm glad you asked me that," I told him, "I had an excellent chance—"

"It's certainly interesting to get your slant," he said, "because my nephew delivers groceries to Ike's relatives at Boone." He got off at the 5th floor.

I cornered a chap, reputed to be a good listener, at the water fountain, with the casual opener.

"One evening I was flying over a Russian jet fighter airstrip near Dessau—" I began.

"Egad!" he exclaimed. "You lead a fascinating life! Over a Red air strip, eh? My wife & I were in KC & saw this girl at the joint near the Muehlbach do her strip tease—"

"How many miles did you fly on your trip?" demanded the man at the barber's. "20,000? 30,000?"

"Well, let me see," I said winsomely. "It was 4,400 from Washington to Paris, & then—"

"I'd rather ride a train myself," he replied. "Flew over to Cedar Rapids 2 years ago & my ears kept crackling for 6 days."

"One evening I was swimming in the Bosporus—" I begin.

"We had a swim in Dick Koss's pool before he sailed," they say.

"One evening I was sitting with a blonde Roman girl in the ancient Colosseum—" I say.

"That reminds me—I'll betcha Michigan State goes to the Rose Bowl," they say.

"One evening I was munching some halvah at Stamboul—"

"My uncle runs a pizza palace in Stamford, Connecticut," they say.

I don't think it's fair to make speeches about your travels. Then people have to listen, especially if it's a lecture with slides.

My 25th reunion

Tomorrow I'm driving up to Iowa State College for my 25th class reunion, if I can get my chores done in time. Many of my classmates now own their own farms, with well-paid hired hands. They haven't milked a cow in years. I have to milk my typewriter 7 days a week. (No automatic milker for it has yet been invented.)

Ah, bright college years! That glorious day when I helped move 2 pianos at 50 cents an hour! Those fruity, eggy dishes I washed, under a romantic impulse to work my way through school! I even tended furnaces long enough to vow that my first one would be a gas furnace, & it was.

I was only briefly a member of the class of 1924, only long enough for ISC to get under my hide. Tomorrow I hope I can recognize a few of my erstwhile classmates, especially the ones who were too light for football & are now too heavy for golf. I hope they all look as young as they act.

College was full of disappointments for me. I wanted to be an engineer, & turned out to be a columnist. I thought I was quite a halfback, & the freshman coach put me to work at guard. He lined up Frank Gotch & Strangler Lewis opposite me & told me to knife through between 'em.

That was really why I became a campus columnist. It gave me an honorable alibi to get away from line-bucking practice. When those 2 oafs converged on me, my left ribs pierced my right elbow. I ached all over. After football practice it used to take me 40 minutes to lace my shoes.

You probably saw me at the Iowa State track meets. Remember the wiry little fellow who broke through on the last turn & won the Missouri Valley quarter mile? That wasn't me. It was Deak Walters. I was the guy who carried the hurdles on & off the track, dragged the cinders & fetched the starting blocks for the high-toned sprinters.

One girl I hope comes back for the reunion is the girl who used to wear a sheepskin coat with a red beret. I hope the years have dealt gently with her. She always smiled & said hello on the campus, & for months I tried to get up nerve enough to invite her to have a banana split with me. If she reads this I hope she can still dig up the red beret.

Ah, the cherry pie à la mode they served in the old college cafeteria! They'd call it a double-double today. Where's the Sig Alph who used to win all the bets in Prof. Brindley's economics class, on how many times the prof would say "on the other hand" in each lecture? He's probably a White House adviser on economics today.

My best event in track was the pole vault. Remember the first time an ISC man ever cleared 12 feet? Well, I was the guy sitting on the tall step-ladder beside the standards, replacing the crossbar every time the other athletes knocked it down. In some ways it was the best job I ever had. I like athletics, & I also like to sit.

After football practice one day an athlete took me to his fraternity house for dinner. I was limping badly, but a free meal's a free meal. "The boys wanta look you over," he said cryptically. ("Zattso!" I muttered.) So I was on my best behavior; ate only 3 pork chops. With the prunes-for-dessert they all "Pick 'Em Up & Lay 'Em Down." I've always hoped they meant nothing personal.

One day a very lovely coed invited me to my first sorority dance. I shaved closely till I bled, & went fearfully. (There was a lot of talk about those wild sorority girls.) That evening I blacked out, from bashfulness, like an amnesia victim; can't remember a thing that happened. . . . If she's on hand for the 25th reunion I hope she'll tell me what I did right.

Ah, bright college days! I took a psychology elective, a class in intelligence testing. Frankly skeptical, I was assigned, with the prettiest girl in the class, to test a pair of 8-year-old twins who lived west of the campus. Each of the twins turned up an IQ of 124, & my faith in science was restored. College is a brief reprieve from, I mean a splendid preparation for, Life.

I'll never escort 5 girls to El Morocco again

How it happened is a separate story. One thing led to another, & I found myself signed up to take 5 girls to this tiger-striped night club where everybody else is a celebrity & the women wear mink lingerie.

All 5 of my girls were lovely & nice. Four of them were from Iowa, where every girl is nice. Most of 'em had never visited the place & wanted to get it out of their system. We had been drawn together by the baleful magnetism which draws Iowans into a huddle in New York.

El Morocco is a place where the *haute monde* seeks refuge from the *haute monde*. It's the 3rd most famous of New York's night clubs, & by some mysterious process that makes it more exclusive than the 1st & 2nd most famous.

Its head waiters are trained judges of the hoi polloi. I had heard that a folded $5 bill, held tightly in the moist palm, tends to influence their judgment. "I'll have a table in a moment, sir," said the head waiter, & I could have sworn that he glanced at my hand out of the corner of one eye.

Hastily I folded a $5 bill surreptitiously behind my back & held it in my palm. My girls had deployed around the doorway, & I felt a fierce pride at being selected by fate to be the escort of such a bevy of dazzling creatures. While I tried to hypnotize the head waiter, they were getting a quick eyeful.

It wasn't like being stranded on a desert isle with 5 girls. That I could have handled with greater éclat. El Morocco's bar was lined 9-deep with people waiting for tables, & the foyer & doorway were jammed with hoi polloi who knew how to push. I felt like Earl Carroll, or Mr. Powers with a basketball team made up of his models, just one short. "It'll be just a moment, sir," said the major-domo.

I stealthily folded a $10 bill & hid the vulgar $5 bill, & watched for a chance to slip it to the man without embarrassing him. Somewhere I'd heard that a $10 bill is stronger magic. I needed it, for so far as I could see every table was filled, with people sitting in each other's lap & showing no signs of departure.

Now, I suffer from storkophobia, or fear of being bruised in a night club, as well as Scott's disease, or dread of being confronted by a $70 night club check. Caught in such a dilemma, I mutter an incantation, "You only live once," & vow inwardly to balance the budget by going without lunch or new books for several months.

The girls were enjoying it more than I was, though one or two looked at me questioningly. I wanted to walk up to one of the larger tables & say, "Folks, it's time to go home & let somebody else carouse." A biblical quotation about a camel & the eye of a needle popped into my head.

With a poker face I concealed my $10 bill in my pants pocket & replaced it with a crisp $20 bill. It struck me that if the head waiter was really watching the tables with one eye and ogling my palm with the other, he ran the risk of going cross-eyed.

"I'll have a table immediately," said the maitre. With a shudder of gratitude I lunged toward him purposefully, trying to slip the $20 into his willing paw. A big rancher type barged forward, blocking me off. "We've seen enough," said one of my more eager maidens. "Let's go someplace else."

With a powerful yank, like a unicorn withdrawing his foot from a trap, I rescued the $20 from the head waiter's questing claw. "Are you *sure?*" I asked, galloping toward the checkroom & feigning reluctance. "It's stuffy in here," said my little minx. "Here's a table for you, sir," said the head waiter. But I didn't hear him. I was scrutinizing the deputy hat check girl to see if she was a *nice* girl.

My dad almost bought a ranch

When my dad settled in DM in the 1890's, he was an optimistic young man, confident he'd soon be rich. But his heart wasn't really in it, & in later years he enjoyed telling us what he did wrong. Chiefly, (1) he didn't scheme enough & (2) he was too often contemptuous of rich men.

Once when I was 6 he took me to lunch at the old Hotel Savery & afterward we sat on two of the comfortable oak sidewalk chairs. He knew a few of our town's go-getters, & told me what louts some were. "Don't lean your chair against the wall," he cautioned me. "Only the bums do that."

Later he conceded that he had a weakness for buying the wrong real estate with his meager savings. "These morons & lowlifes are luckier," he told me of men whose investments turned out better. "Or else maybe they're smarter than I am." But they liked to listen to him philosophize.

One of his favorite spots was the boat house just above the Center Street dam. He took me fishing there occasionally. His role as outdoor man caught me offguard; when I discovered that he was a better marksman than I, it was a profound shock. To this day I have a deep respect for fathers, not shared by many.

My father always felt close to the pioneer days. One of his neighbors once told him over a beer that *his* father had, as a youth, sailed up the DM river on a steamer from Keokuk. From then on my dad awaited impatiently the revival of navigation. He suspected the railroads of blocking the ships.

One day Dad showed me proudly his "25 prompts" in the DM credit rating book. He was a stickler for paying his bills promptly; on the 1st of the month if he was flush, on the 10th if he wasn't. I often wish I were prompter; but the b.w. jogs & nudges me till I pay 'em.

Against his better judgment, he finally yielded to my pleas when I had the measles & bought me a 1,000-shot beebee rifle. He was right the first time; he soon caught me aiming it at my sister, seized the ramrod & hid it, rendering the weapon inoperative. Anyhow, I didn't have any beebees.

The panic of 1907 scared him, though my mother confirms that around the house he maintained a stiff upper lip & a brave front. But the use of scrip for money in the Golden West puzzled him. "There are burglars in the corn, Son," he said. "We are helpless." He pondered how he could free his family from the risks of depression & panic.

His research took several years. Then one summer day he announced he was boarding a "landseekers' special" to Colorado to inspect a homestead. "If you behave yourself, you can come along," he said. "Maybe we can get a whole square mile of land. Maybe more!"

His father had been a farmer & operated a flour mill; Dad liked the wide open spaces. But when they told him the only nearby water flowed in an underground river, we hot-footed it back to Iowa. Yet we had seen coyotes & antelopes from a buckboard on the Great Plains; he contended the trip was worthwhile. So did I.

After a burglary in the neighborhood my father always kept a pistol locked in his trunk. It was unloaded, & he kept the ammunition hidden elsewhere, & the key to the trunk hidden, too, lest we rummage for the gun & shoot ourselves. Any burglar would have had a long start on him.

My father never got rich, but we forgave him, my 3 sisters & I, because he took it so philosophically. He was a great reader & a deep thinker; in his later years he reached the conclusion that the accumulation of great wealth was indelicate & somehow blameworthy.

But he saved a little money always, & bought himself the most expensive hats & shoes available. He was a hard man to buy a present for; he never wanted gimcracks lying around. On my first trip to Europe I foxed him, though; I bought him a retractable solid gold toothpick in Paris. He locked it in his trunk & took it out & looked at it occasionally.

❋ ❋ ❋

That lovable curmudgeon around the corner confides he's clocked his wife, discovers she spends more time on the phone gossiping than at housework. "If you count overhead," he grumbles, "she costs me more per hour on the phone than my wild ducks!"

"Some men drive three thousand miles to Florida and back," muses Peter Comfort, scattering some rock salt in his driveway, "and spend a thousand dollars just to avoid shoveling a little snow. Yet more tourists die of heart trouble in Florida than of snow shoveling in Minnesota."

One of our town's more confused husbands has decided to buy his wife a mink coat instead of offering her a divorce. "But if we get a divorce," he argues, "she ought to deduct it from the alimony."

As I shaved this morning my thought-of-the-year popped into my head: why isn't there a beautiful woman or two at the big table of every four-power conference? Their gentle intuition might make sense when male pugnacity doesn't.

Alas, we husbands no longer ride out with our lances level against the Black Knight for our Lady Fair. But we *can* carry the garbage out to the submerged can in a blizzard, after we've helped wash the dishes.

At our lunch-club round table the more sensitive souls are worried that the Texas millionaires are plotting to annex the rest of the Republic. "I only hope they elect a Texan as leader," says our town's legal eagle, over his pie à la mode, "not some furriner from one of the other forty-seven states."

Egad, my Dream Girl has contrived a tasty dessert of cranberries and ground-up oranges, sweet but with almost no calories. Now, if we could only find a calorie-free substitute for French-fried potatoes.

After a trip through Europe with his wife and daughter, the home-spun nabob in the next block now favors the UN, and even a United States of Europe. "We've gotta fix it up," he says, "to eliminate this frontier and customs tommyrot, and so we can use American money or the same kind of money in all twenty countries."

"I'd hoped that Kinsey's two books would solve sex," muses Betty Comfort, exposing some angel-food-cake crumbs to the birds. "Especially the one about women. But here we are, still up in the air!"

Our neighbor in the big remodeled stable suspects his wife of double-crossing him. "When she wooed me," he recalls, "one of the big points in her favor was her master's thesis on Edith Wharton. And now she needles me for reading the *Atlantic Monthly!*"

I'm on the alert constantly for signs of age in myself; as for example, when I find myself arguing that a great sonnet memorized does a school child as much good as a day's discoveries in "social studies."

Cheerful thought at a high-school basketball game: we can't be so tense about Russ bombs as we imagine if we get this much fun out of watching young men throw a ball through a hoop.

FOR MEN ONLY [VII]

When our youngest catches me scratching my head at my desk and asks if he can brew me a cup of tea . . . or Junior invites his young brother to week-end at the university to see the sights . . . and our daughter reveals an overdue gratitude for inheriting my red hair . . . or my wife unexpectedly offers, to my confusion, to scrub my back in the tub . . . then I'm left with little to act soulful about and confess I'm as happy as a man can get.

8
Military life

PROLOGUE

Our unknown soldier

He lies on a hillside southwest of the Potomac. Below him airplanes rise from the drome in the lowlands & fly above the small boats in the river—a thrilling sight against the Washington backdrop—if he could but see.

On the left, beyond the formal terrace, beyond the river, the gray stone buildings of the Government march from the Lincoln Memorial past the White House & the Washington Monument to the voluptuous dome of the Capitol.

There the messages were written, the speeches uttered, the laws voted with ayes & noes, and signed; there the military commands went forth which sent him across the sea to die in a foreign war, the Unknown Soldier, this most singular enigmatic hero of our century, under the marble slab in Arlington.

Hundreds have stood here whose son he may have been, whose lover or husband or father perhaps he was. Did he leave a son behind? An eager, militant, warlike son? A son with a bitter hatred for war? His son is trench-size now.

What manner of man was he? Probably he was in his middle 20's—24 or 26. Was he a volunteer? Was he drafted? Did his heart leap or sink as he put on his uniform the first time? Was his blood racing with high adventure as he climbed the gangplank?

Was he a tall, slim, silent, drawling son of the West? Was he short, husky, garrulous, passionate? Was he of Revolutionary stock or the son of an immigrant? Was he blond, dark-haired, red-haired with blue eyes? Was he shy & withdrawn, or was he the life of the party, always kidding? Was he an aristocrat, like Quentin Roosevelt, or was he the obscure son of an obscure family, as unknown in life as in death? Was he a lieutenant or a noncom or a private?

What was the way of his death? Did it stalk him & find him in his trench? Did he go forth to meet it crawling in the wet murky dawn through the stubble of some inauspicious yellow field? Did he go toward it with a rush, invincible, invulnerable, immortal?

By what sudden quirk did his death overtake him? Did he swerve to left or right to tighten a gap in the line? Did he avoid one bursting shell & praise his luck star, only to run into another? Did death come to him with merciful swiftness? Did it torture him for agonized hours seeming like eons? Did he lie for weeks in some thicket or shellhole, half buried?

Had he ever seen this Washington, his capital, which now lies spread out below him? Had he wandered through its avenues as a tourist with a camera? Had he once looked down from the Monument toward this Virginia hillside where he would one day lie in enviable but anonymous glory?

Had he ever strolled among these graves in Arlington, a little awed & depressed by the reminders of the illustrious dead, faintly troubled by the uneventful happiness of his own obscure, peaceful life, who is now honored for a multitude, beyond them all?

Would he smile if he stood now on these broad stone steps, watching one of his 4,000,000 buddies pose uncomfortably but stubbornly against this marble slab while a proud fortyish wife snaps a camera & the sentry marches past eyes front toward the canvas sentry box, & the greenhouses of the experimental farm in the valley below glisten in the westerly sun?

His last hour— The top sergeant says we've got 'em on the run. Next week the war will be over. Anyhow, we're due to move out tomorrow. Damn this mud! Maybe two weeks' leave in some dry sunny place in the south of France? Haven't been dry for 3 days! Maybe a bottle of wine with a pretty French girl? Home before Christmas & a parade down Main Street! The job & the girl— The hero's homecoming— So much to tell—so much left to live.

AFTER THE WAR IS OVER

Right in the colonel's face

Of the 4 army officers I swore to punch in the nose some day after the war, I have now met 2 face to face in civvies. I punched neither of 'em in the nose, nor in the jaw. In fact, we had quite an amiable reunion in each case.

I still have 2 to go, & 1 of them is the man I most enthusiastically want to punch in the nose or kick in the pants. I know I'll encounter him some day. But I fear that when we meet again, my fist will be unclenched.

Alas, when you meet an old comrade, no matter how you hated his guts in the army, you find you've so much more in common to reminisce about than you have left to bicker about, that it's perhaps too easy to let justice fall flat on its face. (But maybe I'll punch one of 'em yet, I hope.)

It's odd that I'd want to punch a colonel in the nose. After all, I reached a rank where others were presumed to want to punch me in the nose. But when exposed to a ruthless bully, I felt exactly as a buck private did with a roughneck sergeant. I used to say, "They can't do this to me!" But they did.

The first officer I ever swore to punch seemed a beetle-browed bully. He was a major & soon a lieutenant-colonel, but he behaved like a roughneck sergeant, or tried to. He wore a perpetual scowl & thought it made him look like Napoleon, & he tried to be more military than Hindenburg.

He was not my C.O., but he managed to make life unpleasant until one day I exploded and told him where to go &

what to do, in lingo unbecoming an officer. Next day he invited me to lunch. We met a few months ago & in civvies he's as sweet as a lamb, tries to be a lovable character.

So far I've never met the one I wanted to punch the most & hardest. He's an officer I saw only one day, on a mission with the British. He was the only West Pointer I ever knew to behave like a boor. Three times in 1 day he bawled me out because the British (who didn't like him either) had snubbed him.

Later I learned he was sweating out promotion to brigadier-general, & was also suffering from a liver complaint, all of which curdled the sweetness of his true nature. (Later I said the wrong thing in the right place—to the effect that I didn't think he was fit to be a brigadier—& to my horror my words were used against him. He never got his star.)

I've often wondered why I ever wanted to punch No. 3. He was an engaging cuss, with more charm than the other 3 combined; whimsical, likable, capricious, & ruthless in a brilliant, magnetic way. Bit of a genius. I met him 2 years after the war, & he took us to the Colony Club for dinner. Pleasant in civvies, painful in uniform. Another reason I didn't punch him was that his wife is a delightful lady. (And he might have pulled a knife on me.)

The 4th officer I half swore to punch was a crusty poseur. He was determined to behave like Bismarck or Pershing or somebody. When you walked into his inner sanctum (he was a general), he'd look at a memo on his desk with deep concentration for fully 120 seconds, ignoring your presence. (Once I caught a glimpse of the memo: "Get candy bars at PX.") But he's getting too old & fragile now, & we'll probably just drink a toast.

In civvies they often turn out to be fairly good eggs, these men you swore to punch. It was their rank that went to their heads, & their amateurish ways of playing Napoleon. The officer who gave me my worst headaches overseas later sketched a portrait of my wife in crayon.

Well, I'm not at all sure a punch in the nose is the answer. Maybe a good stout dig in the ribs is enough. Possibly it wasn't the man we wanted to punch in the nose; maybe it was the arbitrary power he had over us, which we didn't know how to challenge.

Oh, yes. There was another man I wanted to punch in the

nose. He was the stupidest & most confused colonel I ever saw, & he added to the crazy chaos at the Pentagon so much that I demanded overseas duty. I met him overseas & we had coffee together. Later I ran across his grave. Turned out not to be a bad egg after all.

Heroes from Main Street

So you think the people on Walnut Street are humdrum people, eh? You could be mistaken. That young man with glasses flew the Hump 42 times. That heavy-set lawyer was an adviser-observer-expert at Frisco when the UN was born. That young woman's husband went down with a submarine.

That little boy staring into the Utica window—his father died on Omaha beach 6 weeks before he was born. These crowds on Locust are flavored with heroes. That plumpish man in earmuffs had 14 months Air Force duty in Greenland, lonely under the northern lights.

You'd be surprised how few of 'em are ordinary. That tall, solemn gent with the doctor's bag—he was a Navy surgeon on jungle Guadalcanal, knee-deep in sawed-off limbs & gore. The husky hombre with the briefcase was present in a small room when a fat-jowled German general biting his nails surrendered Paris to the Americans & General de Gaulle.

See that lad eating a candy bar—he's a hero, too; tailgunner in a B-17 on 4 Berlin raids. Get that red-haired golfer to tell you of the week he crouched all night in a slit trench with a German corpse. Don't look now, but that gal in slacks dished out doughnuts at a Roer River pontoon bridge.

Heroes seldom look heroic. That worried slim Jim there—he put in 40 days under the kamikaze divebombers off Okinawa. The guy with the 3 books under his arm—in the beachhead he slept in a cot occupied by a Storm Trooper the night before. This is a nation of ex-warriors—& future warriors.

How do you know that elderly woman in the red coat isn't the one from the east side who lost 2 sons in the war? That shorty getting out of the taxicab at the Savery—he was born while his dad was overseas in World War I, & his son was born while he was overseas in WW II.

Don't sell these baggy-pants pedestrians short. The one with the box of candy under his arm—an incendiary bullet set fire to his blanket in an orchard near Eindhoven, Holland. Those 2 highschoolers in those gaudy green-&-gold dragon-jackets—they've each served a year in Korea.

Wars are won by baldies like these—the one at Katz's sodafountain—from Dover's breakwater he watched us & the Germans exchange bombs & artillery shells across the straits—saw 'em exploding at both ends. That tall character dressed like an actor was twice wounded.

Look quick—the handsome chap with the mustache (blue storm coat with gray fur collar) was captured in Africa. And the trim poker-face there—medium height—commanded one of those woeful isles in the Aleutian chain.

Did you notice that slim, patrician type who just passed—bit of a swell—he skidded a flat-bottomed landing craft all over the Pacific. That handsome matron wrote her husband 743 letters while he was overseas. At the skyscraper portal—you recognize him; a lawyer: he lost a leg at Chateau Thierry.

Across the street—looking at the neckties in Zuna's window—he was on the Missouri at Tokyo Bay. His great-grandfather fought at Gettysburg. See that chap who reminds you of a Peter Arno bartender? He spent some hot nights at Anzio.

You'd never mistake that shot-putter type for an acrobat—he climbed down the battleship Nevada's 60-foot landing nets off Utah beach in full pack. And there's a screwball, the one gazing into Jack Smith's flower store—had a cushy Pentagon spot & wangled overseas duty.

Oh, Locust & Walnut Streets are speckled with heroes & warriors full of memories. At the next table I overheard one telling of the day he reached the Siegfried line. He had a snapshot of Patton baptizing the Rhine. His companion tossed a hand-grenade into an Aachen cellar & emptied his carbine into a machine-gun nest behind a picture window at Chartres— How humdrum they look in their overcoats. But they ain't humdrum! Not by a long shot.

Old soldier looks back

Over thirty-five years ago he had more pep & cockiness than any World War II vet has today. Now his tummy leans heavily on his belt. His hair line has deep indentations & he can no longer chin himself 10 times on a German castle's fancy chandelier.

"Gad, we'll never get flabby like that!" the cocky new crop of vets mutters. . . . But they will. In 25 years or so, they too will be too tired to throw paper bags full of water out of hotel windows or kiss thin native girls at conventions. Remember the rhythm of the 1917 convoy going over, the crusader's thrill?

Ah, the biggest moment of his whole life, that day in '17 when he walked down the gangplank to French soil. The electric excitement at Le Havre, first time he kissed a French girl. (By the third kiss it was very much like kissing an American girl.) The first boom of distant bombardment as he went up to the lines, the sudden vagrant thought: "Those people want to kill *me*!"

Now that little shudder that comes every time he remembers the first American blood he saw in France. His first visit to a French village, & the manure heaps at every door. (That first stiff angular German corpse.) The first French meal of raspberries & an omelet of 6 eggs at a country *estaminet*.

How different it tasted from the scrambled eggs the company cook made in a wash boiler. The letters from home, no V-mail that time. The little airplanes like dragon flies, the Spads & Nieuports. Those colossal German bombing planes made of wire & canvas. They say you could still see the first war's scars while flying on a mission in World War II, old scars & new.

So this is November 11, 1955. It was 37 years ago today he hitch-hiked from the front into Paris on the first Armistice Day to celebrate, with the French girls dancing around him in circles. The one who snatched his cap. The church struck by the German Big Bertha shell that yanked 250 to kingdom come.

Shucks, there's nothing new, we're in a rut—a German V-2 hit a chapel in London 26 years later & killed 200. His first kiss in Paris, by its ruins. Next war maybe they'll hit First Methodist in Des Moines or Aimee's temple in LA. The Navy next time, or maybe sit one out? Oh, the mud & the rain & the barbed wire. The old-fashioned war.

He's glad he was a lot younger than the average, just a kid out of high school. Remember that camp out at the fair grounds before the outfit went overseas? And the folks coming out to visit & looking doubtfully at the rows of khaki-blanketed cots? Gad, it's hard to think they really got old Pat & Mac. Do they still make men like that? I guess they do. He shaves & meditates.

"Hell's bells. I'll never forget how it feels to cross the ocean in a convoy. The silly camouflage on the ships, the destroyers weaving in & out & the cruisers up front. No aircraft carriers in those days. The guys who think they see periscopes & the 7-mile shots at drifting wreckage.

"And, oh, the lifeboat drills, Mary, you shoulda seen 'em. Some of the guys wouldn't break up the blackjack game, & drew KP. The moonlit night when the big Zeppelin came over & fell 12 miles from our camp. Wonder whether I've still got that little scrap of aluminum from her? See if you can find it, pet.

"I've never told you, darling, about that little English girl at Southampton, the one who sat on my lap at the cinema—Carter was her name? What was her first name—Betty? Joan? Marjorie? No, it was Ethel. Somehow those things all get telescoped. She was a sweet little thing."

He never thought in those days he'd ever be a grampa. Always thought of himself as a rootin' tootin' roué till his 49th birthday. Still does, sometimes after a good night's sleep. Shucks, he used to think maybe he was a kind of hero, secretly & ashamed, maybe while listening to a patriotic speech. Now he doesn't know. Maybe he helped hold back the tyrants another 30 or 50 years—who knows?

※ ※ ※

Nothing flabbergasts one of our town's solvent pairs, on returning from a month or six weeks in Florida or the West Indies, to find all their neighbors with better sun-lamp tans than they've brought home for $2,000.

Nowadays when I get a letter written in a clear, legible and handsome handwriting, I jump immediately to the deduction that the writer is over thirty-five years old. Or have any of the younger people learned to write decently?

Now we don't need to worry how to plan our summer vacation. Both our boys are motel enthusiasts, and since they saw a list of America's "10 best" motels, they simply want to drive around and spend a night at each of 'em.

My big discovery of the year: that a wife gloats so innocently at the sight of her husband in a kitchen apron that he's a cad if he doesn't don one now and then long enough to wipe two or three spoons.

My Lady Love now has recipes for as many different kinds of meat loaf as you'd encounter at a P.T.A. supper. She humors me, but still thinks I'm crazy when I say roast beef is O.K. when you can't get good meat loaf.

Some of our town's solidest citizens remind me of the Russians, the way they both hate the United Nations. At moments in a UN skirmish at the country club you'd think you were in a locker room at the Kremlin.

UTAH & NORMANDY BEACHES

First night ashore

During the war I was on the expendable battleship Nevada off Utah beachhead. Her big ruddy captain sat on a tall wooden stool behind the steel-plated rail on the bridge directing fire at the German guns toward Cherbourg. Everyone wore helmets & awkward lifebelts & nibbled at K rations. Ten of my sharper memories:

1. My heavy-laden awkwardness as I climbed down the big rope landing net hanging over the Nevada's towering sides. My canteen, Colt .45 & musette bag kept dangling in my way. Halfway down I clung by one hand & tossed the musette bag to a soldier in the landing barge far below. "Hi, Harlan!" he said a moment later. "I'm from Mason City, myself."

2. An officer was peeking out of a cave in a sand dune ashore. He held a list in his hand, & had the preoccupied look of an ISC man at an alumni picnic. "These Heinies certainly left a mess!" he said. Down the beach a truckload of something was burning. Up the coast their 8-inch guns boomed too late. "I hear it's tougher over at Omaha beach," he said.

3. Prisoners were shambling, arms up, hands sagging near their ears, beachward down the narrow road, eyes down as they passed us between the flooded fields. In the 11 P.M. double daylight dusk the landscape was grim, forbidding, unfathomable. A few bodies lay twisted at the water's edge. "Let's see, 8 hours difference; back home they're drinking mid-afternoon coffee, & it's the last week of school."

4. It was dark when we reached the stone-walled courtyard of the old Norman farm which was the command post. I bruised my knee hitting the dirt when a bomb landed 400 yards away. Behind the blanketed doorway officers were at the field phones. "We're making contact with the airborne," one of 'em said. An Iowa boy showed me the battered hayloft as if it were the royal suite. (Wish I could remember his name.)

5. The night sky was laced & rosetted with tracers, flares & explosions. We were acutely aware of the enemy in the darkness ahead, & the Channel water not far behind. Somebody tossed a grenade down the road & it sounded like an artillery shell. I left the hay to the rats & went out under a tree near the pump.

6. I couldn't sleep & made some cold coffee with the K ration crystals. At the pump I ran into Joe O'Malley, an officer who'd been stationed at Fort DM in the days of Sunday horseback rides, weekly bridge & polo. Tonight he was at the high point of his army career here in the beachhead, at the heart of the greatest military exploit of all history.

7. More sentries were posted; small groups of Heinies were

infiltrating into the beachhead or trying to zigzag out to their own lines in the dark. Everybody was trigger happy. Soldiers shot their carbines into the dark sky at planes whose motors thrummed with an alleged German rhythm. I fumbled nervously at my .45, trying to feel valiant.

8. At dawn we could see our shattered gliders at the next crossroad. I counted 11 with crumpled wings which had knifed through the trees. A Norman farmer complained someone had thrown a grenade into his milk room. At the edge of a thicket an American parachutist in mottled green & tan camouflage uniform knelt upright, in full pack, stiff in death.

9. Amazement & triumph sang through our veins; we were alive; we had a firm foothold. Fortress Europa was a sham. No endless concrete wall with guns every few feet; no rivers of blood. It dawned on us: if a conqueror spreads out too much he cannot hold his conquests. I wasn't quite so lonely.

10. Half the Frenchmen in Carentan were watching us throw a pontoon across the river. That line of nervous soldiers crouching in the ditch was our front line. The Germans were 800 yards away up the slope across the lowland meadow. (If they're as efficient as we've heard, why don't they pepper the crossing? What a bottleneck, what a target!)

I visited Utah beachhead again last year, & the whole landscape said, "Not guilty, this isn't the place." I even found the walled farm with the haymow & the pump; they didn't look the same either; nobody shooting.

Bedtime in Normandy

At this point the beachhead was almost 5 miles deep. That afternoon we captured another village, and about 11 P.M. our outfit moved forward toward the sagging German line. I got involved in one of the strangest nights I ever lived.

It was D plus 4, & the narrow space between the enemy line & the Channel beaches still seemed skintight. A few of the new H-bombs would have destroyed every living thing in the whole beachhead. The water over our shoulders had a Dunkirk flavor.

We had landed less than 100,000 troops so far. Hitler had ordered his armies to throw us back into the sea. It was not until 3 days later that Eisenhower felt secure enough on the beachhead to utter his famous "Now let the so-&-so's push us into the sea!"

It was nearly midnight when my jeep reached its objective, & the late dusk of double daylight summer time had fallen across Normandy. Our troops were mopping up in the village, & I was trying to find a place on its edge better than an apple orchard to sleep in. And I didn't want to spend the next hour digging a foxhole.

Just as it was getting too dark to look much longer, I stumbled into the gateway of a large walled farmhouse. Across the road in the side of the embankment were 2 German foxholes, curving with the entrance to another farmyard. Above them in the hedge were the remains of a German machine gun, with a body beside it.

For a moment the ready-made foxhole tempted me. Then I explored the house cautiously with brief beams from my flashlight. It seemed empty. On the ground floor was a tackle room with some straw on the floor & a battered cot in a corner.

I lay down gladly, placing my flashlight, pistol & helmet on the floor within reach. Through the large window with the shattered glass the nightly fireworks display was beginning. Brilliant flares lit the sky as enemy planes cruised around dropping an occasional bomb.

Our boys at the anti-aircraft guns were still trigger-happy & the darkness was laced with the colored ribbons of tracer bullets. Now & then a bomb burst with a flowerpot splash of flame, always too near. Half the time the dark room was lit up.

I began to long for company. In the dusk we had become separated, & the others had found other places to sleep. My imagination got to work, & I began to see stray Germans lobbing hand grenades through the broken window at the ground-floor level.

By the light of a floating flare I looked at my wrist watch. It was only 12:45, & I had thought it must be nearly 3. I decided that if I wasn't asleep by 1:30 I'd move out to the foxhole. It would be getting light soon after 3 A.M. I couldn't sleep, & I hadn't had much sleep for several nights.

The danger of bugs began to worry me. Many of these German posts were lousy, & this looked as if it had been a Jerry company c.p. & billet. I began to feel imaginary nips from imaginary bugs, but that reduced the menace of imaginary hand grenades.

Through the shattered window the sky reminded me of a Fourth of July celebration at the fair grounds. After a long, long spell when time seemed endless I looked at my watch again. It was 1:10, & I suddenly remembered that with double summer time it would not be light till after 5 A.M.

"Well, I can't take four more hours of these bugs & hand grenades," I said to myself. I picked up my helmet, pistol belt, musette bag & flashlight & moved out to the foxhole. A flare over the far edge of the village lit my way. That foxhole now seemed as attractive as a suite at the Ritz.

I sneaked a quick look with my flashlight, hand on my pistol. It was deep & dry. It seemed to have another occupant. He wasn't stirring. He was beyond restlessness & fear. I moved over to the second foxhole & settled down with my head on my musette bag. I couldn't sleep but I was below the ground level, below any flying bits of metal. Only a direct hit could bother me.

* * *

One of our more flirtatious belles has a new definition for social activity. "It's aimed to calm and placate," she says sweetly, "the suspicious wives of the men I like."

If I tote an early cup of coffee and some orange juice upstairs to my wife first (and drink some myself), I find myself losing fewer arguments at the breakfast table.

I've told half the matrons in our little coterie to read Clifton Fadiman's essay, "The Decline of Attention." Some of 'em, of course, look on the sunny side and tell me about the enormous increase, among our children, of inattention.

I suspect that one reason so many fashionables in New York and Hollywood wear sun glasses is to veil their eyes and conceal the fact that they aren't listening to what you're saying.

Our deep thinker at the club is alarmed at Senator Bricker's brazen attempt to steal Ike's striped diplomatic pants with a constitutional amendment. "It's the Lilliputians trying to hog-tie Gulliver," he snorts, "that's what it is."

One way to improve the looks of a room is to saw off the legs of some or all of the furniture. This cures the taller old-fashioned pieces of their overwhelming and awesome quality and makes rooms seem larger and roomier. (You can burn the legs in the fireplace.)

"Maybe I'm too sensitive," broods Peter Comfort, "but every time I begin to tell a story my wife begins to worry whether the room is too warm or does somebody want more coffee or a cooky or is that light shining on their face."

DRAFT AGE

Army life won't ruin him

Recently I've begun to think quite a lot about Junior's next birthday. He's 18 in May & the Army will be reaching for him. If he's away 27 or 30 months I'll miss him like blazes, but I decline to let myself get worked into a tantrum about it.

    The b.w. takes it all calmly too. She loves him as much as other mothers love their young sons, but she hasn't written, phoned or telegraphed her senator. Nor does she bluster about making 30-year-old patriarchs with 9 children go first.

    He himself faces the barracks & drillground with admirable equanimity. He isn't enthusiastic about chopping this big slice out of his young life, but he isn't maudlin with self-pity either. He seems to feel equal to whatever comes his way. I admire his guts.

We don't fear that the Army, Navy, Air Force or Marine Corps will corrupt or ruin him. I think he's a boy who won't ruin easily, & I don't think the Armed Forces are much rougher on a boy's morals than any shopping center or beer joint or ice cream dive.

Maybe the Armed Forces will do him good. Our well-heeled neighbor down the hill swears the Navy improved his boy wondrously in 2 years. "He was just a half-baked kid when he enlisted," he says, "but when he came home he was quite a man."

I don't think he'll get out of the notion of going to college later. Of course, I hope he squeezes in his freshman year first, but even after 30 months away I think his good sense will still bring him back to his school books.

Among the things he's wanted to do the next year or two are: (1) work in a lumber camp; (2) go to Mexico; (3) spend a summer in France; (4) drive coast to coast with 3 other 17-year-olds in a flivver, & (5) sail to the Argentine in a 24-foot sailboat. He loves travel, & the Army runs quite a travel bureau.

My wife and I have talked it over & agree that any harm he might come by in the service could happen in civilian life at home. He'll meet some strange varieties, but his chums at home aren't exactly choir boys, & I think the flavor of unusual types will do him good. They'll teach him humility, & maybe he'll end up with pride, too.

Father-love & mother-love can be more painful than the mumps, but we don't want to try to keep our children in diapers. We can't buy him a big chunk of freedom & hire a Hessian to defend it for him. He understands that, as quite a few of his ancestors understood it before him.

We know a few hysterical mothers who pretend that 18-year-olds are babes in arms, but I think these estimable ladies are still playing with dolls. I wish to heaven neither their boys nor ours had to go. But it's a world neither he nor I made; we merely have to cope with it.

I rely on Ike Eisenhower when they ask for 18-year-olds. Maybe Junior won't fight in '52 or '53 but it's sensible to train him so he'll be ready in '54 or '55, still at the romantic heroic fighting age.

In my weaker moments I wish they'd handpick the more robust of the 4-Fs & let them fight side by side with Junior. But I'll try to trust Ike about that, too. I don't want Junior ever to share a slit-trench with a weakling or a screwball. That would be tougher & more dangerous than the night I spent in a foxhole with a German corpse.

Is it easy to be so calm about Junior? No, not entirely. But it helps if I face the facts. Junior is a natural soldier, like the 18-year-olds who added up to two-thirds of our soldiers in the Civil War. If he trains, his chances to become a father & grandfather in a free land are vastly better.

To a raw recruit: a little advice

Bud, Old Boy:
Your mother wants me to write you a letter. She cherishes an illusion that advice does some good. Well, you really plunged in; enlisted without telling Dad & Mom, & now you're on your way to Marine boot camp in California. Good outfit, fellah.

They'll look you over, & the quickest way you can get in dutch is to talk too much. Silence is probably the easiest of all short cuts to prestige & popularity. So don't talk too much. This applies equally in the Army, Navy, Air Force & even in civilian life.

Remember, the more letters you write the more letters you'll get. And what those letters come to mean to you when you're overseas! Even before. And what your letters'll mean to those back home who love you. I tried to write home at least a note every day I was overseas, & the b.w. wrote me every day, 757 in all. Letters are tops for your morale & theirs.

If you want to rate your fellow soldiers in the order of importance to you, I think they'll line up in this order: (1) the privates, (2) the noncoms, & (3) the officers. This reverses the order of the apple-polishers, but in the long run it's the realistic order in your army life.

To the officers, I hope you'll be neither subservient nor rude, servile nor surly. You can even learn how to say "sir" in a semi-scornful way, not quite an insult, that'll put bad officers in their place. I know men who in 2 wars learned how to say "sir" like a whiplash, so it sounded almost like "chump."

Be appreciative of the noncoms' rank, but don't overdo it. It's a mistake to treat a sergeant as if he were the Commander-in-Chief, but it's also a mistake to affront his self-esteem. And sometimes the nearest corporal can loom bigger in your life than the Chief of Staff.

You'll be a buck private longer than you think, chum, & all the other privates are your blood brothers. Treat 'em with as much respect & considerateness as you treat the officers & noncoms, & with more affection. In fact, treat everybody in the Army as an equal, from generals down. The rank & brass is laid on just to help 'em do their chores.

You'll grouse a lot, & at times you'll be convinced that everybody from the nearest corporal to the Big Brass in Washington is your enemy & trying to snafu everything for you. But in a strange, secret way you'll be happy, elbow to elbow with other courageous men in a great crusade, even if you deny it.

Don't clutter your duffle bag with too much junk. Everything you lug around ought to be useful. I once set off for the wars with a 7-pound volume of poetry in my duffle, but I got rid of *that* in a hurry. Better a small volume of poetry & six good pairs of woolen socks. Never pass up a chance for a bath, & tote some stuff for athlete's foot.

Always carry a little emergency ration in your musette bag & don't eat it except in an emergency. Do you remember the lieutenant in Shaw's *Arms & the Man* who used his pistol holster to carry chocolate? Keep your canteen filled. Catch a few winks of sleep at odd times. I used to carry both sleeping pills & stay-awake pills, yet I'm not too sold on 'em.

But I do remember, after 3 sleepless nights in the beachhead, when a big pill (a bromide) made a foxhole seem like a featherbed. Try to find out the peculiar way the Marines do things; a smart lad gets familiar with his environment. Read the manuals & poop-sheets, get familiar with your equipment, find out your rights as a soldier.

Son, you may be scared, but you won't be afraid. Maybe that's too complex, but put it in your own words. Every soldier knows that fear & courage coexist, side by side. You'll experience your share of both.

Don't succumb to loneliness, son; that's the occupational disease of the young soldier—& the older one, too. When the yearning for your loved ones, for your home, becomes a physical pain, the companionship of your comrades will save you. You'll stave off loneliness by chatting with your relatives & friends in the letters you write, by re-reading the letters they've written you. And sooner than you think you'll be back home again.

❋ ❋ ❋

Our youngest is a demon for modern furniture; each piece we buy to rejuvenate our living room ends up in his bedroom. But he graciously lends 'em back to us when company comes.

A well-rounded husband should devote two hours twice a week to outdoor sport; an hour twice a week to a hobby; and read 100 pages a week in good books or magazines. (Of course he must earn a good living, too, and not neglect his household chores, or he isn't well-rounded!)

After years of marriage a husband learns that if he wants ham and eggs at midnight, and his wife has sensitive nostrils, he'd better cook 'em on the old gas stove in the basement laundry room.

At the bridge table the other night that insoluble problem came up again: "If a wife could rescue either her husband or her child, but not both, which should she help?" I've never heard a forthright answer; but "The one who weighs less" seems to me a plausible one.

My Lady Love has examined the group photograph on my den wall of us lawn-tennis umpires at last year's singles tournament at Forest Hills. "Well," she said finally, "it's not as athletic a group as I'd expected." Alas, brains and judgment don't show in a photo.

I suppose we've taken 500 snapshots of the five of us in this family; but only three of 'em portray each and every member flatteringly enough. What we might need is one of those phony "composite" photographs they sometimes use in political campaigns.

* * *

FOR MEN ONLY [VIII]

When your youngest across the room consults you every thirty seconds about his lessons . . . and Junior ponders his future over scrawls on his college clipboard . . . or your daughter quotes from Doc Spock to prove how mistakenly you reared your infants . . . and your wedded wife knits at a sweater she vows her old beau will get if you don't mend your ways . . . then you don't really live in the "Age of Anxiety," stranger, no matter what the country-club oracles of doom are saying.

9

Husband & wife

PROLOGUE

Tips to a groom for his honeymoon

If you don't want to come home from your first road trip in last place, be on your toes for every contingency. Instead of arguing damply with an innocent hotel clerk for an air-cooled room, reserve one a month ahead. (Even if he wins, no man looks good to his new queen while arguing with a room clerk.)

Always know in which pocket your rail tickets are hidden. Don't fumble; women hate a fumbler. Don't spend 15 minutes looking for a parking space, & above all don't try to back into a space a yard too short for your car.

Don't be a prude on your honeymoon, but it's none too soon to begin to practice bathroom privacy. Even if you have to get up 30 minutes before she does. Even a maharajah's bathroom is not a good setting for more than one person.

Be ultra-masculine; let your bride win all the minor arguments. That's 19 out of 20, & no more than her due. But you better win the big ones, chum, & without too many words. Or you're in 2nd place from there on in. (Like double bed vs. twin beds or apartment vs. cottage.)

By more modern doubletalk, bride & bridegroom are not one but two persons. So don't try to act as if you two were just one person. Allow her free choice & scope for her personality & goofy ideas wherever possible. (If she doesn't want grand opera or ham & eggs don't force her.)

Next to love it's respect that makes close quarters endurable for two people. But don't let woman's natural abhorrence for exercise keep you both from hiking 5 miles a day, or a swim or golf or some tennis. (At heart women are just as lazy as men.) Better spend an hour or 2 apart each day. Even if it is your honeymoon.

At least 5 times a day put yourself in her place. If you were a woman would you think that big oaf fascinating? If you've got some foibles that irk her (even if she hides *how* irksome), shed 'em. But if some of *her* mannerisms irk you, don't let on; just razz the same mannerisms in *other* women.

You'd better talk frankly about sex beginning the second day out. Nobody knows all about it; even the experts don't agree. They used to say it took 10 years for a man & his wife to become sexually harmonious; but people are quicker nowadays, & not so patient. Ask the smartest doctor you know for the best book on sex.

A honeymoon is a time to get acquainted. You ought to tell your bride a lot about your boyhood & early family life, & the truth, too. Don't brag or pretend or gloss over; if your dad never earned over $18 a week don't be ashamed to say so; all the more credit to him & your mother for raising such a big shot.

Don't be a traitor to your sex. If you let your wife dominate you, or walk over you roughshod, or get away with murder, her example can infect all her friends & acquaintances & make it tougher for all the husbands you know. Start on the honeymoon to be the 51% stockholder; but let your wife vote the other 49. Oh, yes; on your honeymoon don't undertip. There'll never be another time when an extra dime or quarter or half-crown will get you so much reward.

The first morning I had breakfast with my bride I wondered what we'd have to talk about for the next 50,000 meals. Well, you'll find plenty. But at first, talk about all the people you both know. That's the best topic. You'll find you agree about most of 'em, & that'll be a great bond; nothing draws you together so much as disliking the same people.

Bring her a flower every day of your honeymoon; not necessarily a big bouquet; just one. Be good company; don't gloom, don't mislay your sense of humor at *any* moment of your honeymoon. Use your brain; that's what it's for. Whether driving or ordering a meal or handling your baggage or paying a bill or cuddling or quarreling, be self-possessed; keep your wits about you. It'll comfort her to know she's married a man who thinks 24 hours ahead & who's likely to take good care of her.

※ ※ ※

My wife is a woman of action. One evening a chum gave her a recipe for potatoes with corn flakes, garlic and cream. Next evening we had it for dinner. Third day I devoured the leftovers, best in the icebox. (As if good old potatoes really need any such fancy treatment!)

I suspect Marilyn DiMaggio's married life won't be all hugs and home runs, if she persists in covering doorknobs with chinchilla. Wait till Joe touches one in the dark and screams and threatens to haul it into court!

In those new cottages near the open fields they pass around their maternity blue jeans and ballooning party frocks among expectant mothers, and save themselves a pretty penny. A baby can use even a modern chrome-legged yellow high chair for next to nothing if its pa and ma are clever about scheduling.

Maybe I'd better not mention any names, but I'll wager there's no greater courage than that of a fourteen-year-old boy phoning the prettiest girl in his ninth-grade class for a date.

One of our town's sports wears colored hatbands that look like one-time diagonal-striped neckties. "Black bands look like a Frenchman's mourning band," he argues. Maybe if the hatmakers adopted colored hatbands they wouldn't be pursuing their bare-headed ex-customers!

"We always invite both our mothers-in-law to dinner the same evenings," confides Betty Comfort, drying her hair outdoors the first sunny day, "and encourage 'em to exchange advice and philosophies. It's like a Fountain of Youth for both."

THE ALMOST PERFECT WIFE & OTHER LIKE TALES

The almost perfect wife

Eighty-nine days out of 90 she is gently tolerant of her husband's eccentricities. About 10 times a year she fears she is losing her independence, or her identity, & puts up a brisk argument on a surprisingly minor point. She almost ignores his worst weaknesses with angelic tact, but he knows she's aware of 'em.

His bosses, she is convinced, do not appreciate his real worth. Some of her dresses fall into disfavor after a week & disappear mysteriously into the rear of her closet. She is totally unaware of a prejudice in favor of the foods she ate in her college days, & her husband eats 'em perforce & likes 'em.

She is more gracious to the straitened than to the affluent. Periodically she fears her husband is too hard-boiled in some minor episode. She pretends to be helpless with figures, but her husband is sure her arithmetic will prove adequate when she's a widow.

One of her greatest charms: she wakes in a good humor, like a child. She is astonishingly efficient when she can persuade herself to concentrate on the household chores she deems dull. For tradesmen she is an easy mark, & her husband is convinced they unload cats & dogs on her.

She treats small children as equals & cannot easily adopt a disciplinarian's attitude. She gives away most of the flowers she grows in her garden. Occasionally her husband notices an elusive haunting resemblance to her late father. She preserves her figure with almost religious zeal.

Feminine subtleties (which her husband scarcely perceives) move her deeply. After a party she often volunteers a complete play-by-play account of her evening, with every vanity humorously underlined. She mends all the family's clothes except her own, and her husband has scant faith in her stitches.

Each period of economical self-restraint leads to an outburst of little extravagances which revive her like a tonic. Like many beautiful women, she has surprisingly little conceit, if any. In emergencies her courage & poise are superb, & she could doubtless repulse a tiger with a kitchen chair.

Once she made her university's swimming team & she'd still rather swim & sunbathe than eat. Unlike most women she has no tolerance for cads. She cannot quite persuade her husband that unattractive women are "pretty" & interesting because of qualities which elude him. . . . But she tries hard. . . . In her company her husband is unconscious of the passage of time, & they enjoy twosome dinners downtown.

She has a deplorable weakness for spoofing her husband when he least enjoys it, in the presence of others. And likes to pretend she is unworldly & impractical, but in a crisis she is staunch & remarkably resourceful. When aroused by bad behavior she can be far tougher than her husband, & slower to forgive.

When asked to sew on a button, she accepts the mission with the solemnity & resignation of a diplomat bearding the Russian foreign minister. She is hearty with caddies & delivery boys. But politely allows strangers to impose on her. She admires the quality of agreeableness as if it were the top virtue.

She becomes most vivacious at parties where her husband is bored, to balance things. Her love of violets is almost mystical. Occasionally she behaves like a child, but rebels when she is treated like one. Her husband insists that when she's miffed, her snub nose moves one-eighth inch northeast.

She insists she'd prefer a business career to keeping house, on the assumption that a "career" consists largely of smiling bewitchingly at enraptured males. She is seldom the life of the party, but spends considerable time sympathizing with nervous husbands.

No man ever feels quite worthy of an almost perfect wife; merely as worthy as any other male.

Slightly imperfect husband

He has a yen for gaudy neckties, but controls it. His clothes closet is as orderly as a West Point colonel's. When tanned, his hair, eyes & skin are the same color. He's never quite so somber as he seems.

No surgeon is more hygienic. He disapproves of long hair on men & would like to clip his. He soaps it daily in his shower & probably will lose his red thatch prematurely. Three times he's sworn off cigarettes for a year or more.

He flinches at another's blood, but once took 32 stitches in his hand without anesthetic. His physical endurance is uncanny, & 5 hours sleep is often enough for him. For a realist he's amazingly optimistic.

His voice is one of the softer voices, & he can sleep on the floor almost as comfortably as on his bed amid piles of books & magazines. When the kids awake him between 2 and 5 A.M., he doesn't seem to mind.

First time through he seldom rewrites a word, but with his pencil edits 3 times with minute changes. When he's lost in thought his scrawl is illegible, but when he concentrates it's microscopic but clear.

He's apt to be awkward, in moments of absorption & shyness, & bump into things, but his recovery is graceful. Even on Sunday he can't sleep after 8 A.M. Criticism he enjoys more than praise; at least it embarrasses him less.

Public appearances excruciate him, & he'd rather speak sitting down or from behind a screen. He's bothered by anything ugly, but is a pushover for charm, & overestimates its importance as a personal trait.

Mimicking a military friend, he's taught his infant sons one trick: to punch Daddy in the nose with a boxing glove. Since his marriage his chin juts out at least a half-inch more, & he argues that a happy marriage strengthens the jaw or else.

He prefers a sprained ankle to stupid conversation. When he does talk, even his casual remarks have subtlety & completeness. He has a mania for brevity. Dirt in any corner bothers him. Nowadays he scribbles his suggestions to the household.

Brains & good taste, he argues, & patient shopping make a family's inadequate income buy more. He collects books, maps, phonograph records & copies of good paintings. Many of the pictures on the walls he's framed himself. Nowadays he doesn't rearrange the furniture as often as he did.

When he feels flush after an unexpected check, he buys gadgets & threatens to start a private museum of useless things he's bought. He still feels he'd have done better at football with thicker wrists & ankles, & is the best speller & word-definer in the neighborhood.

At a guess, he wades through 50 books & magazines a week, & never walks across the room without a book or magazine, old or new, in his hand. He likes bridge, but claims he's too poor for poker, & doesn't want to lose our meat money.

After a loud heavy frown at the grocery bill he'll buy his wife perfume or black lingerie in penance. He reads in bed, with 3 pillows, & falls asleep nightly with the light on. Seldom does he swear, but then he's forceful with it & apologizes.

His preference is for light wine. Why the kids don't like eggs or fish he can't understand, & their dawdling with food puts a heavy strain on him. Otherwise he's firm but gentle, & seldom loses his temper.

He claims that more than half his conversation is intended humorously, & that he's often taken seriously in error. In view of his innocence of bridge technique, he wins oftener at the game than he deserves.

The chores he did as a boy, he believes, were his best training for work. He spends more time at his typewriter at home than most business men or execs spend at their desks. . . . His wife occasionally admits that he's fun around the house & that she's never had a bored moment. But sometimes a caged panther might be cozier.

Man's doom in a brave new world

One moonlit night on a semi-tropical isle in the Bahamas, at a memorable picnic, the most brilliant & fascinating woman I know shocked & stunned me with a proposal which nothing in my masculine experience prepared me to hear. If I'd worn a hat that night, she'd have knocked it off.

She proposed, in short, that a man who works full time at a job downtown must help his wife substantially with the household chores, even if his wife doesn't have any job at all outside their home. I covered my confusion by tossing some driftwood on the fire.

Nor did she mean that he should merely help her wash or wipe the dishes. Oh, no; she didn't let the men get off that easily. "He should perform *more* than half the household chores," she said, taking another sip of champagne. "Preferably he should try to take care of three-fourths of the household work."

Unfortunately, this lovely & charming creature is under no illusions about how hard men work downtown. She herself has a responsible high-level job, & she knows how lightly men get by at the office, & she told me so as the steaks broiled.

Their work, she has observed, is often more fun than anything else they could do if they were mere playboys. Anything burdensome or disagreeable is usually attended to by their secretaries. I hastily offered her a bit of crabmeat & said I don't have a secretary.

I listened attentively, nervously sipping my unaccustomed champagne too quickly. "He should help with the dusting & vacuuming & cooking & dish-washing & making the beds," she averred. "My, doesn't that striped lighthouse look lovely beyond the palm trees?"

"Women nowadays," she went on, as we watched the dinghy come in zig-zag from the small white cruiser in the dusk offshore, "work much harder than their grandmothers or their mothers did. They're under much greater strain. They've problems on their minds that Granny never dreamed of. Often they work twice as hard as their husbands."

Then, while the moon idly blazed a rippling scar across the

water, she enumerated. Modern wives take their kids regularly to the doctor; they transport 'em to & from dancing class; they bake cakes for PTA, canvass the neighborhood for Red Cross & take pulses at the Blood Bank.

I watched the reflected glow of the driftwood fire on the white sand beach as she went on. Grandma didn't have to consult child guidance experts nor plan birth control meetings: she didn't have so many things to shop for, nor so many letters to write; nor so many guilds & auxiliaries on her neck.

By this time the lovers of rare steak were forking theirs off the grill. "Grandma didn't go to meetings of the League of Women Voters or university women," she went on, "nor work at the polls, nor prepare exhibits for the garden club, nor meat loaf for church suppers, nor organize elaborate birthday parties for tots."

Blithe spirits were razzing us for chattering so seriously, but we ignored 'em. "They never had to dust venetian blinds," she said, "nor phone or pursue repair men to resurrect 19 different gadgets, nor play canasta with sorority alumnae, nor report to the USA on how much money they'd paid their laundress."

I'm omitting the bulk of it, but I remember her punch line. "They didn't worry about their children's psychological adjustment, nor were they saddled with their husband's neighborhood relations, nor with the kids' tennis or swimming lessons, or allergies, or teeth straightening."

I capitulated; she had convinced me. Her steak was getting too well done, & mine quite well. I reminded her of the Navy's Commander Bill Lederer, who'd once done his wife's work in 2 hours when she broke her leg, & won fame with an article on how women could better organize their work. "He's the writer," I advised, "to shame us men into doing three-fourths of the home work." Or was I being kidded by an expert?

Your 2nd husband may be worse

While I was at dinner the phone rang & a woman told me she knew 4 DM couples who're talking divorce. "If you write a column about it," she said, "you might head 'em off, make 'em change their minds. For 2 of 'em it'll be irrevocable after Saturday."

I doubt anything I can write will make 'em change their minds. If they're fools enough to rush into divorce, they won't listen to reason. Some of the happiest couples I know have been talking divorce off & on for 15 years or more.

One reason why I don't mention divorce oftener is that I had a significant experience with a paragraph about divorce I wrote in the 1930's. Six different couples I knew thought I meant them. Only 2 of 'em ever got divorced.

I've noticed this about people who're divorced. About 9 times out of 10, either the wife or husband or both are sorry they ever agreed to divorce. And about 9 times out of 10 they have a sadder & not a happier life afterward.

Quite a few divorces begin conversationally. "Maybe you want a divorce, huh?" Or: "If you don't do what I say, you can get a divorce!" The opener is as silly as that, & neither side has enough flexibility to back down. It takes guts & wisdom to back down.

My own observation is that most people who make a flop of one marriage are incapable of doing any better with another marriage. They'd probably do better to continue with the spouse they already understand a little. If they use their heads, who knows?

(Too often a 2nd divorce & a 3rd one follow the 1st divorce. Many recent divorcees are the children of divorced parents. Most juvenile criminals are children of parents who've been divorced. Almost half the people who divorce have fumbled with juvenile courts.)

My guess as to the chief reasons for divorce: money, temper, sex, nagging, stubbornness, jealousy, stupidity. Most or all of these deplorable hurdles also occur in every happy marriage. They result in divorce only when neither wife nor husband has enough intelligence to cope with 'em.

Now I'm talking directly to the couples who're taking the dive this week end. Give yourselves another 6 months. Go to a movie once or twice a week. Take long walks. Have picnics with the kids. Play bridge. Arrange a signal for ending your quarrels.

Okay; let's assume your husband's a dolt. He can't earn $75 a week, or $500 a month, or $10,000 a year. What makes you think you'll ever land a man who can? Maybe he could earn $5,000 a year if you'd inspire him to devotion & courage.

All right; your wife is the worst housekeeper you've ever seen. She can't even cook well out of tin cans; she even spoils frozen french fries. She nags you; she's untidy; she snores. How do you know your next wife won't, twice as badly?

Ah, he's unreasonable about sex! How do you know? Are you an expert? Very few people are really experts on sex. Even Don Juan & Casanova could have learned from a bright doctor. I've heard complaints about both of 'em.

Temper, temper, *temper*! Your spouse has a beastly temper. But look at yourself. Are you a smug, complacent, velvety inciter to bad temper? Do you ever give in on anything? Or are you always right, & self-righteous about it, too?

Maybe the Catholics have the right slant on marriage & divorce. It may be better for the marriage to continue. If a selfish hussy is married to a jealous, stubborn dolt, why turn the job of civilizing each other over to somebody else?

I've tiptoed into the divorce court occasionally, & based on what I've seen, here's a warning to its graduates: the chances are 10 to 1 that neither Prince Charming nor the Queen of Sheba will be waiting for you outside the big doors. If you can't make a go of it, they don't want you either. Next time I'll try to be sweeter about it.

※ ※ ※

From my friskier cronies I've won quite a few bets each year since 1947 that we wouldn't be at war with the Russians by the end of the year. Now I'm prepared to bet modest sums that we'll still be at peace by New Year's Day of 1960.

Maybe the deplorable side of living in an apartment is that there are so few chores for the children to do. . . . But we'll be glad if you cliff dwellers will send your kids to our old homestead to share the chores our youngsters neglect.

Oddly enough, my Lady Love reproaches me for shooting rabbits in November (the only matron in town who can cook 'em is a

Frenchwoman). But she goads me into shooting 'em in May, when they nibble at her bulbs!

Our locker-room wit at the country club has defined a small-town biggie. He's a man from whom you're glad after church to get the big hello in front of your wife and kids. (Alone you wouldn't care.)

When we eat giant hamburgers and salad off a tray in the living room, Junior and I look at each other in amazement. I marvel that he can eat his meat so raw, and he marvels that I like it so well done.

WHO CAN WIN?

How wives pamper husbands

I don't know when the report first got around that I like black bean soup. It didn't begin with me; at the time I'd scarcely tasted it, if ever. But I can remember the b.w. saying, in the first year of our marriage, "Wouldn't some black bean soup taste good?"
    As an agreeable husband, I surmised it would. Probably I even smacked my lips, and took part in a spirited argument of whether it's improved if you squeeze lemon into it. The b.w. was enthusiastic about lemon, but I held out against any lemon in mine.
    Maybe that's the way the word got around that I was a man who took his black bean soup straight untainted by lemon juice or Worcestershire sauce. On Thursday & Sunday evenings black bean soup appeared more & more often, the b.w. aglow with the bright visage of a woman who's doing something that pleases her husband.

My fondness for black bean soup began to assume fabulous proportions. The b.w. would even put some in a thermos bottle to take on picnics. Word spread around that any picnic would be a flop for me if I didn't have my regular ration of black bean soup.

I tried to remonstrate. "You're spoiling me," I'd say. "Black bean soup is a rather exotic dish. I'd be content with white bean soup." After all, I didn't want to be selfish about it, even though I was learning to like it.

Also, I hinted that I was terribly fond of broiled octopus or broiled goose, a weakness alas only too true; it didn't really matter too much which. Secretly, I hoped the b.w. would put some of *that* in a thermos bottle & take it out on picnics, too. But the b.w. thought I was just spoofing. (Sometimes she suspects me of a rather raucous sense of humor.)

One day, to my shocked surprise, not to say horror, I discovered in the storage room a whole case of black bean soup, 144 largish tins. That assured us of black bean soup once a week for almost 3 years, unless I could force the kids to take second helpings.

While I was overseas the b.w. frequently slipped a tin or two of black bean soup into my parcels. I had become known as the best-parceled man in Ike's army; nobody got more parcels than I did, according to a story which made the rounds. Certainly nobody got more black bean soup.

When I returned we had black bean soup the first picnic of the summer. The b.w. had learned to like it, too; perhaps she always had. I poured a second helping of it out of the thermos bottle & drank it out of a cup as I gazed lovingly at her. I could have drunk a gallon of green thistle soup to please her.

Now, the unvarnished truth is that it's white navy bean soup I like, the kind they serve at the US Senate restaurant in Washington, DC. To my knowledge I have never voluntarily ordered a dish of black bean soup in any restaurant.

But I had become known definitely as a Black Bean Soup Man, & I could scarcely blurt out "White bean soup!" without stumbling clear out of character. I've tried to get up enough courage to say to the b.w., "Wouldn't some *white* bean soup taste kinda nice tonight?" but never quite made it.

On one unforgettable evening my mania for compromise

led me into an indefensible position. I suggested that we blend a tin of black bean soup with a tin of white bean soup & see how it tasted. The b.w. gave me the inscrutable look she always gives me when I'm not nearly so funny as I think I am.

Up at the Okoboji summer cottage last week end I noticed a dozen tins of black bean soup on the pantry shelf. All week I have been brooding about it, between week ends, as I subsisted almost entirely, while batching it, on a diet of white bean soup, morning & evening. Somehow I must absolve myself of my predilection for black bean soup. Next week end I may take a dozen tins of white bean soup up to Okoboji.

Husband loose in a supermarket

I persuaded one of DM's most piquant matrons to go shopping for groceries with her husband & report the results to me. He's one of those curmudgeons who's always squawking about the grocery bill & asking embarrassing questions like "what do artichokes cost this week?"

Guess who bought more costly, luxurious and useless victuals?

He bought a beef tongue for $1.63 out of curiosity. She bought 80 cents' worth of pork tenderloin, 5 pieces for supper. He bought 42 cents' worth of calves' brains, for a gag. She bought 2 dozen eggs for $1.04—"We've only 3 left for breakfast!" He bought a beef heart for $1.23—"Wonder how it tastes?"

So he bought 18 cents' worth of kidneys—"The English like 'em." She bought 2 bunches of rhubarb for 46 cents—"Season's first rhubarb!" He bought a peculiar braided loaf of bread for 17 cents— She said, "Darling, the breadbox is full of bread!" She bought 2 grapefruit for 19 cents—"A half for each of us." He bought a novelty "instant potato mix" for 33 cents. She smiled!

In a fit of whimsy he bought a 4-ounce bottle of liquid sweetener for 79 cents—"Non-fattening!" She bought a carton of cigarettes for $2.09. He said, "We'd save $200 a year if we quit smoking!" He bought a new kind of ketchup for 21 cents because the bottle has a screw-top. She bought a tin of coffee at 89 cents.

She bought a 30-cent sack of macaroons—for him. He bought a 1-pound can of corned beef hash (40 cents)—"Like to keep a can in the car if they haven't anything I like at a roadside hasherie." She bought 2 glasses of cheese spread for 56 cents—"We need fruit juice glasses."

With wrinkled brow he bought a tin of roast beef hash (57 cents)—"I never remember the difference in taste." With a guilty look she bought a tin of mushrooms, 30 cents. He bought a 16-ounce tin of chili for 36 cents. She bought a can of chocolate syrup at 19 cents—"Biggest bargain in the store." She likes chocolate.

Puzzled, he bought a 15 ¾-ounce tin of chili for 39 cents—"Wonder why it costs more?" She bought 2 tins of canned corn for 33 cents. With a sentimental eye glint he bought a tin of spam at 45 cents—"I was the only man in the army who liked it." She bought a big tin of tomato juice at 29 cents—"Let's try a new kind!"

He bought a can of pork sausage for 48 cents. He bought a can of chicken gumbo soup for 18 cents. He bought a can of gumbo creole soup for 18 cents—"I don't really think there's any difference." He bought a can of split pea soup— She said, "Darling, we have a dozen cans of it home!"

She bought a tin of green gage plums for 24 cents & said, "Let's go before this cart collapses." He bought a 4-ounce glass of lumpfish caviar for 49 cents for company. He bought a 2-ounce glass of lumpfish caviar for 29 cents—"Just a snack for us." He bought 2 glasses of red salmon caviar at 45 cents each—"I don't think any of that caviar at the cocktail parties is *real* $1 an ounce caviar."

She'd quit buying, but he bought 3 tins of ravioli for 81 cents—"Good to have on hand." He bought 2 big bottles of ginger ale for 31 cents & 2 quart bottles of tom collins mix also for 31 cents—"I like 'em better with nothing mixed in 'em to spoil the taste!" She said, "Darling, you're extravagant!"

He bought a paperback copy of *The Dream Merchants* for 35 cents off the rack—"Gosh, that's a new one, about Hollywood!" She nudged him toward the cashier exit & he asked, "How'd you like one of these inlaid wooden slicing boards at $4.45?" "We've got a slicing board," she said patiently. So he bought a pound of butter crackers for 37 cents.

All in all, the two of 'em spent $20.01, according to their figures, or $19.97, according to the store's. "Mine could be mistaken!" he confessed. This included a 20-cent bottle deposit & 33 cents sales tax, not to mention about $1.40 tax in the cost of the cigarettes.

Their boxscore shows she bought 13 items at a total cost of about $7.58, while the old curmudgeon (the denouncer of grocery bills) bought 25 items at a total cost of about $12.08. "This stuff is nice for a snack," he explained. "And with the liquid sweetener we can make some non-fattening soft drinks."

"Like the tom collins mix, you mean?" she inquired sweetly.

Doctrine of alternative objectives

I happen to be married to a highly efficient (though charming) woman, who plans every detail in advance, reserves Pullman berths far ahead, can locate in her desk the address of a college chum she hasn't seen in 14 years, & by consulting her diaries can ascertain which movie she saw on her 11th birthday.

So she finds it difficult to understand how I can start off on a trip without every reservation nailed down, & not quite certain which parts of my journey will be by air, which by train & which by water, nor exactly which towns I'll visit for how long, nor the precise day of my return.

There's nothing harum-scarum about such travel. It's based on my Doctrine of Alternative Objectives, which I evolved during a period when I didn't know whether I'd spent the next night in the attic of a bombed chateau, a haymow or in a shallow foxhole under a hedge.

Actually, the uncertainties of travel nowadays are somewhat exaggerated. I've seldom failed to find a seat on any train, nor a berth if I wanted to sleep, nor have I ever had to sleep on a billiard table, nor missed a train I didn't want to miss.

On a recent trip I had to stop at Iowa City first. "If the

dinner there ends in time," I told the b.w., "I'll drive up to Cedar Rapids & catch the plane to Chicago. Otherwise, I'll catch the late Rock Island train. . . . At Chicago I'll either catch a plane to Boston or take a train, depending on how things work out."

She gave me an unfathomable look. But things worked out okay. The dinner ended in time; I was driven to the CR airport by one of the 10 most attractive women in Iowa City. Between planes at Chicago I wrote a column (11 P.M. till 2 A.M.), reached La Guardia Field in time for an early breakfast, & Boston in time for a late breakfast & a shower bath.

I've tried to explain my Doctrine of Alternative Objectives to the b.w., but unsuccessfully. It boils down very simply to this: if you don't arrive where you're headed, you arrive some place else, & reach your destination a little later. I'll admit that this doesn't work out quite so well when you're traveling with a lady. Nothing makes a lady so resentful as waiting several hours in a depot or an air terminal between trains or planes.

Sometimes my Doctrine is a positive advantage. Recently it saved me $4 on a hotel room. Unable to get a room at a certain self-important hotel at a top-heavy price unless I waited 2 hours, I merely telephoned & got a better room at a better hotel for less money. Wives can't understand this hazy, fatalistic approach to travel in husbands who've traveled the Army way. There were often times when not only did we not know where we were going, but neither did anybody else within hundreds of miles.

When perplexed or baffled by the incidents of travel, I like to think of the important colonel who was ordered overseas immediately. By one of those peculiarities of Army orders, his sergeant flew across & arrived in 2 days while the colonel waited 2 weeks for space on a ship & didn't arrive until after his sergeant had become engaged to get married.

Such experiences make it comparatively unimportant in these piping times of peace whether you arrive in New York on a Sunday or a Tuesday. If you really have your heart set on Sunday at 10 A.M., you'll probably make it without a motorcycle escort. And in spite of all the moaning I've heard about travel in the States during the war, I doubt there was ever a train that didn't have an empty upper.

Oh, by all means make your reservations weeks in advance.

I yield to the b.w. when we're traveling together, & flaunt a long railroad ticket with even return reservations we'll probably have to change later, & I enjoy her smile of approval.

※ ※ ※

I'm aghast at a shirtmaker's boast in a letter that his customers own an average of "forty-nine wearable shirts" apiece. I own an average of eight wearable shirts, five of 'em pre-empted by our two sons, while I get along by wearing my countless unwearable shirts.

We might improve modern discipline and morals if our scholars copied twenty-five times such gilt-edged maxims as "Honesty is the best policy." Even if it didn't improve the 1955 pupils' behavior, it might improve their handwriting.

Our youngest's new hobby (photography) is turning out to be more expensive than I'd expected. He spends more money photographing our neighborhood's dogs than it cost Brady to photograph the Civil War.

The deep thinker at our big round table waded into the school board at lunch again. "They think they merely need to seat the pupils in rows and keep 'em awake," he said, flattening the sphere of ice cream on his cherry pie, "even if teachers have to make faces at 'em."

A professor of our local college attacked comic books at a meeting of the P.T.A. at our son's school. The most embarrassed listeners in his audience were the parents who read comic books themselves.

When a dizzy, tone-deaf teen-ager buys a tune or plays it on a juke box, he disturbs only those nearby. But when a disk jockey adds 'em up and plays them as "top tunes," he annoys innocent millions over radio and TV. Possibly he's even guilty of committing a public nuisance.

DO IT YOURSELF

Husband: handyman in a crisis

A few of us husbands were discussing how to act when the wife yanks us into the limelight to repair something around the house. It's an emergency, & she's slightly excited & feeling her oats. Her eyes flash; she points at it; her voice is authoritative.

All the same, she's pessimistic, too. She knows we can't light the new doo-dad heater, or replace the washer, or detect the wounded fuse; we're too dumb; but she'd enjoy seeing us try. She'd like to get it fixed, but she'd bear up if we flunked.

We husbands agreed on a few points:

1. Don't try to keep calm. That may feed your masculine ego, but it'll only irritate her. Get excited; roll your eyes; do a little tribal dance; dash into corners, look at the ceiling & then the floor, & behind doors.

2. Don't suggest that she phone an electrician or a plumber. She'll suspect you of 2nd degree cowardice & 3rd degree inefficiency. Tell her *not* to phone for an electrician. "Sheer extravagance!" you snort. "I can fix it myself in a jiffy." So she'll probably phone.

3. Sneak to a phone & summon an electrician yourself, just to be on the safe side. Give him your wife's name, or somebody else's name, but be sure & give the right address. If it comes to a showdown, you can convince her that *she* called the electrician.

4. Arm yourself with plenty of tools. Pair of pliers in one hand, a hammer in the other hand. Don't attempt to placate her bare-handed. She'll feel more victorious if you brandish plenty of tools. You can even send her next door to borrow a left-handed forceps.

5. Put on an act. If it's the heater that won't light, then act

as if the glacial age were descending; we'll all freeze in 3 hours. If it's a faucet, put on your hip-boots, phone for a canoe. If a fuse has blown, scatter lighted candles all over the house & tell her to order 3 dozen more.

6. If the electrician is slow coming, find your hunting coat. Put different tools in each pocket & in some of the ammunition loops, sticking out; all kinds of screwdrivers, pliers, awls, wrenches, slide-rules, spirit levels, bits & braces, triangles, compasses.

7. Lunge at things. Practice lunging from the refrigerator to the gas stove, from the sink to the washing machine. Glare a little. Let your fingers be pinched or bruised; if you bleed a little she may soften into sympathy. Again, she may not.

8. Take drastic action. Turn off the water all over the house so she can't take a bath or make any coffee. Pull the master switch so the refrigerator goes off. Phone the druggist for 10 150-watt bulbs. Ask her if she can cook dinner on a charcoal grill.

9. Collect as many giant, oversize tools as you can. If necessary, borrow 'em from the neighbors. Get a crowbar 5 feet long, a stilson wrench that weighs 30 pounds or so, wrinkle your brow, scratch your head & mutter something about the TV set short-circuiting the automatic dryer.

10. By this time the plumber should have arrived. Tell him it's the wrong address, & probably a mistake, but he can look at several things. Talk to him half as authoritatively as your wife talks to you, & she'll think you know what you're talking about.

I wish I could understand why a wife enjoys imagining her husband is an ignoramus about machinery. We have 2 tricky butane gas heaters in the Okoboji cottage, & I've lit each one of 'em easily the first time I tried. But in vain.

One of her favorite stories is about how we have frozen to death several times at Okoboji because I couldn't figure out how to light those confounded heaters. One of these days I plan to get into the act when we have guests & the temperature suddenly falls from 80 to 40 degrees, & it's too late to phone for anybody. I'll just pretend I don't know how.

How I do my chores

I was standing on a short ladder putting new light bulbs in the carriage lamps outside the front door when the b.w. said the wall can opener in the kitchen was maladjusted. As I climbed down to get the oil can from the basement, I noticed the rain gutters on the garage were full of leaves.

So I got a longer ladder & poled most of the leaves out. From this vantage point I noticed the garage doors were covered with small paw & finger prints. On my way to get the solvent to wash 'em off, I found the oil can & lubricated the can opener.

When I finished this the b.w. asked me if I'd carry the empty bottles from the back porch into the car, so she could return them, & as I did so noticed the driveway drain was partly clogged. I unclogged it & began to pick up nearby candy bar, cigarette & gum wrappers, which led me on a long trek all over the yard.

Near the tennis court terrace I discovered a wheelbarrow full of old leaves, so I wheeled 'em back to the pasture. I saw a long wire tangled in the fence so I went after the wire cutter, but on the way paused to carry a big load of garden furniture to the basement.

There I collected the solvent & washed the finger marks off the garage door & noticed the latch on the gate was bent, so went after the pliers, pausing to find a razor blade to scrape some caked paint off the storm window glass on the side door.

On the cellar steps I observed a stack of papers, which I carried out to the garage to remind me to phone the Salvation Army to pick 'em up. My sleeve caught on a nail in the cellar stairs, so I got the pliers & pulled it out & fixed the latch on the gate.

Near the gate lay a shingle from our roof, so I made a mental note to ask the b.w. to remind me to phone the roofer to repair it. Quite by accident I stepped on a rake & it rared up & hit me in the elbow, so I took it to the garage, where I re-draped the garden hose on its reel.

That reminded me of the other hose in the garden, where I rescued it & removed some gravel from a flower bed. Near the cellar steps I filled an old dog hole & noticed that the brickwork needed pointing up, & finding the pliers still in my hand, I tightened the hand rails on the cellar steps on which the kids have been swinging, & found I needed a hammer.

I traced the hammer to the attic, where I repaired the loose leg of an old cedar chest after getting some nails from the basement, & carried a pile of wire coat hangers downstairs to the basement, where I stenciled my name on an old favorite suitcase & took it to the 3rd floor.

On the way up I noticed a hole in the upper staircase plaster where Q had driven a nail, so went to the basement for some putty & fixed the hole, & carried a stack of magazines to the basement. There I got some wood & laid a fire in the fireplace & measured the fireplace for the 'steenth time for a new screen.

I now found the wire cutter in my hip pocket, so trudged to the back fence to trim the dangling wire, stopping on the way to shoot a few baskets with the small fry. They had partly uncovered the non-waterproof garden furniture, so I replaced the tarpaulin, & found a second bulb in my pocket & inserted it in a front door light.

Now I found the piece of picture wire I'd hunted for weeks, & strung it in my bedroom closet so I can hang on it my clean shirts which this household no longer has time to fold & put in my dresser drawers. Among my shoes I found one of Q's electric train units, so took it to his room where I discovered my missing electric razor, enough to make the whole day worthwhile. I got a lot acomplished, just in a casual way, & ended up with that good sanctimonious feeling of fatigue you get from doing some chores. I could do nothing but minor chores for several years & never catch up.

* * *

I'll applaud modern schools again when our ninth-grade son, instead of wangling aid with his algebra, helps his mother balance our family checkbook.

"Even if I do bring my wife her breakfast in bed on a Sunday," says Peter Comfort, hiding a Christmas package in his garage, "that's no admission that I behaved badly on Saturday night."

At a wedding reception recently the bride told me she had never cooked a meal, but expects to learn how the day she returns from her honeymoon. "In three days," she said, "I can learn to cook better than they do at the places my husband's been taking me."

Over a two-hour lunch at the club we agreed that a modern man needs outdoor sport to survive the pressures of modern life. (We also agreed that if a man can't participate, the next best thing is to watch it or read about it.)

A Frenchman who visited in our town was tolerant about American food. "Your bread," he said, "is quite edible if you toast it, butter it and spread enough conserves on it."

When we were first married I was browbeaten by Emily Post and my Dream Girl into letting her choose all the guests to invite to our house. But I've staged a plucky comeback; often I am allowed now to name as many as one-third of 'em.

I've resurrected the twenty-year-old living-room drapes it took us two years to pay for when we were married. After a long exile in the attic they now adorn my den with all their faded splendor.

※ ※ ※

FOR MEN ONLY [IX]

On the serener days—when Junior tells me I ought to play more golf . . . or our daughter demonstrates how well she's resisted my attempts to spoil her . . . and our youngest shows me an essay nearly as good as William James wrote at his age . . . or my Princess of Sheer Delight tells me I have the handsomest pair of legs on the beach . . . then I bless the early inklings I had of the horrors of bachelorhood, such a lonely and parlous estate.

10

Men & women

ST. VALENTINE'S DAY COMES & GOES

To all our secret loves

That's what Cyrano de Bergerac said to a lady he admired, & that's what a man should send his adorable & adored ladies on Valentine's day. But you can't send 'em all flowers without being misunderstood or bankrupted, & it's the wrong weather for plucking armfuls of loose bloom.

Yet so many of us are absent-minded that while I think of it I'd better order flowers for some of the girls I admire, & some I'd better not identify too clearly. (Who likes tedious explanations?) From all the men of our Great State to all their girls, too.

So I toss at the b.w.'s feet ten bushels of imaginary violets, which she prefers to roses. And armfuls of carnations to Leah & Fannie, a peerless pair of grandmothers. And a duffle bag full of chrysanthemums for the b.g. (With maybe a few snapdragons.)

Fill a rucksack with amaryllis for Annabelle, warm & gentle. Stack a bandbox high with hyacinth for Maude. And a pipkin of tuberoses for gracious Anna, and just repeat that order for Shirlie.

A large vase of royal coconut palm blossoms for Helen, whose head hath a regal tilt. A creel of mountain daisies for Roberta of the fetching freckles. And a vat of dahlias for Isabel, the animated darling.

For Lois a ton of Etoile de Holland, all done into leis. A whisket of peonies for Helen Jane & her calm radiance. And a pannier of gladioli for Esme, or a whole conservatoryful. And for Marcie a musette bag of gardenias.

What flower shall we fling at the iridescent Valene: a reticule of tiger lilies? And for ever-smiling Patricia—perhaps a corbeille of shamrock. Ah! Just the dish for elusive Barbara—a chalice of mignonette.

For Catherine, a parachuteful of green Irish bells & yellow carnations. A jardeniere of "Golden Charm" roses for Ethel, who radiates a glow. And a canister of "Red Radiance" for vivid Mary Esther. And a hamper of "Golden Ophelias" for scintillating Dorothy.

Pile the saddlebags with azalea for Elizabeth, nimble-witted & profound. Load the quiver with daffodils for gentle Norma. And a bowl of narcissus for Gertrude of the questing mind, & fly in a row of potted tulips for Betty.

Arrange a vessel of mixed blossoms for Julie. And a tall crock of hydrangea for Ruth so soulful & wise. Raid the greenhouse for a chest of hyacinths to send to generous & unselfish Mary.

Pluck a punchbowlful of jonquils for Virginia the serene. And a pitcher of tall iris for Jane. And have that jorum of sweet peas for Maggie delivered at the house not later than 6 o'clock, & a pikaki lei for Marijane, too.

Fill a wide-necked carafe with tulips for Grace. And a tall flagon of stock for stately Loretta. Heap high a tray with primrose for Janet. And mind you, a graceful salver of forget-me-nots for Ingrid.

Float a tray of camellias for Beatrice the delectable. And adorn a firkin with cattleya orchids for Fleur. Fill a whole carboy with larkspur for Mildred, & find out Marjorie's favorite flower & send her a dozen.

And a cruse of delphinium for Jeanette. And a tall umbrella stand of apple blossoms for Ophelia. Fill carefully a punnet of purple lilac for Agnes. And a flaring copper pail of cherry blossoms for Fran.

What's more, on behalf of all the men of Iowa (besides the hereinbefore mentioned) I hereby dispatch a fragile & graceful orchid to all their secret Valentines & sweethearts, be they bobby-soxers, debs, career girls, matrons, dowagers or femmes fatale of more or less mature vintage.

On second thought, why be stuffy about this? Boy, take a loose mink coat to each & every one of these girls, sacred or profane, & a bracelet of square cut diamonds, & a quart carafe of their favorite perfume, & a magnum of sparkling burgundy, & to the b.w. a pan of lobsters & a kilo of imported bon bons, too, & a big thick steak topped with caviar in the fashion of Malibu.

Valentines for old flames

When I watch a musical comedy on Broadway (or at KRNT here) it's easy to pick the one girl in a chorus of 16 I'd rather be shipwrecked with on a small fertile Pacific isle—if I were condemned to be shipwrecked with a girl, of course. (Why not on a small isle in the Mississippi, within an easy swim of either shore?)

But in real life you get closer to 'em & it's harder to pick & choose. You choose eventually above all one Permanent Valentine, but before that, you collect a variety who haunt you a little around Valentine's Day. So I send heart-shaped clusters of orchids to:

Bianca: She could make a man feel witty, gay & important. Her grandparents were English & German, but she reminded you of an Italian princess. . . . The windy day we drove to cover the Tama Indian pow-wow I telegraphed my story in Hiawatha-style blank verse.

Liz: Her mind flashed like summer lightning, yet her legs were worthy of her $5 stockings. She seemed moderne, but underneath her lowcut dresses her backbone was pioneer woman & her heart doughty & devoted.

Ann: Her nose turned up but couldn't escape the freckles all around. She was Scotch & her father was a preacher & her brother joked about his role as ne'er-do-well, & she warmed you with her queenly shyness & her radiant smile even when she caught you going barefoot.

Ingrid: A blonde changeling who could transform herself

from a slim adolescent girl in a bathing suit into an overwhelming Valkyrie in 20 minutes, with the help of high-heels & a hairdo. Her excellent mind underestimated her fine profile.

Minerva: It took the combined strength of 6 generations of Puritan ancestors to keep her passionate nature in check. Her destiny: to become a suburban matron; but she'd blurt out a few rebellious words on dark nights from her wild heart.

Julia: A rare girl who didn't object to silences, didn't think them awkward. She hid her innermost thoughts except when cornered or surprised; they were always worth the chase. I hear she married a placid go-getter.

Katinka: A blend of the milkmaid & the sphinx. You could breathe into her any shape of fanciful creation, & there she was, radiant, until you listened for the echo. Ere she was 16, somebody must have told her she was "all woman."

Honore: Winsome and sweet-faced, & almost the last unsophisticated girl I ever knew. She was embarrassed because the boys thought so well of her. Why did she ever have so many babies? With a touch of birth control her beauty might have outlasted her synthetic rivals.

Imogene: She was the patrician of the lot; she could take a Cadillac as easily in her stride as most girls take a bicycle. She made you feel as if you were sitting with her on the exact center of the universe. The richest, she cared least about money.

Maria: Airiest & wispiest & most elusive of all these female creatures, I hear she became the earthiest, & as sensible as Jurgen's wife. No man would try to run away from her, back to a certain Wednesday. Claims her garden's still haunted by faeries, & I fling her armfuls of loose bloom.

Isabel: She could do more to a man with a side glance & a curve of her cheek than some girls can with 6 highballs & a roast turkey. Of all these girls she snagged the most husbands, & I hear they were all baffled.

Diane: The all-round girl. From early on she reflected the dawn light; the crusader, the female athlete, the sharp wit, the dancer & actress; & she entered a room like a peacock with a Ph.D. Her Yale boy friend called her the most "wantonly wholesome woman" he'd ever known.

In a way all the girls I've ever valentined were these, or

bits & pieces of them, or these same girls in various combinations & arrangements. I suppose the girl you fall for in the 5th grade is a prophecy of the one you'll marry, the best blend of the lot. You give your own true predestined one a valentine every day; she can't begrudge you a day dream on Valentine's Day. So double that stack of orchids, Florist.

* * *

"Love, courtship and marriage are so accidental!" philosophizes Betty Comfort, trying her hand-made Christmas wreath on her front door. "Isn't it a marvel so many marriages endure happily for twenty-five years and more?"

They've made our Junior the scholarship chairman at his college fraternity house, as well as pledge trainer and social chairman. In fact, they've got more work out of him in two and one-half years than I have in eighteen.

Some of our town's best people are still lukewarm to four-lane toll roads. At times they don't seem quite reconciled to the invention of the wheel, to the three-car family and to people's silly ambition to drive coast to coast.

This is the year we're inviting all our young one's teachers to dinner. Over the dessert I'll try to put across the idea that if he learns to write legibly, to spell and to read books enthusiastically, I'll yell for a $5,000 minimum salary for teachers.

Last year I again issued my ukase that the neighborhood boys who use the basketball goal in our back yard must paint the backboard green. As usual, I've relented and painted it myself.

CLOTHES MAKE THE MAN

Revolt against the haberdasher

You've mislaid your stickpin, eh? How long since you've worn one? It's vanished—& it's a minor item among the stuff we men used to wear proudly but wouldn't be caught dead in now. I still have a gray spat in the cellar.

Never before have so many changes in men's clothes happened in one short lifetime. No more long socks, unless you're set in your ways. Only short socks, & no garters. Even at 5 below zero I counted 11 hatless in one block on Locust Street.

At the Y gym, out at Drake fieldhouse & at the high school locker rooms, it's amazing how few males now wear undershirts. Clark Gable's fad, begun when he was undershirtless in a movie. Alas, this haberdashery once so essential!

All men & boys once wore suspenders, either over or under their shirts. Now only dogged traditionalists or exhibitionists. In the transition era some cautious men wore 'em with belts, too. . . . Do you realize how impatient you get when you put on a pair of pre-zipped pants?

There are men still full of zip & romance who could hardly wait till they were 18 so they could buy a derby. And now they've gone brave-new-world on us & sniffle bareheaded into Kleenex in this wintry weather instead of a handkerchief. How long since your wife forgot to sew a button on your shorts?

That's only because shorts are buttonless nowadays; elastic instead; not even snaps. All this must have been tough on the button magnates. I'm told 1 shirt in every 4 is sporty enough to wear without a necktie, & some senior members even show up necktieless at the club on hot days.

What's become of the seasoned traveler who always packed a tweed cap on top of his valise? Does he try to get away with a beret? Or one of those low-brow, long-visored caps? Hardly! How long since you've anchored a loose, separate, unattached collar to your shirt?

Down the street from our house lives a man, still young, who once went wooing in a Norfolk jacket—remember, pleats running up the back & over the shoulder & down in front—& a turtle-neck sweater! (He occasionally wears these days a turtle-neck sweater & nylon shorts as pajamas.)

Two or 3 men in our town still wear white piping around the V-opening of their vests. Several others should. But who ever hunts collar buttons under the bed & who knowingly lets 'em starch his shirts stiff? We're mostly too civilized. You can't buy a vest with your suit unless you insist, or unless you pay extra for a loud one.

Men wear fewer and lighter clothes, in rooms always overheated for half-clad women. And only 1 man in 30 ever wears rubbers; probably more have galoshes. Even at the club & the C of C you scarcely ever see a pair of ankle-high shoes, unless they're cowboy boots at the Jr. C of C.

Remember how much thought you devoted, the year you got out of high school, to the choice of exactly the right tie-clasp, maybe shaped like a scarab? And maybe a tiepin, or a horseshoe? Now girls make earrings of their dads' tiepins.

And were you the last boy in your school whose thrifty ma made him wear out his knee-length short pants after the other boys switched to knickers? Or wear out his knickers after all the fellahs put on long pants? I'll bet you still have some ancient plus-4 golf knickers kicking around.

And when the Norfolk jacket was passé (FDR continued to wear one at White House press conferences), there was the pinch-back jacket, the belted jacket, & the belted-back jacket. They sold Norfolks in New York briefly after the war. I saw a DM advertising man in long underwear at a party!

Remember the rubber sleeve-bands your pa wore if his sleeves were too long? And the cuff-guards at the office, to keep the dust off his cuffs? And how tight the pants used to be, & how form-fitting the jackets, & how loose they've become? And how the village banker had a big "break" in his pants at the ankle, & how his son at Yale wears his pants shorter, no break, just to his shoe top? And how pants & jacket always had to match at a party? Men, I think we've gained ground, at that!

When a man dresses: 32 steps

What the average American does in his own bathroom to beautify himself is his own business, if his family has another bathroom or two. But it's a mistake to think the modern American male is far behind the old Roman of 2,000 years ago in complex care of his face, hair, hands and body. Some men do more to themselves almost every morning than a girl getting ready to dazzle the Junior League charity ball.

There's a diplomatic attaché in Washington who is reliably reported to submit himself to 37 distinct operations in his morning toilet. After a little research, guarded inquiries, & bathroom prowling, I'm convinced some of our self-conscious males in DM aren't far behind him.

Here are some of the steps in the beautification of the male:

1. Washing of the hands & face.
2. Brushing of the teeth.
3. Explorations with dental floss.
4. Gargling with mouth wash.
5. Lathering up for the unavoidable shave.
6. Scraping off of the beard.
7. Application of shaving lotion.
8. Sprinkle of a masculine variety of talcum powder.
9. The plunge into the tepid tub.
10. Polishing the spinal column with the long-handled brush.
11. Stoical exposure to the more or less icy shower.
12. Foamy shampoo of the remaining hair.
13. Massaging of the scalp with the rubber-pronged brush.
14. Application of the aromatic tonic.

15. Some add a dab of stickum to make the hair stay put.
16. Maybe eyebrows have become bushy & need removing.
17. Some men use electric razors to remove the faunlike growth of hair from the ears.
18. Several men I know have little cylindrical gadgets for trimming the luxuriant growth of hair in their nostrils.
19. In cold weather some men use hand lotion regularly.
20. Some men use clippers to remove excess hair from their chests.
21. About 49 men out of 50 do their own manicuring.
22. The toenails require a secret ritual.
23. Yes, more men than you suspect add a dash of toilet water.
24. He combs his hair, trying hard to place the part where the barber does.
25. Some of those corns need trimming.
26. He has already taken a cold pill with a glass of water.
27. Then, in deference to his doctor's advice, he swallows a glass of warm water.
28. If he's really streamlined, he takes a couple of vitamin pills.
29. If he has remembered, he has bent down & touched his toes 20 times or more.
30. If he's a real devotee of fitness, he has stretched horizontal on the floor to raise his legs from the hip 20 times.
31. Then he scrunches back on his shoulder blades & pedal-kicks his legs up & down 100 times.
32. Now he is ready to brush his hair, face his ham & eggs & the world.

(I could run this up to 50 or more if I listed rituals I've observed in army barracks, like removal of wax from ears, or safeguards against athlete's foot.)

Some men, of course, put eyewash drops in their eyes, get under the sunlamp, siphon nosedrops into their nostrils, dab at their ears & armpits, & even make their skin & scalp tingle with an electric vibrator. A few have monstrous machines to retain & restore their hair.

By this time he's almost even with the Washington diplomatic attaché, and is lucky to reach the office by 9 A.M.

And by 5 o'clock he feels like a rag again.

※ ※ ※

Maybe my Dream Woman has solved the problem of diverse eating tastes in our family. At one meal she served five kinds of precooked meat pies—turkey, beef, tuna, chicken and lamb; no two of us were eating the same proteins.

Junior has introduced a new college and Army phrase into our peaceful household: "No sweat!" It seems to mean that when he favors a certain decision or solution, the rest of us should fall in step without argument.

"A wife who's acutely jealous of her husband if he so much as lights a girl's cigarette twice, is apt to be an incorrigible flirt herself," whispers Peter Comfort cautiously, scraping ice off his windshield.

In our block the baby of the girl who married the boy next door has two sets of grandparents; around its play pen they look daggers amiably at each other; each suspects the others of mishandling the infant, like a halfback fumbling on his own two-yard line.

Rattling around in a sixteen-room house since their children married, our neighbors around the corner decline to move into an apartment. "We can leave the Christmas tree in an unoccupied room," they agree, "and keep it around till the Fourth of July, or keep an indoor sand pile in another room to lure our grandchildren.

Our plumber says he can go to Florida for the winter if he wants to. "But I get in more swimming at the Y.M.C.A. pool," he says placidly, "and more sun baths, under the lamp, than my boss does around Sarasota."

Our youngest and I are both almost convinced that the best diet to lose weight must include a couple of padlocks on the pantry and the refrigerator. On a baffling day around the house a nervous eater can easily tuck away three times as many calories just between meals as he ought to eat all day.

Even homely babies in our town seem to be treated as if they were beauty queens; their "cuteness" is half innocence, half serenity. But a truly handsome infant reigns like Miss Universe; I've seen strong men neglect grown blondes to dandle such an infant.

After a twenty-year prowl for a modern sewing cabinet for my Princess of Sheer Delight, I've finally found a superb and tricky Swedish blond model with retractable trays. Now maybe I'll get my argyle socks mended the same winter.

"Who objects if eighth-graders are taught how to organize a precinct caucus or conduct a disarmament conference," demands our town's second oldest fogy, "if they'd also read Gulliver, Crusoe, Alice in Wonderland and Huck Finn!"

CAESAR & NAPOLEON WERE SHORT

One of the few millionaires I know intimately (remember when millionaires were bigshots?—we now have 150 or more in DM) exclaimed recently, "I'd give a cool million, Slim, just to be 4 inches taller."

This shocked me. He's short & chunky, but he's regarded as somewhat arrogant & self-satisfied on the surface. He acts as if short men were superior to tall men. (He calls me Slim because I'm just a few inches under 6 feet tall myself.) I'm amazed it bothers him.

But I've always known that short men secretly suffer (perhaps needlessly) because they're 5 or 6 inches shorter than tall men. At 100 yards' range the difference is slight. A 6-footer is only 9% taller than a 5½-footer. But ah, the difference to short men, 10 times a day!

Probably other people don't notice it much if a man's short. But I saw somewhere that a half million men bought deceptive shoes last year that'll make 'em look 1½ to 2 inches taller. They take seriously what boy-crazy Empress Catherine said: All 6-footers are handsome.

On NY's Broadway practically every affluent short, dark man you see has a girl by the elbow who's 4 to 6 inches taller than he. It's notorious around Times Square that when a new 6-foot blonde chorus girl opens in a new show, 10 to 9 she'll be married to a rich 5-by-5 in 90 days.

If you're one of Iowa's 100,000 men under 5 feet 7 inches tall, don't stay awake nights brooding about it. Winston Churchill is shorter than you are. (I know he's shorter than I am, because I've been close enough to him to measure our heights surreptitiously.)

Stalin was shorter than either you or Churchill (or me, for that matter). I have that from a reputable Iowa eyewitness, Mike Cowles, who sized him up at the Kremlin one day.... Mike says that when Stalin drew himself up to his full height, chest & shoulders up, tummy in, & teetering a little on his toes & the balls of his feet, he reached just below Mike's chin.

I don't need to tell you that Napoleon's field marshals called him "Shorty," behind his back. That's translated "Little Corporal." I once measured myself alongside a lifelike, realistic wax statue of Napoleon at Madame Tussaud's, in Paris. I was several inches taller.

By this time you're probably glad you're short, like Fred Astaire & the Duke of Windsor. Of course, where it matters most is with the girls. They like men tall, so they say. But I've noticed that about half the pretty girls who rave about tall, dark men tend to marry short, fair-haired men.

I almost forgot to mention that Julius Caesar, too, was shorter than you are. Yet Cleopatra fell for him, and how, brother! I'd bet an inflated $ that she wore low ballet slippers when she had a date with Julius. Incidentally, if you're under 5 feet 6 & eager to find out how a tall girl feels about you, here's the way. See if she wears low-heeled shoes when she's with you. If she wears high heels, better look for another girl.

At the sorority houses at Iowa State, Drake & the state university they have a system of signals for girls upstairs awaiting the arrival of a "blind date," as they picturesquely call a young man they've never seen before but who may try to kiss 'em before the evening's over.

A freshman girl is stationed at the front door. If the "blind date" is tall, she buzzes a buzzer once, which means "wear high heels." If he's short, she buzzes twice, which means "wear low heels."

Two of the brainiest & most beautiful girls in DM who happen to be very tall have a cute trick which I admire enormously. When I approach 'em, they somehow, by a magical trick of compression, manage to lose anywhere from 3 to 6 inches. This is a sweet & tactful recognition that I'm under 6 feet myself.

If you're short, don't take it to heart. Sometimes the right girl may even take off her shoes just to make you feel tall & masterful. Girls are far shorter barefoot. Short men have a lot of punch. They're fierce, zealous, ambitious & masterful. They often get famous, rich, powerful. But they'd still give a lot for another 6 inches of height.

※ ※ ※

"Since all the books of guidance for parents seem to be so loaded in favor of the kids," says our town's most shameless unnatural mother, "I wish somebody'd write a book for children on the coddling of nervous parents."

Some people like better a treatment by a masseuse or a chiropractor or an osteopath; what relaxes me the most is either (1) watching my wife wash the dishes or (2) admiring her as she brushes and primps at her dressing table.

I was the most surprised man in the house when my Lady Love presented me with a hand-knit tennis sweater for Christmas, with red, white and blue stripes at V neck and waist. I'd stumbled on it many times, but I'd estimated she'd finish it for Christmas, 1959.

"Complain all you like about modern schools," says my favorite P.T.A. matron, "you must admit they do teach the kids self-assurance?" Yep, I admit; if the matron weren't so cute I'd ask her if it might not be better to teach the pupils "I don't know" occasionally instead of "I know it all."

FOR MEN ONLY [X]

When I find pasted in my daughter's album every post card I've mailed her from overseas . . . or our youngest gets up thirty minutes early so he can listen to Gordon Jenkins' "Manhattan Towers" before school . . . and Junior supplies four facts in half an hour that I can't remember in our endless father-and-son debate . . . or my wife and I tend to phone each other nightly when separated, if the tolls aren't too forbidding . . . then my chronic husbandly "inner rebellion" subsides from a boil to a simmer to a placid self-congratulation, since man needs but little here below.

✳ 11 ✳
Literature is what you make it

MIDDLEBROW'S CHOICE

100 poems to read aloud at picnics

If you can get away with reading poems aloud at meals, outdoors, or indoors, here are a few your family listen to without a barrage of egg shells. Carol Haynes' "Any Wife or Husband," Henley's "Invictus," Newbolt's "Vitai Lampada," Holmes' "Chambered Nautilus," Bryant's "To a Waterfowl."

In a sentimental moment try 'em with Tennyson's "Sweet & Low," Kipling's "If," Markham's "Man with the Hoe," Coleridge's "Kubla Khan," Fitzgerald's "Rubaiyat," O'Shaughnessy's "Ode," Milton's sonnet on his blindness.

Coax 'em to take turns reading: Bryant's "Thanatopsis," Gray's "Elegy," Sill's "Fool's Prayer," McCrae's "In Flanders Field," Holland's "God Give Us Men," Edna Millay's "Elaine," Elinor Wylie's "Let No Charitable Hope," BLT's "Canopus," Wordsworth's "Ode on Immortality."

But never more than 50 lines at a meal. Ficke's "View From Heights," Hillyer's 3rd sonnet, Tom Hood's "A Plain Direction," Shakespeare's 29th, 71st, 87th, & 94th sonnets, Keats' "To a Nightingale" & "On a Grecian Urn" & "La Belle Dame sans Merci," Pope's "Ode on Solitude," Blake's "The Tiger," Wordsworth's "World Is Too Much with Us."

Memorized, these 100 are worth $10,000. Swinburne's "Garden of Proserpine," Dowson's "Cynara" & "They Are Not Long," Emerson's "Concord Hymn," Longfellow's "My Lost Youth," Whitman's "O Captain My Captain," Emily Dickinson's "A Wounded Deer Leaps Highest," Santayana's "In The Midst of Battle."

Or even between meals. Frost's "The Runaway," Millay's "Euclid Alone," Carroll's "Walrus & the Carpenter," King's "The Pessimist," Whittier's "Snowbound," Lowell's "Vision of Sir Launfal" & "First Snowfall," Tennyson's "Charge of the Light Brigade."

You can memorize 'em from kindergarten through high school. Seeger's "I Have a Rendezvous," Brooke's "At the Victory Ball," Kilmer's "Trees," Byron's "Waterloo," Shelley's "The Cloud," McGinley's "Tirade on Tea," Thayer's "Casey at the Bat," Poe's "Raven."

Let each member pick his own poem to read. FPA's "Columbus," Abe Lincoln's "Memory," Foss's "House by the Side of the Road," Longfellow's "Children's Hour," Sill's "Opportunity," Spender's "Thoughts During an Air Raid," MacNeice's "Aubade," Auden's "Look, Stranger!" Schwartz's "All Clowns Are Masked."

Not highbrow poetry; just memorizable & recitable. Louisa Thomas' "What is Charm?," Field's "The Duel," Morton's "Who Walks with Beauty," Browning's "Incident of the French Camp," Arnold's "Forsaken Merman," Tennyson's "Lotos Eaters," Saxe's "Blind Men & the Elephant," Longfellow's "Village Blacksmith" & "Day Is Done."

By unanimous consent you can read more'n 50 lines. Byron's "Destruction of Sennacherib" & "Isles of Greece," Milton's "L'Allegro," Buchanan's "L'Envoi," Shakespeare's counsel of Polonius, Wordsworth's "Daffodils," Read's "Sheridan's Ride," Browning's "How They Brought the Good News."

You can find most of 'em in good anthologies. Tennyson's "The Brook," Longfellow's "Hiawatha's Childhood" & "Evangeline," Hood's "I Remember, I Remember," Heman's "Landing of the Pilgrims," Williams' "The Elements," Jeffers' "Roan Stallion," Hoffenstein's "No Army, No Navy," Lindsay's "Factory Windows," Eliot's "Hollow Men."

You needn't read or memorize *all* of any long one. E. B. White's "I Paint What I See," Wylie's "Eagle & Mole," Huxley's 9th philosopher's song & Frascati's, Marianne Moore's "Silence," Masefield's "On Growing Old." And what's the pair by Bliss Carman we once read?

These aren't the 100 best poems, by a long shot. Nor are they printed in the order of their excellence. Does some of it seem corny to you? But any poetry is better than no poetry. The moderns are less tuneful. These 100 poems contain music & love, wisdom & beauty, & any man who memorized 'em between his 5th & 18th years would be richer than a playboy with 2 yachts.

My 50 favorite books from the Army's paperbacks

Probably the most sensible list of 1,324 books ever compiled for male Americans was the Army & Navy wartime list of little paper-covered books. More than 120 million of these were actually distributed to our Armed Forces overseas. You saw 'em everywhere from landing craft to foxholes. I brought home enough for a modest library in my own private basement bathroom.

In my opinion, this was the most spectacular triumph in mass education ever achieved, next to (maybe ahead of) the GI's free college courses. But the books weren't highbrow, though they included plenty of solid stuff.

The Army & the publishers deserve a loud 19-gun salute, which I hereby tender.

Today I'm naming my 50 favorites among the Army books, & I'm not including any of the 160 westerns, 122 mysteries nor 30 sports titles, because you're better at choosing those.

I'm concentrating on the more modern books which can be read without undue brow-wrinkling or mumbling, but which are by no means a waste of time.

First you may be interested in a quick summary of the other chief categories the Army & Navy sent all over the world: adventure, 33; aviation, 8; biographies, 86; classics, 23; cartoons, 6; contemporary fiction (of a rather high quality), 246.

Countries & travel, 45; current affairs & the war (Lippmann to Ernie Pyle), 20; drama, 7; fantasy, 26; historical novels, 113;

history, 20; humor, 130; music & arts, 11; nature, 16; poetry, 28; science, 32.

And sea & naval stories, 28; self-help & inspiration (like *How to Think Straight*), 16; short story collections, 92. The most popular & most numerous groups—fiction, historical novels, humor mysteries, short stories & westerns—total 863, or roughly two-thirds of the grand total; but very few of these (if any) are definitely lowbrow. Perhaps you could call 'em middlebrow.

Of course, they made a few mistakes. No book by Thornton Wilder, but 18 by Ernest Haycox! No *Rough Justice* by C. E. Montague, but 18 by Max Brand! Nine Zane Greys, no Whitman & just one slim Bernard Shaw! If I brooded over this long enough I'd find other gripes. But I must get at my 50 favorites.

1. Adams' *Education of Henry Adams*. 2. Marquand's *Late George Apley*. 3. Bemelmans' *Hotel Splendide*. 4. Michener's *Tales of the South Pacific*. 5. Wilbur Steele's short stories. 6. Heggen's *Mister Roberts*. 7, 8 & 9. *New Yorker's* "Reporter-at-Large," "Profiles," & "Baedeker." 10. Jack London's short stories. 11. Edna Millay's lyrics & sonnets. 12. Cather's *O Pioneers*. 13. O'Hara's *Pal Joey*. 14. Kantor's *Author's Choice*. 15. Clarence Day's *Life with Father* & *Life with Mother*. 16. Wechsler's *Looking for a Bluebird*. 17. Vardis Fisher's *The Golden Rooms*. 18. Steinbeck's *Grapes of Wrath*. 19. Dinesen's *7 Gothic Tales*. 20. *Fireside Book of Verse*, Untermeyer.

21. Clark's *Ox-Bow Incident*. 22. Brogan's *American Character*. 23. *Yankee from Olympus*. 24. E. B. White's *One Man's Meat*. 25. Wolfe's *Look Homeward Angel*. 26. Jackson's *The Lost Weekend*. 27. Kober's *My Dear Bella*. 28. Thurber's *Let Your Mind Alone*. 29. Schuster's *World's Great Letters*. 30. Saki's short stories.

31. Thurber & White's *Is Sex Necessary?* 32. Strachey's *Eminent Victorians*. 33. Lewis's *Babbitt*. 34. Tutt's *Yankee Lawyer* (Train). 35. James' *Andrew Jackson*. 36. Hemingway's short stories. 37. Cozzens' *Last Adam*. 38. Mansfield's short stories. 39. Maugham's *The Summing Up*. 40. Franklin Adams' *Innocent Merriment*.

41. Mencken's *Happy Days*. 42. St. Exupery's *Night Flight*. 43. Ellen Chase's *Windswept*. 44. Lane's *Let the Hurricane Roar*. 45. Betty Smith's *A Tree Grows in Brooklyn*. 46. Forester's *The Ship*. 47. Guthrie's *Big Sky*. 48. Kains' *5 Acres & Independence*.

49. Guedalla's *Wellington*. 50. Ross's *Education of Hyman Kaplan*.

I wonder how many thousand Iowans brought some of these home in their duffle bags? I've been collecting 'em since the war, & will gladly trade some of Junior's thrillers, old comic books & even some science fiction for 'em.

* * *

Our town's young bloods who once beseiged the dime stores for dates with the pretty girls are baffled to hear that one of Woolworth's great beauties of the past is a doctor's wife in Tennessee, one a missionary in Africa, one a nurse in Texas, and five have moved to California.

I've argued that broken Christmas toys contribute to the modern child's sense of insecurity. Or are the young moderns more violent toy breakers? We've always returned indignantly any Christmas toys which fell apart by New Year's Day.

We can't bring ourselves to throw away photographic holiday cards, they're such a cyclorama of our faraway friends. But too many of 'em are oversold on pictures of their young, and much too modest about using their own pictures.

We argue occasionally at the club how we can show resentment toward states which send low-grade senators to Washington to become nationwide nuisances. "Maybe we can refrain from buying gasoline in such states when touring," says our club wit, "but that hardly seems enough."

Our basement shelves and nooks are alive with the b.w.'s narcissus, amaryllis and hyacinth bulbs. She's forcing 'em into innocent green stalks and wondrous bloom among the stacks of soap and canned salmon. How magically they shrug off a blizzard!

Our two sons' feet grew bigger so fast that before I knew it my wide assortment of shoes were all too small for 'em. Now I can wear some of their outgrown shoes by inserting a thick insole. (It helps pay their college expenses.)

My harassed friend next door tells me he's given his wife an ultimatum: she can have her kitchen modernized or a trip to Europe, but not both. "But you watch and see," he says darkly, "she'll *get* both."

BOOKS & MORE BOOKS

10 books for my desert isle

So far I've been too lazy (I mean too busy) to select my 100 best modern books, as I've promised. As a substitute I hereby offer my list of 10 best anthologies to take ashore in case you're planning to be shipwrecked soon. Be sure to keep 'em dry as you swim through the surf. (These are the 10 books I keep at my bedside always.)

1. *A New Dictionary of Quotations*, by H. L. Mencken. He's a good man to cull wisdom. Here are more than 50,000 tidbits, each of 'em good for a moment's sleepy meditation. Especially if you've been shipwrecked alone. In my opinion Mencken has influenced American writing more than anybody else now alive. 1,347 pages.

2. *Great Short Stories of the World,* as chosen by Clark & Lieber. 180 stories from 37 countries, ancient Egyptian to American. Of these, 18 are British, 19 French, 16 Italian, 10 Russian & 16 by US authors. Many of these I've read a dozen times. You would too, if you were marooned long enough. 1,075 pages.

3. *Reader's Digest of Books,* compiled by Helen Rex Keller. About 3,000 books in condensed synopsis. Each averages about half a page, though some get more than a page & others only one-fourth. All the books you've ever heard of, & a lot I've never. Runs the gamut from Halevy's *Abbé Constantin* to Van Druten's *Young*

Woodley. Barely enough on each to give you a rough hint or clue. 1,447 pages.

4. *World's Best Essays*, chosen by Pritchard. Voila 229 separate essays averaging about 4½ pages each, with 27 countries represented. The British are far ahead with 51 samples of their meditations. It's hard to prevent an Englishman from writing essays. 1,012 pages.

5. *The Great Confessions*. What 5 men & a woman thought of their own lives. Cellini, Franklin, St. Augustine, De Quincy, Rousseau & Madame Pompadour. These reveal more than most writers generally do about themselves, & frankness is the great virtue in autobiography. 1,136 pages.

6. *The World's Great Speeches*, as chosen by Lewis Copeland in 1942. One blessed advantage—you can walk out of the hall whenever you please. The 231 orations include everybody from Pericles to Lady Astor, Harold Ickes & Mark Twain. Shorter than you think; just over 2 pages each. 738 pages.

7. *A Treasury of the Theater*. In the opinion of Burns Mantle & John Gassner, these are the 34 greatest & most typical plays from Sophocles to George Kaufman. Probably the biggest money's worth of the lot, though it involves 1 or 2 which may not last as long as Euripedes'. I have spent over $250 seeing some of these on Broadway, & often enjoy them more when I read 'em. 1,640 pages.

8. *A Modern Reader*. A highbrow collection by Walter Lippmann & Allan Nevins. What 72 of our deepest thinkers think about it all—politics, economics, world changes, war, science, religion & morals, education, literature, art & dear old America. This practically brings you up to date. I scotch-taped up my brow. 765 pages.

9. *Great Short Biographies*. The lowdown about 50 greats & near-greats, written by 50 who were no slouches, either. Edited by Barrett Clark, & full of fascinating glimpses & angles from Socrates to Bismarck. Remember, even on a desert isle you need some history. 1,407 pages.

10. *The New Yorker Book of War Pieces*. By far the best single book about the war I've seen. From Mollie Panter-Downes' brief bit about London on September 3, 1939, the day it all began, 70 items in all, to John Hersey's *Hiroshima*. Lots of Liebling &

Kahn, too. Superb journalism, & not a trace of gee-whiz. 562 pages. (Liebling is my choice as World War II's top journalist.)

This, of course, doesn't include the best anthology of all, the unabridged dictionary, or even better, the abridged college dictionary which eliminates the tiresome & repetitious forms of words. The beauty of this list (11,000 pages, $30 or $40) is that it's good not only on desert isles, but also on non-desert isles & in places that aren't even islands. I think I'd rather read these 10 anthologies than any list of "100 best books" I've ever seen.

Bookless room: uncivilized?

I've made people mad at me recently by asserting boldly that a living room without books in it is uncivilized. Well, maybe I'm right; but all I intended to do was to provoke the bookless into buying a few books & perhaps nailing a few shelves on the wall for 'em. Books do make a room seem civilized.

It irks me to see DM's new bookstores so full of new books, & the 2nd-hand bookstores on upper Walnut Street & near Drake university so full of cheaper used books, & the drugstores & groceries & depots aglow with the paper-backs, & yet thousands of Iowa living rooms with scarcely a book in 'em.

When my weekly allowance rose to 25 cents a week (on my 14th birthday) I became a bookbuyer at Fike & Fike's, the old 2nd-hand bookstore on 4th Street, about where the Moose Hall is now. At 10 cents a week I hadn't been able to buy many books. But Fike & Fike's, the predecessor of Homer Hanson's, had a 2-for-15 counter.

Ah, great day (!) when I discovered Joseph Conrad's *Nigger of the Narcissus* on that counter, & bought it with another book to present to a friend on his birthday party. As I strolled out skimming through the book, I fell so enamored of Conrad's prose that the birthday boy got only one of the books. The other adorned my bedroom.

Later I bought another copy of the same book, also for a present, but this time it was titled *Children of the Sea.* You could buy Frank Merriwell's thin thrillers 2 for 5, used ones, and Alger's printed on a sort of wrapping paper for a dime. You can still buy a 5-foot shelf of books for a few dollars.

Civilized or uncivilized, let's look each other squarely in the eye & confess: it may be a vulgar motive, but you know darned well that a few books in your living room impress your neighbors & your guests & give the less vocal of your callers something to talk about when they're desperate.

Maybe we've carried this notion too far in our house. We have better than average libraries in 2 rooms & the bathroom in our basement; in 2 rooms on our 1st floor, all 4 bedrooms & the hall on our 2nd floor, & in what Junior calls the attic & what I call the 3rd floor, where he eventually sequesters my favorite books.

I am morally certain that $25 worth of books (either a few new hardcover books, or a lot of 2nd-hand & paper-backed volumes) can do more to adorn or "interior-decorate" a room than a $1,000 painting or $500 worth of draperies. Maybe what I really mean (the b.w. argues) is that books warm up a room.

You've seen rooms with $10,000 worth of genuine handpainted oil paintings in 'em that looked cold & impersonal. We have 2 walls in our living room covered with bookshelves filled with books, 10 shelves high, clear to the ceiling. The room may look slightly shabby-threadbare or cluttered or frumpy at times, but it never looks cold or impersonal.

Some of the fabrics people use for draperies cost up to $20 a yard, especially when they're lined with expensive fabric, too. A few yards of books will, at under $100, in my opinion (but it's only one man's opinion) do more for your parlor than a modernistic designer's rebellion against a distortion of a Gobelin tapestry.

These ornamental books last forever, even if you read 'em. So far we've talked only about the external phase of books; maybe a stretch of novels or biographies or Harvard "classics" used in lieu of an engraving of the Parthenon or the Colosseum. But how about looking inside 'em occasionally?

Our parents & gramps kept their books inside bookcases with glass doors. That made 'em cold, remote & forbidding. Nowadays we keep 'em in open shelves. And whenever you're bored with the rut you're in (or with your own ideas, as I often am with mine), just a gesture lassoes for you a companion from among the 100 greatest or most amusing minds of all times.

Let me confess candidly: I'm trying to trap you into buying books as interior decorations, which I do with a clear conscience, because they *are* decorative. What I'm really after is to trick you into reading your decorations oftener & oftener. Without books we don't become civilized much faster than the Ubangi.

✻ ✻ ✻

Our town's most eligible bachelor has a tricky way of judging a girl at Valentine's Day: Would she prefer a dozen red roses to just one yellow rose with an Edna Millay sonnet pinned on?

"I'm haunted by the suspicion," reveals Betty Comfort, removing her shoes at the front door after a party, "that people who love to discuss sex publicly in mixed company are the same ones whose private sex life is a problem."

Our town has become a gastronomical melting pot. When you dine out you're apt to encounter 1—pizza (Italian), 2—curry (Indian), 3—blintzes (mid-European) or 4—chow mein (American). Each appears in such infinite variety as to crowd hash or stew toward oblivion.

As I gather it, the college set is inclined to question the existence of such a thing as "romance," even when they've just parked three & a half hours in a wind-swept driveway with the temperature around zero.

Both ladies at the bridge table the other evening denied vehemently that there's such a thing as intermittent warfare between the sexes. I've noticed that women who deny such male-female strife are the very ones who're content with the way the battle's going.

I'm horrified that our town's school children no longer memorize Lincoln's Gettysburg speech. For most of us this and "The Chambered Nautilus" and "To a Waterfowl" are the brightest mementos of our school days.

To most of us men an early-morning shave or a quickie with an electric shaver seems primping enough—unless we happen to encounter by candlelight an especially lovely woman.

Some of our town's soundest men with haberdashery have remained leery of the vogue for masculine pink and black, yielding to it only for bed or underwear, or when at least 1,000 miles away from home.

We read heart-rending post cards daily from friends wintering in Florida and California, complaining that the weather isn't quite like August at home. This breaks our hearts; what can we do but shiver or bleed in sympathy?

I smile secretly at the shocked newlyweds in our block. They behave as if they're the first ever to encounter the high cost of play pen, high chair and baby bed as unbudgeted expenditures.

A brand-new baby has established a dictatorship in our family, and I notice that anyone who charms a smile from him seems more elated than a spellbinder at a roar of applause in Madison Square Garden.

MUSIC DEPARTMENT

Music soothes a savage

My first big bonanza I sank in a bicycle ($22, an Iver Johnson), but when I made a second killing, at the age of 16, I bought a metallic green phonograph for $13.50, a hand-winder. It was worth months of self denial; no candy or sundaes. Music has been a minor passion with me ever since, & I've left a trail of abandoned phonograph records all over the world.

I can't remember whether that first tin phonograph of the long series had a horn; probably not, though I like to imagine fondly that it did. But I'll never forget the first time I ever played my first record, "Poor Butterfly," in the privacy of a holy moment alone with a lovely pigeon-toed Irish girl named Enid.

A $2,000 Capehart couldn't equal that thrill today. Music isn't so simple as it was with that green tin machine. Should I be content with a machine that turns the records over & plays all day? Should I wait till music is recorded on wire or paper or plastic tape, & you can put most of Brahms, Bach & Beethoven in one cigar box?

I have been sorely tempted by the Seeberg Selectomatic, the big blond machine with the 100 green & red disks standing on end waiting to play from now till the end of time, like the one at Rocky's roadhouse when you push the magic button. But the b.w. argues that there isn't room for it anywhere in the house except in the basement.

Now comes a whisper from Santa that a big handsome $400 music box is coming to our house for Christmas, but not too big for our living room. It'll play our old records & the long-playing records, too, the ones we don't have yet, a stack that goes on & on for 240 minutes.

It'll receive either AM or FM radio, & can be expanded next year to involve the unknown & breathless delights of television in our own home. Also, you can put a bowl of apples or walnuts on top of it, you can batter it with a vacuum cleaner, & sooner or later some jolly soul will char it with a lighted cigarette.

Gradually all our old short-playing records will be broken, & the problem of buying the new ones will become more & more formidable. When I first began to buy records you could (with luck) buy some passable ones for 35 cents, but the new 12-inch unbreakables cost 17 times as much.

They may well be worth it, provided:

1. That they don't make you buy a whole album of 'em to get one composition you want.

2. That a 21-minute record offers 7 of the old 3-minute tunes.

3. That they don't put repulsive, ear-rending cats & dogs on the reverse side of a cherished tune.

4. They don't ever, ever sell us sub-standard recordings or inept orchestras.

May I whisper to the record magnates that 3 minutes of "Star Dust" or "Vienna Woods," much as I love 'em, will be enough for me on a long-playing record, as it always has been on the old records? I hope they don't drool it out for 8 or 10 minutes.

All the long-playing, slowly revolving, non-breakable records I've heard so far have been enchanting. The recordings are consummately accurate, delicate & faithful; no distortion, no mechanical rumble. I shudder to think how I'll flee to the attic when our young put a stack of 12 boogie records (240 minutes) on the changer. But even boogie may be gentler in the new version, I hope.

Music refreshes, music is a joy, music is medicine. I know nothing that restores serenity more quickly. Especially if the record wizards let us buy singles as well as albums & keep on hand copies of our worn-out old favorites.

So phonograph records are no trivial detail in civilized life. I can't imagine a quarrel with your wife while one of your favorite tunes is playing; nor spanking a child in the middle of Victor Herbert's "Indian Summer"; nor even Molotov spitting in the world's eye to the tune of the flower waltz from the "Nutcracker Suite." Maybe they ought to open all sessions of the UN with prayer & with music.

* * *

One of my sedate neighbors was shocked to discover at Mount Vernon a large chest in which George Washington carried twelve gallons of rum when he traveled. He should remember that this was before the invention of modern mouthwash; and travel was slower then.

"After years of marriage," confides Peter Comfort, dusting snow off his mailbox, "my wife is surer than ever that artichokes, hollandaise sauce and oyster stew are my favorite foods. By a queer coincidence they do happen to be hers."

My partner at the bridge table bawled me out because, instead of getting set by playing my hand the orthodox way, I made game with a lucky crossruff. She's good-looking enough to get away unscathed with such guff.

Suddenly the great world has overflowed our town's quiet social life. Out in the suburbs somebody had visitors from Denmark, and a neighbor served thick coffee and nougat in honor of a guest from the Turkish embassy. Our curved little fingers stuck out a mile.

FOR MEN ONLY [XI]

When our youngest begins to use my stiff-bristle hairbrush six or seven times daily . . . and Junior breaks down under heavy pressure and consents to wear a hat in blizzards . . . or our daughter tells me she has a boxful of her red hair saved up for my first toupee . . . and my wife suddenly tables potato pancakes for dinner even when I haven't mentioned 'em for over a year . . . then my morale jumps seven points and I kid myself into thinking I may yet amount to something when I grow up.

12

Nature as I like it

THE FOUR SEASONS

Hurrah, another spring!

Eagerly the early April wind blows on the exposed scalps of the men's short spring haircuts. And the b.w. fiercely chases a young rabbit from the tender new shoots of her tulips, green tinged with red. In the Walnut Street lobby the lone traveler angles a questing look at the prim girl at the marble table, in muddy toeless shoes. "Waiting for somebody?"

Spring is 9 days old & my canniest neighbor retrieves his grass cutter from its winter hideout & phones the sharpener with prideful foresight. Not a vestige of ice lingers in the northern shadow of your house, & you fish in your drawer for thinner sox to wear ere Iowa's final blizzard.

On Locust Street the thin-clad nymphs hug themselves against the wind as they scurry for mid-morning coffee. Dry leaves rattle in your driveway from the unkempt hedge down the block. It is light when your alarm clock rings & still light after your early dinner, & life is cheerier with more daylight than darkness.

Your cherubs have hung away their ice skates for another year & now it's the roller skates you stumble over on the cellar steps. For a few days basketball & baseball overlap incongruously as some kids throw baskets while others toss a baseball against tingling finger tips & palms.

Exactly when will your Dream Girl demand that you remove the storm door on the back porch & put on the screen, so at her kitchen tasks she can taste the balmy breezes from the south? But the breeze that whisks off another shingle or 2 isn't yet balmy, & all night the house shakes, rattles & groans.

Ah, this is the year the vegetable garden will be bigger, the great year of healthier lyre-shaped pear trees clinging flatly against the brick wall, the year to clip the overhanging branches that block the life-giving sun from the anemic grass near the western fence.

You peel the removable lining from the inside of your topcoat, & eye catalog pictures of the dwarf watermelons: "Will they grow in our tainted & ambiguous soil?" And hidden in the garage rafters you find the spray tank for your battle versus weeds & poison ivy & the mayor's mosquitoes.

Between the window & the storm window the giant imprisoned flies buzz menacingly, & you wonder if they'll be immune to fly spray this year. Each evening your young trek home with their pants caked with mud, & little girls jump rope prematurely in the street in their chilly cotton plaids. Our Town's trucks scrape off the winter's curbside crust of debris.

Ah, a fragrance in the breeze opens a new chapter: 1955's early picnics. Will your Dream Girl simplify those outdoor meals, or will they be more complex & multi-coursed than a Waldorf-Astoria banquet? You recite to her in your corny way, "A loaf of bread, a jug of wine & Thou, beside me singing in the wilderness . . ." But she'll insist on pickles & olives & celery, too.

Yet as you sniff the breeze something in your bones tells you there's another sudden snow lingering between you & the northern Rockies. The first intrepid sports cruise around in their unroofed convertibles, & a faint memory of boyhood troubles you, a leftover from your 10th year or your 20th.

What was so supernatural, that forgotten day, that vanished morning moment in your childhood, when life & the whole sparkling world opened up like a flower? You rummage in your closet for the baseball glove; you find in a cedar chest the Spanish shawl she wore (that other she) to the freshman dance, with the explosive embroidered roses. And in the corner hangs the old jumping rope.

And now the honeymoon carpet is wearing thin, & maybe you must cover its middle with a rug. There, where your youngest & his chums have left their shoes & the clods of vernal mud. Will the lilies-of-the-valley bloom again amid the candy-bar wrappers beside the front door? For a moment you adore even that lifetime's clutter in the front closet. The breeze *is* balmy, snowstorm or no, & spring makes you immortal again for a moment.

Midsummer rhapsody

Across our town drones the somnolence of deep midsummer. Downtown streets end in vistas of green slopes nearby & faraway. Twenty minutes from 6th & Walnut you're on a peaceful dirt road. A pig nuzzles in the weeds of the roadside ditch. Tonight the suburbs will throb with passions of parked lovers.

Sluggish as in a dream back there is the thick-spurting traffic. Across the fields rise the cement plant's white towers, like one of King Arthur's knightly castles. In the weeds at the edge of the golf links a coffee-tanned lady golfer in short pants & frizzled hair hunts her ball.

Drowsy hum & clank of the frenzied aircraft machines at Solar. War & rumors of war, on a day like this? Cows bunch up in a tree's muddy shadow near a tiny pond in a low fold of the southwestern slopes. At the airport a flurry of vacationers & gogetters climb on & off 2 planes.

Behind the coke plant curve the new striving lawns of Wakonda village. Those cherubs have wangled a lemonade stand & its owners outnumber the customers. Why are those enchanting low haciendas huddled so desperately cheek to jowl?

From this hilltop a surprise glimpse of Iowa's golden dome far across the double valley. Those 2 fabulous white horses in the pasture angle, from a fantasy by Chirico. Which storm-tossed soul wrecked that rusted harvest combine in the deep ditch?

"Stop & swat 'em," says the sign at the roadside driving range, & the chunky customer swings like a man bedeviled. High in the empty blue sky hums a tiny plane like a rumor of a dragon. From his 2,000 feet he can see cars on a dozen highways racing like ants.

Let's take a $3 hop & from the air see how the reservoir

spreads, an eccentric starfish amid the fields. Downtown in small rooms people are irked at themselves & at each other. Over the hills echoes the wild goose honk of the Rocket. Somebody is rehearsing to give somebody a piece of her mind, downtown.

Now & then a single cricket chirps; impatient for twilight! Softly a bird twitters; remember 'em at dawn? How calm that white brick farmhouse with the red silo, after your city's elusive fevers. Incredible now the oratory & the TV scowls.

How voluptuous the curves of the golf course fairways! Almost as sexy as the low round hills of Nebraska. Is it moral? Those fence row hollyhocks, more soothing than a triple-bromide. Stop & spy on the critters in the hedgerows.

Look quick, on the skyline; 2 palomino ponies, blond centaurs in tandem. At Walgreen's downtown the man can't find a stool at the counter, & at Katz's across the street the impatient girl is dying for her vanilla malted milk, to quench her midsummer's turmoil.

How calm the ducks on the little barnyard pond! That's the road to Winterset, delight of transcontinental truck drivers. Let's turn on the radio! "La Vie en Rose" sounds best out here in the country.

Under the bridge the locomotive belches black smoke past the haunted eyes of the girls at the factory on the edge of town. Ten miles out your pressure drops to normal. Which is reality, this dusty roadside peace or the clamor of the pavements?

Another cluster of dreamhouses. Those lawn-frisky cherubs —proof that yesterday's midsummer night tamed our roadside lovers. See the tall red & white Equitable tower—there, beyond that patch of purple heather?

Here in no-man's land those weeds don't offend as they do on your own quarter acre. Just plants. Why don't we drive out beyond the pavement 3 times a week. Don't be silly—how can we? We have a rendezvous to fuss & fume in town. The walls fence us in. We built 'em.

Autumn comes to town

And now the early autumn sun hits the great flying horse high on the tall building at 5th & Grand. Naked without his neon. That's not dew on Locust Street, only the sprinkler's damp spray. But it's winy autumn, & more than one old curmudgeon has stuck a small chrysanthemum in his buttonhole.

Last night it was dusky by 6, but this morning at 6 it's already bright daylight. The fog lingers in the 2 river valleys, & on the hills across the Raccoon the leaves are russet through the white locomotive puffs, & at oil stations blooms the anti-freeze.

Every night the neon tubes light the façades of the churches, & the autumnal flight from the godless summer begins. By December it will reach crescendo. Now the neon ice cream cones flash on & off and Junior makes out a logical case based on the depraved sweet tooth of youth.

It's nippy at 8:45 A.M., & the girls seek warmth in their mysterious female way, clasping their arms tightly across their breasts & fingering their shoulders as they tap-tap & undulate along Locust Street. Tonight the neons will shine up luridly to the reddish brown leaves yet unfallen above the hamburger stands.

How futile that householder's tidy gestures with his slender leaf rake against the tides of leaves. How impatient the small boys as they roast potatoes in the burning piles & eat them raw. How soothing the scuffle-rustle of the leaves on the rough sidewalks.

Maybe candlelight would be easier on the nerves than so much neon. Ah, there's the supermarket's neon in the deep autumn night, & Pa on a food spree amid the lush & fertile shelves of the supermarket, he'll teach the little woman what's good to eat & good to linger on the pantry shelves forever.

Lamps shine out into the deep autumn night in the quiet streets between the clustered neons of the shopping centers. On the sidewalks & in the gutters the russet leaves turn yellow & then brown, & under the street lights the small cherubs climb on the shiny hoods of parked cars of bachelors & spinsters dining lonely in neighborhood cafés.

High above the cinema palaces the flying red horse is in his glory tonight, girt in neon & spraying back the darkness from his nostrils. He may be seen plainly from the quiet outer streets where the dry leaves make a wake for the pedestrian. Indoors 4 around a bridge table through a lavish picture window.

Ah, the pedestrian's envy at the golden halos of the living-room lamps shining through the venetian blinds. He has a golden lamp at home, too, but what is this mysterious happiness around these golden lamps of strangers? In the distant silence a dog is barking & children's voices trill like tracer bullets on the dark excursions of run-sheep-run & last-couple-out.

No neighborhood is so poor as to lack its neon-lit hamburger palace. Only yesterday it was candlelight & moonlight in a quiet clearing in the rustling autumn forest. But in a hundred neighborhoods the neon shines proudly on the manmade disorder.

Bright the windows in the high schools with adults at their education. Ah, a trio of bobby-soxers glide through the leaves like fawns in the forest, & the boys in the ice cream heaven press their noses against the insides of the windows. Early evening, & a drawn shade seems secretive & anti-social.

The philosopher on the corner billboard-bench. Believe him, he isn't waiting for any streetcar. High overhead the golden diadem on the state house, & the pennants at the oil station flutter in the restless autumn night, & soon the first ducks & geese flying south through the night.

In the lighted arch at the heart of Drake's campus the pair stands, holding hands, & down the street the neon ice cream cone flashes on & off. The golden glow of the yellow lights is gentler than the blue-white arcs. If I were dictator I'd turn off the neon once a month.

Pretty things, though, those brilliant neon tubes. A pretty sight in the desert at Faid Pass or high atop Mount Aconcagua. Not bad, either, if you stroll from your dark quiet street to a corner where you can rub elbows with your unknown comrades in the dark & rustling autumn night.

Late winter rhapsody

Now descends winter's last assault. On Locust Street the hatless young men are redder-nosed than older diehards with hats. A fortyish Spencer biggie sees frost leaves on his bedroom window & remembers the magic beauty in his boyhood. . . . Quiet shallow ponds & bayous of the Mississippi are still frozen but dangerous for skaters.

Ah, the old-fashioned coziness of winter evenings. Atop a downtown building the flying red horse of neon flashes bleakly on & off. . . . Mom jerks the thermostat up 4 or 5 degrees, equal to 3 or 4 shovelfuls of coal when she was a girl. Defiant local sports appear with fancy fur hats, earlapped. How much better these modern cars start with cold engines.

I leaf through half a dozen anthologies of poetry to find "Snowbound." Whittier makes a frozen New England farm seem fuller of delight than Florida's white beaches. On a dozen ponds the last skaters reminded the spectator of Breughel or Grandma Moses.

In Davenport a fortyish biggie snuggles under his thin warm electric blanket & remembers the joys of childhood's thick quilts & featherbeds. Near Atlantic a car skids on the thin slick snow & sashays into the ditch with a hip-flip. At 9:45 A.M. the thin-waisted stenogs hug their chilled torsos across Locust for morning coffee.

An airplane zings through the crisp sky & 1,000 TV sets flutter in sympathy. A DM biggie dives into the broad doors of The Club and surreptitiously fingers his nose to see if it's actually running. A reluctant adult studies the tracery of the frost pattern on the window: Why have the magic ingredients of life diminished?

Why does the sharp wind turn some cheeks ruddy & some pale? On the long roller-coaster roads across the Great State the traffic rolls on past the windswept farms. In small rural schoolhouses the potbelly stove blazes red & the windows steam up. The racks won't hold all the mid-winter wraps.

And now a Waterloo biggie is worried. Can he & his wife get south of St. Louis toward Florida before the next blizzard? He is attentive to weather bulletins & tells his wife to pack. In the crisp night sky overhead the airplane passengers squeeze noses against shatterproof glass to see 100 neon-lit villages & towns glow softly against the dark land.

With neanderthal jollity men ask each other, "Cold enough for you?" Never did weather influence mankind less, & never were there more bulletins & badinage about it. Godfrey's chubby figure in shorts is flashed from Florida & superimposed on a New York blizzard via a TV screen. He telescopes the whole country cozily, both the electric blanket & the quilt types.

And now Sir Launfal tosses the leper a coin across the snow 10,000 summers old. Vaguely stirs your boyish vision—"the gift without the giver is bare?" Verses later Sir Launfal, no longer the jaunty knight with the butch haircut, shares his crust with the leprous beggar, precious remnant of verses memorized.

On the frozen back-yard turf the leftover week-end ice cubes survive. Indoors the new pale green shoots of narcissus & amaryllis & hyacinth aspire upwards from ugly bulbs to immortality. And 70 isn't warm enough for a non-sweater girl.

But cozily the girls hug themselves as they sortie & scuttle for mid-afternoon coffee. With a metallic rustle the early edition blows across the busy intersection on the bitter wind. Tony, the pride of the Force, must be wearing 2 suits of underwear today. At zero what's as comforting for a girl as a hot fudge sundae? A dish of soup, maybe?

And now the twilight stretches pinkly a little later like a smothered half-smiling yawn. The Rocket pants in on time from its headlong plunge across the Illinois-Iowa prairies, & the old home town greets travelers with the meager blue-lipped pathos of winter.

What a touch of glee or genius it takes to lure men or women from the cozy hibernation of their homes on a winter evening. Halfway between the great rivers the flying red horse gallops motionless above the Capital City. The Great State lies fallow under the twinkling stars, yet man contrives to keep his loved ones cozy. Man has conquered nature again with a cautious retreat to his lamplight.

※ ※ ※

Our kids' grandparents reminisce that in their youth the stereoscope, dominoes and checkers interfered with pupils' homework, too. But these weren't quite so hard on the eyes as TV, and fewer children wore glasses.

I'm wearing my new hand-knit tennis sweater with the red-white-and-blue V neck, proudly as a peacock. But my lady warns me I mustn't wear it to bed even on the coldest nights.

Our worldlier townspeople smiled a little at a series of ultra-"well-bred" divorces which seemed almost too, too sporting. But only until a few rude, ill-mannered divorces exploded in court; then the well-bred ones looked positively chivalrous.

We were startled one evening when a legal eagle at a party told us how big inheritance taxes are likely to be—if we don't take steps. Our only consolation is that we don't have much to leave our heirs anyhow.

Three youngish matrons in our little circle have agreed to live together in the old rambling childhood home of one of 'em, when their husbands die. But what happens if even one of the three husbands turns out pestiferously long-lived?

I'm no expert in the new science of "geriatrics," but from what I've seen of our senior citizens they're happier in each other's company at seventy and eighty than if they rely too much on the uncertain solace of children and grandchildren.

"If our scientists could only rest from their atomic bombs long enough," sighs our club's fat slim-souled man, "to invent something that tastes like roast-beef hash, but non-fattening even in greedy quantities!"

WHY IMPROVE UPON?

What's wrong with crab grass?

One of our neighbors in despair paved part of his shaded front lawn & thus escapes much of his yard work. It was expensive to sod it every year. He gets an extra dividend, too—he has become a 2-car family (more energy for his job) & now parks one of the cars on the paved part of the lawn. It gives the front of his house a festive look.

I doubt that any man really enjoys yard work in his 20's. Even in his 30's he does it with mental reservations. But in your 40's yard work can begin to rival golf, especially if you're not a good golfer. I'm told that in the 50's & beyond yard work can become a positive passion.

We rather admire the strategy of another of our neighbors, who mows a thin narrow exhibition strip of lawn near the front sidewalk, but lets the grass grow farther back. He can take his lawn mower or leave it alone. Several of us in our block watch the governor's lawn closely & follow a policy of not letting our grass get much longer or much shorter than his.

A tough test of character has been passed by a chap I know a couple of blocks away. He can stretch out on a long canvas chair in his back yard, surrounded by his long, uncut grass, & read a murder mystery with total absorption while neighbors on both sides of him are sweatily weeding or pushing their lawn mowers. When they offer to lend him one, he just laughs.

No true nature lover, of course, would touch a sharp revolving blade to God's green grass. The close-cropped lawn, I suspect, is a snobbish British idea smuggled over here long after the

Mayflower. It spread like wildfire among American Anglophiles who like to imagine they're descended from the Earl of Exeter.

A good argument could be cooked up for letting grass grow and go to seed. Especially on the slopes. Still, if you want refuge from your worries about the H-bomb you can find it at the tiller of a lawn mower. I'd almost squeezed Russia out of my mind when a neighbor walked past & allowed that this was the time to drop a quickie on the Kremlin. Now I'm worried again.

As a husband, I think there's nothing lovelier nor more graceful than a woman doing a little yard work, enough to maintain her figure in the pretty curves to which it has been accustomed. Why don't the great minds like Henry Wallace's which gave us hybrid corn & head lettuce concentrate on guaranteed, sure-fire grass seed?

You remember the American who saw an incredibly lovely lawn in England & asked its owner what it took to grow such grass? "Only 500 years of cultivation," said the Englishman, as if he'd taken care of it personally for all that time. Maybe that'll console you for the baldish patch north of your house.

I have discovered an axiom about lawns, known as Miller's 5th law of horticulture: your lawn never looks as bad to anybody else as it does to you. People driving past in a car admire your lawn when you know secretly it's just a mass of half-domesticated weeds. Anyhow, weeds don't look too awful if you keep 'em mowed. Some people like 'em better'n no grass.

What makes me feel underprivileged is mowing the grass around my tennis court while my giddy young friends are playing tennis on it. I'd rather play tennis, too. It makes me feel like The Man with the Hoe. And I wouldn't cut the grass if it didn't get so long that it's hard to find a tennis ball.

Well, when I built the concrete tennis court, it cut down my yard work about 60%. Best piece of engineering I ever did. I once studied to become a civil engineer, & now I can't even adjust the blades on a lawn mower. Should you rake up the cut grass or let it lie?

And next fall I'll be wondering again whether to rake up the leaves or leave 'em all winter to keep the lawn warm. Some of us mow our lawns only when the neighbors mow theirs & make ours look shaggy by comparison. Maybe this *would* be a good time to drop a *blank* atom bomb. Scare 'em a little. You think deeply at the tiller of a lawn mower.

What is so rare?

Was anything more painful than the endless descriptions of "Nature" with a capital "N" in the novels & essays they made you read as a child? Even in *Madame Bovary* & *Mlle. de Maupin,* which had been recommended to me as juicy & scandalous, they drooled on for pages about the rustling of the leaves & the impact of the clouds on the hero's libido.

But those swooning phrases didn't make me hate nature. I still love it, as it unfolds in our Great State's spring, & I've vowed never again to be away from home in May, as I was recently in Argentina, where it was chilly autumnal Thanksgiving weather. Here are my 10 favorite ingredients for a fine spring day, & I hope God's listening:

1. *Light:* When you lift your bedroom shade & draw open the curtains at 6 A.M. your eyes must be gladdened with brilliant gold & blue sunshine. On such a morning I can feel the smile chase away the nightmares from the corners of my lips, especially if I can smell the coffee perking.

2. *Warmth:* The temperature must be between 62 & 79 degrees. Fascinated as Flaubert & Theo Gautier were by nature, watching it endlessly through telescopes from the doors of their favorite bars, they yet never realized how important this 17-degree stretch was. They wore long wool underwear into July.

3. *Buds:* If you're in the upper income bracket, then the days when the buds are just opening are worth $1,000 a day to you. From the bare naked twigs till the dawdlingest leaves are full-grown & gawky is a span of what—maybe 20 or 30 days? If you're a low-income man, each such day is worth exactly what a millionaire pays—$1,000 a day. But you get it free.

4. *Blossoms:* Let's not get mawkish about this. But it's manly to confess that heaven is nearest on the days when pink & white blossoms explode like popcorn on the plum, apple & cherry

trees. Artificial sprigs of pink & white apple blossoms on women's hats almost ruined 'em for me; but my love of nature perisheth not.

5. *Breeze*: Gentle must the wind be, & from the south, with a faint breath of the Gulf of Mexico, if south-southwest, or the Caribbean & the Bahamas if south-southeast. About 8 to 12 miles an hour, with an aroma of bougainvillea & pirates. On such days we trekked as boys to the orchards south of the Army Post & came home with sprays of loose bloom, if in May, & looted fruit, in July & August. It wasn't quite so illegal then.

6. *Twitters*: Unless the birds are twittering it isn't a genuine Tiffany-Cartier day. I don't know exactly how many decibels is ideal; but it should be casual & unrehearsed twittering, without undue emphasis on worms & nest materials. If you can't hear at least 7 different kinds of birds, you're living in the wrong neighborhood.

7. *Blue Sky*: From where you sit you must be able to see at least a trillion acres of blue sky, shading from azure to turquoise. One or 2 clouds are not undesirable, but they must be small & white. Up to a maximum of a blue sky one-tenth cloud-covered. Beyond that I complain to my preacher.

8. *Grass, Hurrah!* A 10-foot square is minimum, like the front garden of an English row-house. Modest grass, like a sweet humble woman. Preferably it should be uncut. When the whirling blades have passed, shades of the prison house descend on the growing boy. Any part of your thin, balding lawn looks good if viewed from a comfortable chair 50 feet away.

9. *Vista:* Incomplete is your splendid day unless your eye can sweep across the land to a faraway skyline & hills ascending. What? A brick wall? No vista? You must stick your neck out to see the river? Go to the park, earth man. The park's your own back yard. You pay for it.

10. *Green Shoots:* Through the damp black soil upthrusting must be a few green shoots (in vegetable garden or flower, who cares?) or I sulk & look at old pressed flowers in an herbarium through a magnifying glass. Nature is a hussy with green eyes & black hair or vice versa.

Ordinarily a modest fellah, today I feel fine & I think this column is as good as a Marin seascape or even a Longfellow poem. The Almighty promises me 50 such days this year, & I'll recognize 'em, even without the Latin names for all the weeds.

EINSTEINS THEORY IN ONE EASY LESSON

If I'm ever to write the simple Einstein column demanded by a bevy of puzzled DM sportsmen, I'd better begin today with a few preliminary violin strokes. Merely an overture, to tune up.

Like a cloud of smoke spins the universe. Through the void spaces whirl the galaxies. Our world is only one clay pigeon among millions. To guess & calculate with Einstein takes more than math, it takes oceans of intuition, a touch of poetry, plus his pain & his sorrow.

Somebody pitched a curve ball. It still sizzles through space between the pitcher's box & the home plate. It curves, it spins, it speeds. To the 3rd baseman it looks different than to the right-fielder.

Like smoke the galaxies spin, like fine particles. . . . You've seen airplanes veer off from each other in curved flight? Each is on schedule, each is lashed to the strings of gravity & magnetism. Even the smoke is a formula in math—x, y, & z.

You know, of course, how a bomb sight must make adjustments for 7 different forces, on a falling bomb, all relative. Neither do I . . . But don't forget the wind, & the rotation of the earth, & the side slip, nor our ovoid path & the sun.

Like a sliced golf shot, see? There stands the golfer, like a fool, hating himself & his brassie; but the ball keeps slicing & spinning on a course neither ball nor golfer can predict. A whiff of smoke in the world's winds.

You know; the way he held his hands, the way his clubhead deviated from a true elipse. Nobody's fault; life is like that. . . . Einstein discovered a lot of spin in the universe.

You ladies know the magnetism that often exists between a blonde & a dark handsome man? Well, that's part of the music of the spheres. It operates also between bodies even more heavenly. There's a strong dash of sex in the universe.

Mathematics sloshes over into poetry, & vice versa. Out in the lonely spaces where Einstein operated, a math formula was apt to nudge a sonnet any minute. Euclid alone hath gazed on beauty bare: that's both geometry & poetry.

Einstein was playing a hunch. He guessed there's no free-wheeling in the universe. Just a hunch, see: that the cosmos & its force & matter are controlled by cosmic law. He proved it for space & time.

He proved it with pencil & paper & his poetic imagination, & others watched eclipses & verified his calculated guesses . . . and one fruit was Hiroshima, & another was television. Same cosmic law brings the Japs a bomb & you TV & Eve Arden.

See the connection? Neither do I, yet. But it's like 2 football teams going down the field, scattering out under a punt or a pass . . . each player plays his own hunch, but he also moves by a cosmic plan: the coach's.

Topspin on the stars & planets, & sweeping curves in the galaxies, & comets whisking their tails past us every umpsteen years, & stars burning up or chilling off & falling, all quite legally, & no sharp angles. Einstein proved it also about matter & energy: E equals mc2.

I must spend a few days at the library: "E equals m times c squared" floors me. It's all tangled up with our little galaxy cooling off, & the ceaseless wind of heaven, & changes of temperature, & the way light curves around the sun & moon.

Einstein resolved it into a not-quite immutable law; he scribbled it down fairly for gravitation & inertia, the way a tennis player can judge a lob floating & spinning high over his head as he runs back & hits it back over his shoulder.

He died a few years too soon. Electromagnetism & gravity he couldn't wed under The Law with his pencil & scratch-pad. Is there then free-wheeling in the universe after all?

Like smoke the galaxies whirl on. What monstrous slugger awaits the sizzling curve at the home plate? Will your body-English do any good? This I must study. (I can't become a 12th who understands Einstein; but can my suspicions stir vaguely & take shape? Is the answer adrift in the heavens? How long must we wait for another Einstein?

* * *

Before I was ten I got the impression that when somebody in our town held "open house," anybody could come who cared to. I wangled cake and ice cream at three golden weddings before I found out different.

Everybody in our neighborhood goes faintly Irish on St. Patrick's Day. Alfonso Bisignano puts on a green necktie, Heinie Weitz wears his Irish-tweed sports coat, and Al Cohen tries to give the Riley tots each a ha'penny he brought home from Dublin.

For a year or so the mothers-in-law of the newlyweds down the street didn't blend any too well; different backgrounds and all that. But you should hear 'em talk a blue streak with each other now, since they became grandmothers of the same baby!

Junior's thin-clad fraternity brother with the runny nose refused to wear a hat till he had to consult a doctor about his persistent cold. "Keep your chest and throat warm and wear a hat," said Doc, charged him $5 and prescribed medicine which cost a little more than a velour.

"Some of the wittiest and most devastating girls in our crowd," reveals Betty Comfort, leaning the old crutch by her husband's skis, "get furious at playing second fiddle to a girl who mostly looks sweet, and smiles, and just listens."

By a horrid coincidence, in the fortnight after Federal income-tax day our local tax collector slugs us with our real-estate taxes. Yet there's one slim consolation: he does all the arithmetic.

One of the young bucks in our gulch spent a cozy evening before his fiancée's fireplace, burning all his love letters from other girls. I'm afraid he'll regret this impetuous act; some day he'll need a few to read to her aloud, to prove other girls liked him, too.

Our town, often called "an overgrown country village" by envious neighbors, had a Turk, a German and a Panamanian visitor all in one week, plus a local traveler who'd been in Bangkok three days before. I guess any town nowadays is almost mathematically the center of the universe.

They're opening a branch bank in our shopping center, but it may have an uphill fight for business; we've all got used to cashing our checks at the supermarket.

My stubborn neighbor who broils under a sun lamp at home instead of in Florida reports complications. "I spread papers on the bed," he says, "anoint myself with sun-tan oil, don goggles, turn on the timer, unplug the phone and finish up with lotion and a soapy shower!"

I've heard the 1955 version of campus romance: he (in bathrobe and pajamas) picks her up twice a week for eight-o'clock classes when he hasn't any; she does his laundry in the sorority-house automatic washer.

EPILOGUE

(Maybe what you need for every day is a personal, made-to-order supplication, to focus on your own faults, virtues & problems like this sample composed by a cynic in our town.)
    Remind me daily, O Lord, that this town & state, too, are the center of your universe, & that life happens here hourly ... let me not reproach myself too cruelly with my failures & disappointments ... Remind me often enough of my triumphs & successes, but with a secret smile, & keep me grateful.

Let me not think too often of myself, oftener of others . . . Nor care too much—but enough—for others' opinions . . . Keep my face serene, so all may see life is good . . . Let not my critics daunt me nor anguish me with their disapproval, and their humors, O Lord, help me enjoy.

Freshen my memory of my travels & adventures which have brightened my life . . . Make me kind to the feeble, the old, the homely & the sore beset . . . In lonely moments remind me of my wondrous friends . . . That they may dance before my eyes in a pageant of wit & beauty fair as a king's.

Guard me from too heavy grief at my shortcomings, for I did not make myself entirely . . . Build no high wall around me, but let me be near to people . . . Never let me take my wife, my children or my home for granted; keep bright their marvel, & help me keep their faces aglow with joy.

Lord, keep me modest about possessions, but thankful for them . . . Let me never forget 'tis sweeter to give away a whole turkey than to eat a club sandwich. . . . Open my eyes 99 times daily for Thy small marvels that fill our eyes with gladness. . . . In every grave time keep me sanguine & tranquil.

Give me courage for both the inevitable & the unpredictable . . . Leave me patient for the joys ahead . . . Console me that I am not handsomer or more imposing . . . Goad me to take risks in good causes . . . Let me not worry too often about our children, but revel in their good traits, which others see but parents overlook. . . . Help me win new friends & keep them.

Refresh for me the joys of solitude which fortifies me as an individual . . . Make me & keep me urbane, deferential, gracious, attentive . . . Help keep my body fit to avoid grossness, & remind me every day that a good life needs daily a sortie outdoors to keep our quandaries down to life size.

Let me not retreat, O Lord, behind a wall of shyness or inertia . . . Never let me lose sight of the likelihood of ecstasy, & strengthen me to deny that life must be tragic . . . Give me small talk for small moments, & deep thought for great moments, & always laughter.

Stimulate me to be generous with praise, but not fulsome . . . And quick to condemn injustice & greed . . . Let me combat tyranny a little each day, & be jealous of my own freedom & my fellow men's . . . Make me condescending to the prideful, & modest with the humble, & aloof enough from the trivial.

Remind me often, O Lord, of all my happiness & good fortune, & the good life I have not always deserved . . . Make me thankful for my comforts, but not too dependent on them . . . Let me not ask more of others than they can give, & help me cultivate a humorous indifference. Disentangle me from too much reliance on others . . . Do not let my runaway imagination undermine or jealousy distort.

Let me not become stuffy or smug, nor irked by smugness & stuffiness in others . . . Save me from loquacity & glibness, & teach me to value a precious silence. . . . Give me sympathy for the secret problems of my friends, so I may admire their secret courage.

Endow me with fortitude, Almighty, to solve my own problems without burden to others . . . Remind me how lucky I am, & make me contented so I will not yearn for the distant places & always the unknown . . . Let me not forget that every answer & each solution must blossom somehow in my own brain, and keep me free and indomitable.

A personal prayer, composed by a worldly & skeptical man who utters it daily. It returns to fortify his soul.

ABOUT THE AUTHOR

HARLAN MILLER has written columns about the light side of family life for the last twenty years—for the *Ladies' Home Journal* since 1949 ("There's a Man in the House") before that in *Better Homes & Gardens* ("The Man Next Door"). He has also written more than 9,000 daily columns for the Des Moines *Register*, the Washington *Post* and Publishers Syndicate, on a wide variety of themes, mostly in a light vein. Most of these columns first appeared in "Over the Coffee," his daily column in the Des Moines *Register*; and Gardner Cowles, who transformed him from a city editor to a columnist, has called him "the best columnist in America."

Harlan Miller studied first to be an engineer and then a lawyer, and his first columns appeared in the Iowa State College campus paper under the worldly title "Bally Rot." He has visited much of the eastern hemisphere from the Azores and Tunisia to Finland and Yugoslavia and Russia and Turkey, has flown twice around South America (including Pan American's pioneer exploratory flight), has visited more than fifty countries in all and aims to see all the rest.

He is a tennis enthusiast and has served several times as a USLTA tennis umpire at the Forest Hills tennis singles championships; on the concrete tennis court in his backyard in Des Moines (which he prefers to New York or Washington) he is known as a dangerous man at the net. Once he learned to fly in four weeks on a newspaper assignment to write four Sunday articles on learning to fly; he soloed just in time for his fourth deadline. He is a fearless advocate of four-lane roads and shorts for warm weather, collects ceramic tiles six inches square, phonograph records and volumes of short stories; he has one of the biggest private libraries in the middle west. His writing has appeared in the *Reader's Digest, American Mercury, Ladies' Home Journal, New York Times Magazine* and anthologies and text books. He likes to brag that he has interviewed Bernard Shaw, H. G. Wells, and H. L. Mencken, the three writers who influenced him most as a boy.